Doing History

Research and Writing in the Digital Age

MICHAEL J. GALGANO
J. CHRIS ARNDT
RAYMOND M. HYSER
James Madison University

WADSWORTH
CENGAGE Learning

Australia • Brazil • Japan • Korea • Mexico • Singapore • Spain • United Kingdom • United States

WADSWORTH
CENGAGE Learning

Doing History: Research and Writing in the Digital Age
Michael J. Galgano, J. Chris Arndt and Raymond M. Hyser

Publisher: Clark Baxter

Senior Acquisitions Editor: Ashley Dodge

Development Editor: Kristen Judy Tatroe

Editorial Assistant: Ashley Spicer

Associate Development Project Manager: Lee McCracken

Marketing Manager: Janise Fry

Marketing Assistant: Kathleen Tosiello

Marketing Communications Manager: Tami Strang

Content Project Manager: Lauren Wheelock

Senior Art Director: Cate Rickard Barr

Print Buyer: Karen Hunt

Senior Rights Account Manager: Bob Kauser

Production Service: International Typesetting and Composition

Photo Researcher: Terri Wright

Cover Designer: Maria Ilardi

Cover Photos: Background globe: Wytfliet's Map of the World, 1598; Greek Temple: © Maria Ilardi; Desk: © Index Open.com

Compositor: International Typesetting and Composition

For product information and technology assistance, contact us at **Cengage Learning Customer & Sales Support, 1-800-354-9706**

For permission to use material from this text or product, submit all requests online at **cengage.com/permissions**
Further permissions questions can be emailed to **permissionrequest@cengage.com**

Library of Congress Control Number: 2007923690

ISBN-13: 978-0-534-61953-4

ISBN-10: 0-534-61953-3

Wadsworth
10 Davis Drive
Belmont, CA 94002-3098
USA

Cengage Learning is a leading provider of customized learning solutions with office locations around the globe, including Singapore, the United Kingdom, Australia, Mexico, Brazil, and Japan. Locate your local office at: **international.cengage.com/region**

Cengage Learning products are represented in Canada by Nelson Education, Ltd.

For your course and learning solutions, visit **academic.cengage.com**

Purchase any of our products at your local college store or at our preferred online store **www.ichapters.com**

Printed in Canada
4 5 6 7 10 09

To all students of history—past, present, and to come

Contents

PREFACE   vi
INTRODUCTION   ix

1   What Is History?   1

The Misuse of History   2
How Much Can We Know of the Past?   2
The Problems of Historical Inquiry   4
The Stuff of History   5
The History of Historical Writing: An Overview   6
Hypothesis and Theory   10
The Varieties of History   13
The World of History   14
The Hard Work of History: Research, Analysis, Writing   15
Suggested Reading   16

2   Locating the Sources   17

Choosing a Topic   17
Prospectus   19
Research Trail   20
  Preparing for the Research Trail   21
  Doing the Research Trail   21

3   Tools for Analysis—Secondary Sources   33

What Is a Secondary Source?   34
Historical Context   34
Historiographical Context   35

Which Secondary Sources Are Best?   35
The Preliminary Review   36
The Internet—Opportunity and Problem   38
    Who Is the Author of the Website?   *38*
Reading the Secondary Source   39
Reading Critically   39
The Past Is a Foreign Country—Reading for Historical Context   41
Reading for Historiographical Context   42
Reading for Sources   45
The Review   46
The Annotated Bibliography   51
Bibliographic Note Card   51
Taking Notes   53
Conclusion   55

4   Primary Evidence   56

What Is a Primary Source?   57
Evaluating Written Evidence   57
    Author   *57*
    Point of View   *58*
    Audience   *58*
    Purpose   *59*
    Tone and Language   *60*
    Significance   *61*
Evaluating Oral Evidence   62
Evaluating Visual Evidence   63
Evaluating Physical Evidence   65
Final Thoughts on Elements of Analysis   65
Source Types and Their Applications   66
    Correspondence   *66*
    Diaries, Memoirs, and Autobiographies   *68*
    Government Documents   *68*
    Wills and Inventories   *69*
    Statistical Records   *71*
    Newspapers and Periodicals   *72*
    Oral Interviews   *72*
    Photographs and Maps   *73*
    Artifacts   *76*
Primary Sources in a Student Paper   77
Conclusion   80

5 Writing 81

Beginning the Writing Process   81
  Early Writing   82
  Prospectus   82
The Jury of Our Peers   83
The Short Informal Essay   83
The First Paragraph   84
Elements of Effective Writing   87
Tips for Effective Writing   87
Types of Writing   90
  Narration   90
  Description   91
  Interpretation   92
  Persuasion   93
Organization   93
The First Draft   95
Revising and Editing   96
The Oral Presentation   97
Suggested Readings   98

6 Finishing the Paper   99

Footnotes   99
  Why Do Researchers Footnote?   100
  What Do Researchers Footnote?   101
  How Do Researchers Footnote?   103
  Historiographic Footnote   110
  Explanatory Footnote   111
Bibliography   111
  Guiding Points   112
  Examples of Bibliographical Citations   113
  Annotated Bibliography   116
  Bibliographical Essay   116
Historiographic Essay   120
Final Checklist   121

CONCLUSION: The Continuing Conversation   123
APPENDIX A: A Reference Librarian's Guide to Historical Reference Works   125
APPENDIX B: The Death of an Ideal City: Rebuilding London After 1666   168
INDEX   185

Preface

For more than 15 years, the three of us have taught undergraduate historical methods from a common syllabus. During this period, we have worked closely together to present a coherent, "nuts and bolts" introduction to historical methodology, which emphasizes identifying all available evidence, weighing and selecting this evidence, analyzing and interpreting it, and presenting coherent history in both oral and written formats. The course has been enormously successful in teaching students how to "do history." Many of those who prepared papers in our Historical Methods course have successfully presented their findings at state, regional, and national undergraduate and professional conferences. Several have won prizes for the best paper in their respective categories. Some of these papers have also been published as abstracts, articles, and in one case, a short book. Whether or not they have continued the formal study of history, most students who completed the course have indicated its lasting influence on their lives as critical readers, thinkers, and citizens.

In teaching this class, we have been disappointed by many of the texts available. Some seem too simplistic, others too sophisticated, and all seem fairly narrow in that they focus on writing, or critical analysis and interpretation, or on style issues; none cover the basics of what a beginning researcher needs to know about how historians think about the past, how they locate and collect evidence, how they analyze and synthesize their sources, and what the writing process entails. In this book, we offer an introduction to all of these in one volume.

The text's most important features include the following:

- an overview of the application of technology to the study of history
- a careful explanation of the research process, and reinforcement of each stage
- an introduction to and instruction in techniques of student peer reviewing, small group tutorials, and individual tutorials

Those who use the text will learn to:

- think like a historian in selecting a topic
- master a thorough and sophisticated approach to using a library with particular emphasis on the most recent applications of technology

- refine a research topic based upon extant and available materials
- develop critical thinking skills needed for the analysis of both primary and secondary sources
- understand the importance of historical context, historiography, thesis, use of sources, and conclusions
- prepare a polished written presentation of their findings through the process of drafting, editing, conducting further research, and rewriting
- evaluate their own writing and that of their peers
- deliver a sound oral presentation of their findings
- review online materials for research and peering
- cite source material appropriately

We are indebted to our colleagues in the James Madison University Department of History for their contributions and inspiration. Their high standards of teaching excellence coupled with their strong sense of collegiality and professionalism provide the perfect atmosphere for excellent instruction. We wish to thank Patricia Hardesty, reference librarian at James Madison University and friend to students of history, for providing her guide to reference works. Our undergraduate students have contributed greatly by showing us that beginning researchers can indeed "do history." We are especially grateful to Jack Sheehan, Sean Crowley, and Darci Mitchell for their examples of student writing.

The thoughtful observations, criticisms, and suggestions of reviewers did much to improve this book, enabling us to refocus our attention in some areas and clarify our thinking in others. We are indebted to the following:

Mark Beasley, Hardin-Simmons University

Kevin Gannon, Grand View College

Marcus Hall, University of Utah

Carolyn Knefely, University of West Florida

Karen Miller, Oakland University

Jessamyn Neuhaus, State University of New York, Plattsburgh

Oliver Pollak, University of Nebraska

Brooks Simpson, Arizona State University

Dan Snell, University of Oklahoma

Eric Strahom, Florida Gulf Coast University

Claire Strom, North Dakota State University

Leslie Tuttle, University of Kansas

Sally West, Truman State University

Any remaining errors are our own.

Special thanks go to our friends at Thomson Publishing. Ashley Dodge has been with us from the inception of this project. It could not have been completed without her professionalism and support. Kristen Tatroe is a terrific editor who patiently guided us through the final stages of the writing and editing process. Her keen insights and steadfast support made this a much better book than it would have been otherwise. Finally, we thank our wives, V. M., Andi, and Pamela, for their love, support, and tolerance.

We are eager to hear from readers of this book. Please feel free to offer your comments about *Doing History* by contacting us at the Department of History, MSC 2001, James Madison University, Harrisonburg, VA 22807, or through our e-mail addresses: Michael J. Galgano, galganmj@jmu.edu; J. Chris Arndt, arndtjc@jmu.edu; Raymond M. Hyser, hyserrm@jmu.edu.

About the Authors

Michael J. Galgano   is a professor of history at James Madison University in Harrisonburg, Virginia, where he teaches courses in European, World, and family histories, and historical methods. He focuses his research interests on the family, religion, and gender in the Early Modern period.

J. Chris Arndt   is a professor of history at James Madison University in Harrisonburg, Virginia, where he teaches courses in U.S. history, the American Revolution, the early Republic, and historical methods. He focuses his research interests on the study of states' rights and economic change in antebellum America.

Raymond M. Hyser   is a professor of history at James Madison University in Harrisonburg, Virginia, where he teaches courses in U.S. history, U.S. business history, Gilded Age America, and historical methods. He focuses his research interests on the study of race and ethnicity in the Gilded Age.

Introduction

The active examination of the past is best achieved through research and writing. In this way, historians employ critical thinking skills and imagination to blend their questions about the subject with existing scholarship to produce their own interpretations. Simply put, the best way to learn history is to research and write it. This book is intended as a "nuts and bolts" introduction for beginning researchers in choosing a topic, identifying all available evidence, analyzing and interpreting this evidence, then presenting their findings in an organized and clear manner. In this way, beginning researchers take responsibility for their own learning.

Undergraduates can perform serious, reflective scholarship if they follow the process outlined in subsequent chapters. In an era when undergraduate research has increasingly become the hallmark of high quality college education, this text will provide beginning historians with the skills to practice history. The research, critical thinking, writing, and speaking skills will also prepare them to be informed citizens and consumers. In addition, since they live in a digital age, the text includes numerous examples of how to employ the Internet and other forms of modern digital technology. This book was written with each of these ends in mind.

This text is designed to provide an introduction to writing history, with the primary goal being the production of an essay modeled after the scholarly journal article. In order to reinforce fundamental skills and elements, there is some replication in its pages. The opening chapter responds to the question "What is history?" It goes beyond simply describing the discipline and the tools necessary to practice it by offering an overview of the rich variety of approaches historians use to study the past. An appreciation of this variety will enable the beginning researcher to better understand the role of analysis and historical context necessary for the writing of history. It also helps readers develop a sense of their own approach to understanding the past. The second chapter guides researchers through the vicissitudes of conducting historical research. Through the "research trail," they learn an exhaustive approach to collecting information in a systematic manner that includes an examination of the basic reference works in the discipline. By examining each in detail, beginning researchers begin to develop an understanding of the significant role that readily available reference materials play in successfully completing a research project. Chapters 3 and 4 discuss the analysis of secondary and primary sources, respectively. Secondary sources introduce beginning researchers to historical context, historiographical interpretations, and methodological approaches. By understanding these works, beginning researchers learn the importance of context, as well as the concept that not all sources are of equal quality. Knowledge of secondary sources enables them to better engage the essence of history—primary sources. The chapter on primary sources examines the different types of primary evidence and the tools used by historians to evaluate them. The fifth chapter offers an overview of writing, discussing the different types of writing and essays that historians employ, with particular emphasis on the importance of drafting, proofreading, peer reviewing, editing/revising, presenting orally, and producing a final written essay. Finally, the sixth chapter discusses how and why historians cite evidence and offers numerous examples of how to acknowledge sources for notes and bibliographic purposes in standard form. The appendices contain a guide to historical reference works found in many academic libraries and an example of writing by an undergraduate researcher, Jack Sheehan. Throughout this book, Sheehan's paper serves as an example of a beginning historian's research and writing. Some chapters in the text are followed by a brief list of suggested readings. For other chapters, the reader is directed to the extended reference guide found in Appendix A. The text will teach beginners to research, think, and write like historians.

1

What Is History?

Every semester in undergraduate historical methods classes across the country, students are asked, "What is history?" Students respond in a variety of ways. "History is everything that has happened in the past." "History is our interpretation of the past." "I saw a movie about the American Revolution last night, but it certainly wasn't historical." "If you know the past, you can predict the future." Each answer may contain some kernel of truth, but none seems to describe precisely what history is. Further reading and class discussion sometimes clarifies, but occasionally muddles, the issue. Perhaps the better question would be to ask, "What is history and why do we seem to care so much about it?" In short, what is history, why is history important, and how has our understanding of the past evolved over time?

Throughout the ages, various cultures have told stories about their past. Part entertainment, part chronicle of events, part myth and popular memory, history might offer knowledge about important traditions and teach a moral lesson, but little more. It was not until the nineteenth century that scholars began to recognize the study of the past as a discipline that could provide a perspective for understanding the world in which one lives. As such, **history is not a collection of facts about the past whose primary value is to improve one's skills while playing trivia games; it is an interpretation of the past based on the weight of the available evidence.** Despite the controversy between those who see history as a science that uncovers universal laws and those who see it as a humanity that engages a combination of reason and imagination to recreate the past, large numbers of well-educated individuals—from political leaders, to businessmen, to lawyers—turn to history for the sense of perspective it provides. Popular claims aside, history cannot predict the future (if it could, professional historians would spend less time in archives and more time at the racetrack), but it can convey a sense of what is deeply rooted in a culture and what is ephemeral, and by extension what is important and what is not. And historical interpretations are subject to change. For example, fifty years ago most American historians believed that the overwhelming majority of colonial Americans were liberal, meaning that they embraced individual rights and participated in early forms of capitalism prior to the American Revolution. More recent research on early America has shown that many colonists placed community values before those of the individual and had only a rudimentary stake in early capitalist enterprises. The informed public has a need to understand how past events gave direction to the historical trajectory leading to the present. Only then can one make sense of the factors that give rise to and influence the way people think and act in the contemporary world. History conveys a perspective that enables individuals to understand how a culture or society arrived at the particular historical moment, how it views itself, how it sees its place in the world, and by extension, the likely range of reactions of a society or culture to future events.

THE MISUSE OF HISTORY

Unfortunately, many seek to misuse historical understanding of the past for their own purposes. In some cases, those pursuing pet agendas—particularly political—seek to twist history to suit their own ends. This often is achieved by the tendentious selection and use of evidence (or cherry-picking the facts), by choosing myths that suit the argument, or by distorting the evidence to achieve the desired end. Such an approach to history is anything but historical, and may involve imagination, but does not include a reasoned or even reputable examination of the evidence. One of the most common misuses of history results from popularly held views about the past. Although certain views of the past may be widely held, they may not be historical, but instead are **popular memory.** Popular memory in Germany, for example, maintains that the German people were not enthusiastic in their support of Nazism, while historical knowledge shows considerable public support for the Nazis in the 1930s. But because of history's powerful ability to legitimize activities or policies, totalitarian regimes such as the Nazis and Soviets sought to abuse history to serve certain political ends. History, which by definition implies historical consciousness, is based on the careful evaluation of available evidence that must be understood within the context of the time it was produced. Such analysis may lead to divergent views from other historians who simply interpret the evidence differently, but it remains an interpretation based on the weight of the evidence.

HOW MUCH CAN WE KNOW OF THE PAST?

In the centuries before the Enlightenment, Western intellectuals conceived of the past as being shaped primarily by God's intervention. The late seventeenth and eighteenth centuries witnessed a growing awareness of the distinctiveness of the historical past and the process of change over time. The period also embraced a sense of progress characterized by a rejection of the distant past. Since the emergence of a modern historical consciousness in the nineteenth century, the question of how much can be known about the past has haunted those interested in the important lessons history can suggest. Historical knowledge is limited in two ways: by the available sources, and by the approach taken by individual historians.

The primary limitation on what can be known of the past is relative to the quantity and quality of available evidence. For some events, particularly those that are more recent, there is a profusion of evidence that can at times be too much for even the most experienced historian to master. For example, anyone studying the role of the Catholic Church in World War II would be overwhelmed by the volume of available primary sources housed in the Vatican Library. But historians' knowledge of the past is more often limited by a paucity of evidence. When dealing with the distant past, or with groups that left few or no records, it becomes necessary to examine the scarce written evidence in new ways or to use different types of evidence other than the written word. For example, there is an abundance of evidence on President Lyndon Johnson's decision to expand United States involvement in Vietnam, but there is far less material discussing the life of a Chinese peasant during the eighth century CE[1] Tang dynasty in China. Limitations in evidence, even when there is a relative profusion, may still leave some questions unanswered. But as much as historians might like to establish a sequence of events and motives beyond a shadow of doubt, the threshold for making claims is not quite this high. Historians often have to infer from the evidence and make guarded assertions about the past of which they can never be absolutely certain. To make such assertions requires a thorough knowledge of the evidence as well as the ability to imagine some details that may not be directly supported by the existing evidence, but which are suggested. Chapter 4 will examine how the historian analyzes such primary sources.

Knowledge of the past is further limited by a long-standing philosophical dispute within the profession. Historians have occasionally made strident proclamations about their discipline, claiming that by employing the scientific method and avoiding personal prejudice, they could uncover historical truths and laws. Still, others dissent, saying that the past has too many variables that allow for little more than the historian's informed impression of the past. Generally speaking, historians fall somewhere on a continuum between these dialectical approaches. At one end of the spectrum are **positivists,** who see history as a scientific endeavor. The positivist approach to history argues that the historian can maintain some semblance of objectivity when evaluating evidence to produce a truthful account of the past that meets a standard for accuracy similar to the hard sciences. The second approach to understanding history is **historicism,** which derives from the idealist school of philosophy and takes a humanistic approach to the discipline. Historicist-minded historians believe that human societies are too complex with far too many variables to be studied like a natural science, and that historians' points of view make objectivity difficult. Instead, historicists

---

[1]CE refers to the common era and is the preferred method of indicating the period traditionally referred to as "AD." BCE refers to before the common era and has replaced "BC" in use among historians.

recognize the distinctiveness of the past and offer an interpretation based on available evidence and the interpretive imagination to offer a carefully reasoned vision of the past based on the weight of the evidence.

Historians from either end of the continuum would agree that an understanding of the **historical context** of a particular time period is imperative. This context, which might be seen as the setting of a period, involves the social, cultural, political, economic, and technological milieu of the day. Among the questions historians should ask are the following:

- What are the values and beliefs of the time period, the economic situation, the political outlook, the social structure, the relationship between genders or differing classes or different ethnicities?
- What are the religious values and mentality of the studied time period?
- What is the basic technological level?

For example, some Civil War enthusiasts muse that if Confederate strategists had followed Thomas "Stonewall" Jackson's advice following the Battle of Manassas in 1861, southern armies could have taken Washington, D.C. While such reasoning seems plausible today with the battlefield only a 30-minute drive from the U.S. capital, such assertions ignore the mid-nineteenth-century reality that reaching Washington would have required battle-weary troops to run the equivalent of a marathon after a hard day of fighting—something few inexperienced soldiers (and fewer Civil War buffs) could accomplish. Only through the establishment of such a context can sound and fair judgments about the historical past be made.

THE PROBLEMS OF HISTORICAL INQUIRY

The failure to place events in their appropriate historical context is one of the greatest causes of an **ahistorical** or nonhistorical perspective. Popular conceptions of history are often rife with such ahistorical perspectives. One of the greatest threats to historical understanding is **presentism,** where the present is read into the past. Such approaches to history are common, but they misread the past by denying what is different or unique about it. Present-minded approaches to history also assume that the circumstances available to historical characters were similar to those of today, and that people in past ages would have reacted to these conditions much as a contemporary person would. England's King Richard the Lionheart should be condemned for his massacre of 2,700 Muslim prisoners in 1191. But one should avoid condemning him for violating human rights, since such concepts did not emerge in Europe until the Enlightenment. Instead, one must remember that Richard's participation in the Third Crusade actually provided some legitimacy for his actions. One might still condemn the behavior, primarily as a violation of the Christian virtues Richard was sworn to defend, but it needs to be done with respect to the historical context.

Another problem for historians relates to **point of view.** A point of view might be something as benign as a mild preference or what one tends to find more believable, or it may be a preference that is closer to a prejudice that influences how one collects and weighs the evidence about a particular event. For example, a historian of American Indians in the modern period would likely possess a very different point of view about Custer's Last Stand than a historian who lived in the late nineteenth century. But can historians balance a point of view with an honest and thorough handling of the evidence? If not, should a historian be allowed to let personal views run amok, interpreting a narrowly selected body of evidence in a way that results in little more than a reflection of the author's own prejudices and self-absorption? Certainly not. But conversely, the holy grail of objectivity is an impossible one to grasp and difficult even to envision. The conflict between subjectivity and objectivity is one of the central debates among historians and one not easily resolved. All historians will always have a point of view, which may deeply influence the way they collect and interpret evidence. Whereas historians might find it impossible to eschew their own point of view, they must be aware of their prejudices and guard against letting these intrude into their approach to historical study. Scholars must also be aware of the point of view of particular sources they read. Just because an author of a particular source has certain prejudices does not mean that the source is invalid; it simply means that it must be analyzed with knowledge of the particular point of view and how it may influence the source produced. The tension between objectivity and subjectivity, and the related question of point of view, is best resolved by conducting as exhaustive a search for materials as possible, and then evaluating that evidence. The evidence might be tested against a **hypothesis,** or **theory,** but one should avoid simply looking for convenient facts to support a pet idea. Historical research and writing requires hard work, self-knowledge and self-restraint, an understanding of historical context, rigid analysis of sources, and constant writing, editing and rewriting before any evidence of historical understanding may be attempted.

THE STUFF OF HISTORY

The methods used by historians to learn about the past are nearly as varied as the number of historians. All historians make use of two general categories of sources. Most students are already familiar with **secondary sources,** which are chronicles or interpretations of events written after the fact. Books (often referred to as **monographs** because they comprise an extended essay written around a central theme), biographies, and **scholarly journal articles** are perhaps the types of secondary sources that students are familiar with, but the list of secondary sources also includes historical dictionaries and encyclopedias, websites, lectures, and reviews. Secondary sources provide historians, both experienced and beginning, with two very important types of information:

- Secondary sources are useful in providing background information about a topic.
- Secondary sources help to provide **historical context.**

Reading a secondary source can convey a strong sense of a time period and the individual, theme, or event discussed. Because no secondary source is perfect in capturing the essence of a moment, it is essential to read several of the best secondary sources on a subject to begin to capture the flavor and feel of a period. A discussion of how to identify and evaluate the best secondary sources will be presented in Chapter 3.

Secondary sources also provide a sense of historiographical context. **Historiography,** or the study of the history and methodology of historical interpretation, is of great interest to historians. A careful reading of several secondary sources can convey a sense of what historians past and present consider to be the important questions for a period, event, or theme, as well as reveal the different ways that historians have come to interpret the event. Evolving methodologies, coupled with changing attitudes and beliefs, affect the types of questions historians ask of the past. Understanding historiography is important to historians in that it shows what questions have received much or little attention, and reveals questions of the past that might be ready for a second look. For example, prevailing views toward the institution of apartheid in South Africa came under global attack during the era of decolonization when historians who were less willing to accept concepts of racial inferiority began to reexamine the topic. Armed with new methodologies that enabled them to go beyond the accounts of white South Africans, this generation of historians revolutionized the understanding of the institution.

Once historians have gained a familiarity with secondary sources, they must begin to locate and analyze **primary sources.** Primary sources are the forms of evidence contemporary to the event or process described. Although secondary evidence is essential to the historian, primary sources are the stuff from which history is written. Most primary sources used by historians are written sources, some of which are published, and others that are in manuscript form. These traditionally included diaries, official records, private correspondence, newspapers, memoirs, autobiographies, tax records, census materials, and wills. In recent years, historians have begun to expand this list of sources to include cartoons, movies, fiction, architecture, art, and other contemporary texts as cultural artifacts. All historians use primary sources to piece together an interpretation of the past that can be supported by the weight of available evidence. It might be best to think of secondary sources as serving as a guide and introduction to a particular topic, but the primary evidence is the actual material from which one can make generalizations and assertions.

THE HISTORY OF HISTORICAL WRITING:
AN OVERVIEW

Although the public generally conceives of history as a nonfiction **narrative** largely devoid of interpretation, historical study requires interpretation. Because of this requirement, historical interpretation has changed over the years. Historical understanding as currently conceived began in the early nineteenth century with the Romantic Movement and the associated rise of romantic nationalism. At a time when German philosopher Georg Wilhelm Friedrich Hegel offered the concept of the *volkgeist* (loosely translated as spirit of the people), it became important to discern what that spirit was. History, with its emphasis on the common experience that bonded a people together, was soon enlisted to support this new ideology. In some nineteenth-century countries, historians played important roles in fashioning how a culture thought about itself, nowhere more so than in Czechoslovakia, where the historian František Palacký became the father of Czech nationalism.

It was also during the nineteenth century that a modern way of thinking about the past and writing history was born. The first to offer a philosophy of history and a guide of how it was to be done was Leopold von Ranke, a German scholar. While Ranke was more interested in looking to the past to discover the handiwork of a Christian god, his sense that each past age was distinct (a concept known as **historicism**) and that past events shaped what came later brought about the first beliefs of history's significance. Ranke argued that while the historian could attempt to understand the past on its own terms, it required a certain leap of imagination. More important than Ranke's philosophical position was his methodology, both as a historian and an instructor. Ranke's method, which in turn became the standard for the profession, rested on rigorous examination and critical evaluation of written primary sources synthesized into a scholarly presentation for a research seminar. This seminar enabled students to engage in careful discussion and further analysis of their ideas.

Ranke's method survived, but his philosophical approach to history came under attack by the late nineteenth century. In an era when science seemed capable of unlocking all of the universe's secrets, historians enlisted scientific approaches in a quest for truth. For example, Karl Marx developed a universal theory for understanding the past based on its relationship to the means of production and class struggle, while Henry Adams applied the Second Law of Thermodynamics to understanding the Jefferson and Madison administrations. The seminar survived, but the earlier historicism of Ranke had yielded to a **positivist** interpretation of history. **Positivism** claimed to be objective, and in the extreme, argued that by using the scientific method, historians could efface themselves of their biases, report what had occurred, and ultimately uncover laws of human behavior. By claiming to be scientific, historians could confidently make truthful claims about the past.

If the positivists were right, ultimately all historians would come to the same conclusions, because they sought objective universal laws. But such a claim would be hard to support. The first serious attacks against positivist-minded historians came from the **Progressive** school. The Progressives included important philosophers such as John Dewey; the most important progressive historians were Charles Beard, Carl Becker, and James Harvey Robinson. Progressive historians, reacting against the certitudes of late nineteenth-century thought, sought to examine the historical roots of social problems. This shifted the attention of historians from the study of politics and the state to the study of society. In addition, the Progressives were attracted to the methodologies of the emerging social sciences. This increasingly interdisciplinary approach, coupled with a shift of focus, led to controversial findings. Beard's *An Economic Interpretation of the Constitution of the United States* replaced the historical orthodoxy that viewed America's founders as great men who disinterestedly implemented the American system of government with an interpretation that the founders pursued a stronger central government as a means to secure their own financial interests. Robinson's contribution to the study of society led to the creation of the new history, which sought to more carefully examine society. By the 1920s, studies of everyday life appeared in both U.S. and European history. The Progressives' skepticism about the scientific claims of earlier historians ultimately led Carl Becker to claim in his 1932 presidential address to the American Historical Association, entitled "Everyman His Own Historian," that history is "an imaginative creation" derived from individual experience. Such statements reveal the growing relativism embraced by historians who believed that the author's point of view often colored the final interpretation.[2]

Historical writing took a decidedly different turn following World War II. The effort required to defeat the Axis powers caused historians to reflect on the common values that united Americans rather than the differences that divided them, so they began to look for that common thread of unity. The events of the Cold War reinforced this theme. The so-called **consensus** historians would assert that despite some differences, Americans had throughout their history been united around the concept of liberal democracy. Louis Hartz's *The Liberal Tradition in America* and many of Richard Hofstadter's works emphasized the basic agreement on core liberal (individual political and economic rights) principles from America's founding to the present. The consensus historians were challenged on a variety of fronts during the 1960s. The growth and democratization of the academy (community of professional historians) generated far more scholarship than in previous generations, and the types of questions being asked changed dramatically as well.[3]

Several schools of thought emerged during the 1960s that transformed how historians saw the past. One of the most important of these was Marxism. Although always evident in historical study, Marxist approaches to history had been something of an intellectual backwater in Great Britain and the United States before World War II. But the splintering of the British Communist party in 1956 enabled new forms of Marxism and Marxist historiography to flourish. Most important among the early British Marxists was Edward P. Thompson. His study, *The Making of the English Working Class,* carefully chronicled the rise of the English working class unified by a class consciousness, persuasively arguing that it was tied to the greater

---

[2]Charles A. Beard, *An Economic Interpretation of the Constitution of the United States* (New York: Macmillan Co., 1913); James Harvey Robinson, *The New History: Essays Illustrating the Modern Historical Outlook* (New York: Macmillan Co., 1912); This essay appeared as Carl L. Becker, "Everyman His Own Historian," *The American Historical Review* 37, no. 2 (January 1932): 221–236; Arthur M. Schlesinger, and Dixon Ryan Fox, series eds. *History of American Life,* 12 vols. (New York: Macmillan Co., 1927–44).

[3]Louis Hartz, *The Liberal Tradition in America: An Interpretation of American Political Thought Since the Revolution* (New York: Harcourt, Brace, 1955); Richard Hofstadter's two most important works that set the stage for the consensus school are: *The American Political Tradition and the Men Who Made It* (New York: Alfred A. Knopf, 1948), and *The Age of Reform: From Bryan to F. D .R.* (New York: Vintage Books, 1955).

structure of production. The importance of this work rested both with its subject matter, which shifted attention from rulers to the less articulate members of society, as well as its dynamic presentation of class relationships in nineteenth-century Britain. The work is also distinguished by the kinds of evidence used to present its thesis. Thompson's work deeply influenced the study of labor in postcolonial societies throughout the world. The emergence of Marxism in British historical writing also clearly influenced a second, somewhat related intellectual movement in the United States, the New Left.[4]

New Left historians in the United States drew inspiration from the Students for a Democratic Society's (SDS) call for the rejection of impersonal corporate society and sought a similarly inclusive, democratic interpretation of the American past. The New Left view of history saw more conflict than consensus in studies that broke new ground in the examination of slavery, race, ethnicity, class, and later gender. Many New Left historians embraced the methods of the social scientists, believing that such methodologies offered greater certainty for historical claims than could be made by previous generations of historians. In particular, the use of statistics and mathematical models held out the promise of realizing the positivist dream of uncovering historical truths.[5]

A third approach to history that challenged tradition was the Annales school. The Annales approach to history began with French historians Lucien Febvre and Marc Bloch in 1929. Rebelling against the focus on politics and government, the Annales school sought to write "total history" that examined history over *la longue durée* (the long term). Their interest in studying the rhythms of everyday life and recapturing the *mentalité* of an era is perhaps best captured in the works of Febvre's student Fernand Braudel. The Annales approach to history influenced a growing number of British and American historians to focus on the history of previously inarticulate groups such as slaves, women, and workers using a new array of sources such as diaries, wills, and census data.[6]

---

[4]Edward P. Thompson, *The Making of the English Working Class* (New York: Vintage Books, 1963).

[5]The term New Left became a popular term during the 1960s to categorize an emerging generation of historians who criticized the consensus school of the previous decade. These revisionists ran the gamut from disillusioned liberals to Marxists. Some of the more prominent New Left historians are Eugene Genovese, *The Political Economy of Slavery: Studies in the Society and Economy of the Slave South* (New York: Vintage Books, 1965); Herbert Gutman, *The Black Family in Slavery and Freedom, 1750–1925* (New York: Pantheon Books, 1976); Gabriel Kolko, *The Triumph of American Conservatism: A Reinterpretation of American History, 1900–1916* (New York: Free Press of Glencoe, 1963); and William A. Williams, *The Tragedy of American Diplomacy* (New York: Dell Publishers, 1962).

[6]The Annales school emerged with the establishment of the journal *Annales Economies, Sociétés Civilisations* (*Annals Economies, Societies, Civilizations*) in 1929. The Annales school is closely associated with founders Marc Bloch, *Feudal Society*, trans. L. A. Manyon (Chicago: University of Chicago Press, 1961); *The Historian's Craft*, trans. Peter Putnam (New York: Vintage Books, 1953); Lucien Febvre, *The Problem of Unbelief in the Sixteenth Century: The Religion of Rabelais*, trans. Beatrice Gottlieb (Cambridge: Harvard University Press, 1982); and Febvre's student, Fernand Braudel, *The Mediterranean and the Mediterranean World in the Age of Philip II*, 3 vols., trans. Siân Reynolds (New York: Harper and Row, 1972) and *Civilization and Capitalism: 15th to 18th Century*, 3 vols., trans. Siân Reynolds (New York: Harper and Row, 1982–84).

Because of the simultaneous emergence of and overlapping interests (and conclusions) of these three schools (Marxist, New Left, and Annales), lines between them blurred as historians from one approach borrowed promiscuously from the others. Combined, these trends helped give rise to a wave of the new histories. Perhaps most significant was the new social history. What characterized the new social history, whatever the approach, was the interest in previously inarticulate groups as a means to both democratize and flesh out the historical understanding of the past as well as identification of new methods for reconstructing the past. Social historians sought to reconstruct lives previously unrepresented, but also to uncover historical social structures as well. Each of these trends that emerged in the 1960s and 1970s initially represented the recreation of the past in an objective manner. But the variability of their findings undermined such claims.

The social scientific approach borrowed by all three schools and the claims of scientific objectivity made in particular by Marxists and New Left American historians soon came under attack. The book that undermined historians' claims of objectivity and truth-seeking was Thomas Kuhn's *On the Structure of Scientific Revolutions*. In it, Kuhn showed that scientific explanations of how the universe works, such as Sir Isaac Newton's Theory of Gravity, were not immutable truths but instead the best interpretations that could be made based on the available evidence. Kuhn demonstrated that over time, scientists uncovered information that challenged important theories of how the universe worked, but the theory would hold with some qualifications until the weight of dissenting evidence forced a reinterpretation. According to Kuhn, the truth was merely what appeared to be true, relative to one's point of observation and available evidence. In challenging the truth claims of the hard sciences, Kuhn created doubt for those making similar claims in history and the social sciences. Such relativism and skepticism opened the door for **postmodern theory** that came into vogue in recent years.[7]

HYPOTHESIS AND THEORY

The public's image of what constitutes history might actually be closer to nonfiction literature than what most historians do for a living. While nonfiction narratives of the past will always be popular with the reading public, few professional historians today approach history as nonfiction narrative. Nonfiction literature alone, while highly informative and entertaining, often falls short of the discipline's claims of offering a critical perspective. The modern historian must do more than merely recite the facts and recount tales of past events. But how does one discern patterns from the complex, convoluted, mix of evidence about the past? One of the most common ways in which historians attempt to make sense of this jumble is through the use of a **hypothesis.** Much like a scientist makes preliminary observations and develops a hypothesis to test in a laboratory, the historian begins to develop a hypothesis after preliminary reading of important secondary sources. **This hypothesis, or central question, must then be tested against the primary evidence.**

---

[7]Thomas S. Kuhn, *The Structure of Scientific Revolutions* (Chicago: University of Chicago Press, 1962).

It should not become an end to be proven by a careful selection of only that evidence that fits. For example, some preliminary reading about the causes of the American Revolution might suggest that a hypothesis focusing on ideological conflicts between Parliament and colonial elites was a key factor in the Revolution. But if an examination of the evidence points in other directions, it may be necessary to modify the developing argument or change it altogether. Ultimately, a hypothesis will evolve into a central argument or **thesis** that is based on the weight of the evidence. But how does one develop a hypothesis? Many historians find theory a useful tool to develop central questions to test against the evidence.

Theory is useful in that it helps to give form to the questions asked of the past, and imposes some discipline on the historians' approach to the evidence. The use of theory remains controversial to some, who assert that theory is often imposed on the past, resulting in selective cherry-picking of evidence to suit the theory. If used responsibly however, such an approach can result in new ways to understand various aspects of the past. Indeed, even historians who eschew the use of theory and prefer to provide a narrative that stands alone often espouse views that are vaguely informed by theory. As such, theory is a tool for understanding, not a replacement for critical analysis and synthesis of the evidence.

The varieties of theory are numerous. Although this text will not carefully review each theory or privilege one approach above another, it is important that beginning scholars have some appreciation of major theoretical approaches. Some of the most important theories employed by historians are rooted in the works of Karl Marx, Max Weber, and Émile Durkheim.

Karl Marx's ideas are often dismissed today because of the economic and political failures of communism in the late twentieth century; but as a tool for understanding the past, Marx has been highly influential. According to Marx, a society could only be understood through examining its means of production. His scientific view of history held that all elements within a society—its values, ideology, politics, social structure—resulted from the means of economic production. Such an approach may seem rigidly determinist, but it does provide a metatheory for understanding the dynamics of a past society. Max Weber was a German sociologist writing in the early twentieth century. His most famous work, *The Protestant Ethic and the Spirit of Capitalism* (1904–05), responds to Marxist claims of economic materialism by pointing out the ideological factors that contributed to early capitalism as a rational form of modernization. Weber's ideas contributed to the emergence of modernization theory, which looked at social upheaval and dislocation as part of a rational process of modernizing. Émile Durkheim, also a contemporary of Weber, responded to problems he saw in Marxist analysis. Writing in late nineteenth-century France, Durkheim's emphasis on changing long-term processes and their impact on individuals and communities provided inspiration for the Annales school.[8]

More recently, historians have turned in other directions for theories to aid the process of historical understanding. Anthropologist Clifford Geertz disagreed

---

[8]Karl Marx, *Capital: A Critique of Political Economy,* ed. Friedrich Engels, trans. Samuel Moore, Edward Aveling, Marie Sachey, and Herbert Lamm (Chicago: Encyclopedia Britannica, 1952); Émile Durkheim, *The Division of Labor in Society,* trans. George Simpson (Glencoe, IL: The Free Press, 1949); Max Weber, *The Protestant Ethic and the Spirit of Capitalism,* trans. Talcott Parsons, with a foreword by R. H. Tawney (New York: Scribner's, 1930).

with the scientific claims of his own and other disciplines. Rather than uncovering laws of a culture through careful observation of methodology, Geertz argued that one can uncover meaning (rather than causation) through careful contextualization, resulting in a "thick description" of a culture. Geertz's ideas provided historians with greater interpretive freedom, and helped to popularize the study of cultural history through an understanding of its symbols.[9]

One of the most controversial theoretical approaches is **postmodernism.** Postmodern theory was largely a French creation most closely identified with the philosophers Jacques Derrida and Michel Foucault. Emerging in post–World War II (and soon to be postcolonial) France, it challenged widely held assumptions about the ability to reason. Amorphous in nature and difficult to characterize, postmodernists often reject historians' ability to produce accurate truth claims about the past. For postmodernists, fragmentary evidence and the inability of an observer to escape his or her point of view makes the past unknowable. Instead, they believe that history is little more than an artistic representation of the past that reveals more about the author than the period discussed. At face value, such claims appear to question the very legitimacy of historical inquiry as traditionally practiced, and implies that the doctrine of rational inquiry rooted in the Enlightenment is something of a dead letter. One of the most common applications of the postmodern approach is seen in the linguistic turn. First emerging with the new literary historians during the 1980s, proponents of the linguistic turn argue that the instability and fluidity of language hides more about the past than it reveals, and that interpretation of narratives reveals more about the author than the narrative in question. Proponents of this approach ultimately deem the past unknowable from the perspective of scientific truth and instead deconstruct texts to recover multiple, often obscure meanings. From their perspective, there is no historical truth.

Although extreme applications of such ideas might seem ahistorical and even illogical, the implications of postmodern theory have actually been important to historians. For example, postmodernists have pointed out the elasticity of meaning for categories of analysis such as gender, race, class, and ethnicity. Many historians influenced by postmodern ideas have begun to more carefully examine the meaning of these culturally defined concepts and the context that defines them, greatly enriching historical understanding. Postmodern theory has contributed to the emergence of cultural history, which also grew out of the Annales school.[10]

---

[9]Clifford Geertz, "Thick Description: Toward an Interpretive Theory of Culture," "Deep Play: Notes on a Balinese Cockfight," *The Interpretation of Cultures: Selected Essays,* comp. Clifford Geertz (New York: Basic Books, 1973).

[10]Jacques Derrida is often called the "father of postmodernism." His major works include Jacques Derrida, *Of Grammatology,* trans. Gayatri Chakravorty Spivak (Johns Hopkins University Press, 1976); *Writing and Difference,* trans. Alan Bass (Chicago: University of Chicago Press, 1978); *Speech and Phenomena, and Other Essays on Husserl's Theory of Signs,* trans. David B. Allison (Evanston, IL: Northwestern University Press, 1973); Michel Foucault, *The Order of Things* (New York: Pantheon Books, 1970); *The Archaeology of Knowledge,* trans. A. M. Sheridan Smith (New York: Pantheon Books, 1972); Hayden White, *Metahistory: The Historical Imagination in Nineteenth Century Europe* (Baltimore: Johns Hopkins University Press, 1975); *Tropics of Discourse: Essays in Cultural Criticism* (Baltimore: Johns Hopkins University Press, 1978); Keith Jenkins, *Refiguring History: New Thoughts on an Old Discipline* (London: Routledge, 2003).

THE VARIETIES OF HISTORY

Because educated people believe that history provides a sense of perspective to understand the present and how society arrived at a particular point in time, there are many different types of history. Traditionally, the dominant area of historical inquiry has been **political history.** Believing that important questions in a society were ultimately determined in the political arena, political historians tended to examine the great statesmen and their impact in shaping events or to look at the rise of political parties or ideologies. Political history practiced in such a way relied on readily available forms of evidence such as state papers, autobiographies, memoirs, and newspapers chronicling the leading figures of a particular period. **Military history, diplomatic history,** and the **history of empire and colonialism** were in many ways derived from political history, with a focus shifted from great political leaders to generals, foreign policy leaders, or colonial officials. Another traditional approach employed by historians was to examine the great ideas that influenced a culture or nation. **Intellectual history** examined the great philosophers to understand the ideas that they contributed. In some ways, the early study of **religious history** fused these approaches in the examination of leading clerical figures, religious institutions, and beliefs.

Each of these approaches offered important insights into the topics they examined, but they suffered from what some would later refer to as a "top rail bias." The problem with focusing on leading figures of society is that often many groups are left out of the story. Historians eager to understand the conditions that shaped past lives often looked to **economic history.** This approach not only shed light on past economic trends and conditions, but borrowing methodology from economists offered a higher threshold of certainty in the claims one could make about the past. In some ways, economic history opened the door to **social history.** Although initially written as a narrative to describe the everyday lives of people, in the last forty years social historians have sought to understand history from the bottom up, as well as trying to understand the demography, social structures, and *mentalités* within a society. Social history eventually wrote many groups into history, including racial and ethnic minorities, immigrants, African Americans, women, the family, workers, and more recently, gays and lesbians. Many of these oppositional histories had, as their opponents often claimed, a political agenda that sought to use history to advance a present-day issue but similar claims could easily be made of the elite-centered history practiced by earlier generations of historians. Simply put, if history helps to provide perspective, then the types of questions raised will always have political overtones. Social historians have made immense contributions to fleshing out the historical record and in offering a deeper and richer context to what is known of the past. They have helped answer the question, "Whose history?"

While the emergence of social history has greatly enriched the understanding of past societies, its main contribution may have been methodological. In order to uncover the history of the inarticulate, social historians turned to nontraditional forms of evidence such as demographic data (census and tax records), wills, and oral history, and employed methodologies from the social sciences to reconstruct the past lives of these groups. The emphasis of many of these monographs has been on group or collective biography. While more traditional branches of history may have criticized the use of such forms of evidence, it was not long before political historians were looking at voting records to determine mass political behavior, military historians were examining the cultural aspects of a nation's approach to war, intellectual historians were carefully setting important thinkers in their social and cultural milieu, historians of colonialism were examining the response of the colonized, and religious historians were trying to discern the faith of the common people. **Cultural history,** as practiced by followers of the Annales school and more recently by proponents of postmodernism, has emerged as an important approach to understanding the past. Their interpretation of cultural artifacts carefully placed within a historical context has offered profound new insights into the historical past. The implications of social and cultural history are perhaps most evident in the proliferation of living history museums and historical buildings that carefully reconstruct past lives for present consumption and have contributed to the emergence of **public history** as yet another field of historical inquiry.

Finally, the areas that historians focus on are virtually unlimited in scope. Some historians carefully examine an event or a specific cultural setting in an effort to better understand the past. Such studies tend to focus intently on the local and the particular, and extrapolate from there. Other historians may focus on a narrow subject, but look at change or persistence over an extended period of time. Yet other historians look broadly at trends within a society that are part of a larger regional or even global perspective.

THE WORLD OF HISTORY

The approaches employed by historians and the types of questions that historians ask about the past are numerous and varied. Most historians' inquiry into the past focuses on some combination of place (such as a region, nation, or subcontinent), time period, or theme. Most historical writing began by focusing on the nation-state. Although **national history** may not be as popular as it once was, in many areas, particularly the United States, it remains a staple of the profession. **Regional** and **local history** is in many ways a subgenre of national history. Some historians have moved past the boundaries of the nation-state to examine historical events from a continental or global perspective. **World** or **global history** has increasingly displaced the traditional study of **Western civilization** as an undergraduate staple, while simultaneously redefining how historians of all types think about their area of study. Focus on global regions such as the Atlantic world or the Islamic world offers historians the opportunity to see a larger picture. The practice of using a particular theme to discern a larger picture has contributed to the growing popularity of **comparative history.**

Historians often categorize themselves by their periods of expertise. Traditionally, historical periodization was pegged to political movements or dynasties, or in the case of premodern periods, broad expanses of time characterized by similar institutions that reflected the idiosyncrasies of a particular place. In the United States, historians claimed to be experts on the Colonial Period or the Gilded Age; in Britain, there are Tudor-Stuart specialists, and in both could be found ancient and medieval scholars. Increasingly, social and cultural historians—with their interest in looking at change over time—have stretched, redefined, and in some cases shattered traditional periodization. Thus, the Age of Jackson has increasingly given way to the Market Revolution, and the Victorian Era has been supplanted by the Industrial Revolution. Many historians refuse identification with a time period. Instead, their primary approach is thematic, leading them to identify themselves as scholars of gender history, economic history, or religious history. Regardless of field or approach, all historians are united in their efforts to add to knowledge of the past through a rigorous approach to historical research, analysis, and writing.

THE HARD WORK OF HISTORY: RESEARCH, ANALYSIS, WRITING

No introduction to the study of history would be complete without a discussion of the requirements of producing a historical essay. Even after carefully reading and rereading the secondary literature, after hours and hours of painstaking research in libraries, archives, museums, government offices, and online, after consideration of the historiography, methodology, and theory, the historian's work has only begun. No serious actor appears on stage after one rehearsal, no serious athlete competes for a championship after one practice, and no serious historian presents his or her conclusions after one draft. The process of producing history is, as the old aphorism claims, "1 percent inspiration and 99 percent perspiration."

Writing history should be thought of as a conversation, with both the secondary and primary sources, and indeed with yourself and what you think about the event in question. The only way to make sense of what one really believes and what can be legitimately asserted about the past is to work these ideas out critically. For the seeds of an idea about the past to bloom into a full blown interpretation, it will be necessary to commit one's ideas to paper in a preliminary way, to constantly test these ideas against the evidence, to subject one's developing argument to other historians who can point out strengths and weaknesses, and to constantly respond to this ongoing conversation through more drafting and editing. But remember, no essay is perfect—at some point, either because of a deadline or perhaps your own weariness, you will have to complete it. However, if you follow the advice found in the ensuing chapters, you will be rewarded with a sense of self-satisfaction that results from a demonstration of acute skills of research, analysis, and synthesis, and mastery of the subject matter.

SUGGESTED READING

Appleby, Joyce, Lynn Hunt, and Margaret Jacob. *Telling the Truth About History*. New York: Norton, 1994.

Brown, Callum. *Postmodernism for Historians*. London and New York: Pearson\Longman 2005.

Himmelfarb, Gertrude. *The New History and the Old: Critical Essays and Reappraisals*. Cambridge, MA: Belknap Press of Harvard University Press, 1987.

Iggers, Georg G. *Historiography in the Twentieth Century: From Scientific Objectivity to the Postmodern Challenge*. Hanover, NH: Wesleyan University Press, 1997.

Molho, Anthony and Gordon Wood, eds. *Imagined Histories: American Historians Interpret Their Past*. Princeton, NJ: Princeton University Press, 1998.

Novick, Peter. *That Noble Dream: The "Objectivity Question" and the American Historical Profession*. Cambridge, England: Cambridge University Press, 1988.

Wilson, Norman J. *History in Crisis?: Recent Directions in Historiography*, 2nd ed. Upper Saddle River, NJ: Prentice Hall, 2005.

2

Locating the Sources

Successful historical research blends imagination and a methodical exploration of the sources. Historians seek to understand what happened to people, societies and cultures, and places in the past. Then they explain their conclusions in a clear, organized, and well-written manner. They are always curious to find more sources while maintaining a healthy skepticism of the sources they do find. One of the first tasks in conducting any research project is fusing historical imagination and rigorous method to define a topic, and to locate the necessary sources. This chapter examines the selection of a topic, the development of a prospectus, and the stages involved in conducting a systematic, thorough search for primary and secondary materials, also called a research trail.

CHOOSING A TOPIC

One way to think about the process of historical research is as a series of ongoing conversations: conversations with yourself, with peers, and especially with the evidence. Whenever possible, researchers should select a topic of their own choosing, that interests and excites them, that has sufficient evidence to complete an effective research project, and that is appropriate to a given task or a particular assignment. Limiting the scope of a topic is often conducted during the research process, as the researcher learns more about the available sources. Thus, the first questions seek to determine an individual's research interests.

- Factors to consider when deciding on a manageable research topic:
  Curiosity—Beginning researchers often draw their first ideas from a curiosity aroused by their readings, coursework, conversations, television, or the movies. For example, the civil rights movement in the United States triggered many historians to not merely examine slavery, but to research the history of slave resistance, organization, and nationalism in ways

never previously imagined. Students should rely on their own experiences in thinking about a topic. The experience of decolonization looks very different to an official in London than to a young boy living in West Africa. The students' curiosity will help keep them intellectually engaged. Less attractive topics will probably be abandoned, faced with less than full vigor, and yield predictably poor results.

Historical interest—Closely related to curiosity is historical interest. What kinds of history interests you? When you read history, what time period, themes, personalities, or ideas attract you? The answers to these questions are the starting point in selecting a research topic. Having a topic of interest is essential since the research process is lengthy, involved, and occasionally tedious.

Imagination—Curiosity and historical interest must be coupled with imagination. The historian's imagination shapes the questions about a topic, the way in which the sources are perceived, and the possible interpretations of that evidence. All that limits imagination are the facts of history.

Narrowing the topic—Students' curiosity, historical interest, and imagination often lead them to broad topics such as World War II, the communist takeover in China, or the collapse of the Roman Empire. While such topics are interesting, they are too broad to be viable. However, a carefully limited idea or question that examines a narrower aspect of these larger themes enables the researcher to satisfy his or her curiosity and engage the imagination while studying a more manageable topic. But how does one do this?

- Thinking about the potential topic:
  After the initial steps in selecting a topic, it is wise to discuss the ideas with others. These conversations sharpen thinking by forcing researchers to articulate what they want to find out about a subject and encourage new questions about the subject and the sources. If researchers can explain what they plan to study to someone else, they are more likely to understand the topic themselves. None of these preliminary discussions needs to be particularly polished, because their purpose is to establish potential interest, build a scholarly vocabulary, and identify questions for study.

  The first conversations are often part of an informal **brainstorming** exercise, during which historians begin to shape a topic. Starting with one or two fairly open-ended questions or ideas, these conversations are likely to be initially vague and roughly defined. The more common questions may relate to changes, causes, consequences, meanings, or connections. To learn some fundamentals about a topic, examine a general introduction to the subject found in a historical encyclopedia, a biographical dictionary, or a textbook. From this preliminary reading, the historian gains a broad understanding of the personalities, places, and events associated with the topic. Such preliminary reading allows historians to generate more refined questions and ideas. Historians are well served if they jot down these initial questions and ideas for future reference.

PROSPECTUS

As researchers begin to record ideas and questions about a topic, they are prepared to produce a somewhat more structured **prospectus.** The prospectus is a conversation in which the researcher proposes a topic and writes focused questions, terms, and ideas to initiate the search of bibliographies and other resources that shape this stage of the research process. These early questions help the researcher develop a **thesis** around which the arguments of a research topic will later be constructed. The thesis introduces the questions that define the argument, provides its context, and organizes each part of the paper. Thus, the thesis at this stage initiates the process of forming more precise questions and setting the project's direction. The thesis will likely be modified as the researcher locates, examines, reads, and analyzes the evidence. The prospectus is a written exercise; the questions will change once the researcher becomes better informed through careful reading and thinking. The prospectus is a natural extension of the brainstorming exercise.

The following is an example of a beginning historian's prospectus concerning Restoration London:

> I'm not really sure what to start on as my topic, and I have been looking at a couple of different ideas. I was thinking along the lines of a social history in England in the seventeenth century because I already have to research information in the field for another one of my classes, and it does interest me. I would like to take a certain period in the century and look at the town atmosphere. How is the town laid out? What are the relationships among people in the town? What are some of the differences between a larger city and a small town? What are some of the occupations? I have looked at *Historical Abstracts* and browsed through *WorldCat* and other sources already and have been able to find a good deal of journal articles written on the general subject. I am still unsure of primary sources. If you have suggestions or guidance, please let me know.[1]

Several points stand out in this first conversation:

- The prospectus is informal. It reflects only the researcher's interest in social and urban history.

- The researcher seeks to blend the research in more than one course by drawing upon previous knowledge and connecting class requirements.

- The topic is broad and amorphous. The researcher suggests some preliminary questions. The prospectus does not, however, have a clear focus. The researcher wants to know more about towns and their citizens in a designated time period without specifying much detail about particular communities, categories of individuals, or social practices.

- The researcher makes some rudimentary observations about the availability of evidence to illustrate that the proposal is feasible. The prospectus does

---

[1]Jack Sheehan, *"Prospectus"* e-mail, 10 September 2002. His paper will be followed through the research and writing process. Other examples of student work will also be used to illustrate specific points.

offer sufficient information to guide initial thinking as the researcher begins to search for primary and secondary sources. It is important to have a peer or colleague review the prospectus and provide constructive suggestions about possible future directions of the topic. By reviewing one's own work and incorporating the suggestions of others, the topic can be further refined. Such conversations should immediately precede a comprehensive search for sources because they provide researchers with a basic vocabulary about the topic and some insights into the kinds of materials necessary. They should also continue as the research proceeds as the questions may change.

The prospectus and the resulting conversations are comparable to studying a road map before beginning a journey. The prospectus provides a general idea of direction; however, like any road map, once the trip is taken, new routes and possibilities may be identified and the original route modified. Similarly, as questions. Once the trip is in progress however, the driver often identifies alternative routes and spots to be avoided become more refined, it is time to begin a careful, systematic search for sources to find as many materials as possible about the topic. This literature search is the research trail.

RESEARCH TRAIL

A **research trail** is the systematic identification and collection of all relevant materials available in print and online necessary to conduct scholarly research on a particular topic. The research trail not only involves an exhaustive search for sources; it offers knowledge and awareness of the topic that is fundamental in shaping it. Since historical accuracy depends upon corroboration of evidence, locating every potential source that might shed light on the topic is important. To avoid embarrassing omissions, successful researchers should follow a careful research trail and list all possible resources. Some of the materials listed in an original trail may be subsequently discarded once particular items are evaluated and compared; yet, the first examination of the literature should be as full as the careful researcher can make it. Since new sources of information appear regularly, the trail is not a static search. Successful researchers check for more updated materials to add to their lists as the project unfolds. Appendix A contains a guide that annotates some of the basic resources used to conduct a research trail. The materials can be found in most academic libraries, but, of course, some libraries house larger collections than others.

The research trail is a multi-step process that proceeds from locating the most general guides to historical materials to the more specific works that lead to the identification of primary and secondary sources pertaining to the paper topic. The research trail has four purposes:

- It helps the historian become familiar with the major reference works in history.
- It enables researchers to compile lists of materials for the specific research project. This is especially important since it helps researchers to better understand what has already been written about a topic and how their own work might consider new questions or add nuances.

■ It provides a working list of materials to be read and analyzed for the project and a rationale for their selection over others.

■ It offers information that helps narrow the research topic and frame new questions.

The steps in the research trail are comparable to a tool box that includes all of the necessary research tools. Some "tools" may never be explicitly used; however, researchers never know what tools they may need. It is always better to have a special wrench that may seldom be used than to need a certain kind and not have it among your tools. Familiarity with the appropriate research tools is essential to completing the project.

Preparing for the Research Trail

Throughout the research trail process, beginning historians should record information about each source—such as author, title, city of publication, publisher, and year of publication—as well as how the particular references that provided the sources are organized. In addition, a comment about what materials they provide and some assessment of their value will be useful as the research advances. It is also wise to list the source and page or URL (uniform resource locator) for online materials. This information may be recorded in a note-taking program or in a standard word processing program, by downloading citations from library catalogs or other online sources, or by writing the information on note cards. Researchers should develop a single method for collecting information and stay with it. While this habit may seem tedious at first, it helps reinforce the researcher's citation skill and facilitate constructing the final bibliography. It also simplifies the process of locating the work again among the myriad of citations and note cards that result from any serious project.[2] Through repetition, the process becomes ingrained and is done more or less mechanically.

Doing the Research Trail

The following steps outline the basic research trail. While it may be abbreviated to suit individual needs or as researchers become more knowledgeable about the contents of individual resources, it is also worthwhile to know something about the basic resource tools of history in order to become more self-reliant and confident. The research trail is the most detailed model for conducting exhaustive research. During the stages of the process, any researcher will have a better idea of whether there are sufficient sources to complete a proposed project, which materials to select, and where to begin reading.

Review a standard guide   For beginning historians the trail should commence with a close review of a published guide. Currently, the standard is Ronald H. Fritze, Brian E. Coutts, and Louis A. Vyhnanek, *Reference Sources in History: An Introductory Guide*.[3] This volume includes fourteen sections that explain the

---

[2]For an expanded discussion of note taking, see Chapter 3 (pp. 51–55).

[3]Ronald H. Fritze, Brian E. Coutts, and Louis A. Vyhnanek, *Reference Sources in History: An Introductory Guide* (Santa Barbara, CA and Oxford: ABC-CLIO, 1990).

basic reference types that all researchers should know as they tackle any research project. Specific sections describe bibliographies, book review indexes, periodical guides, guides to newspapers, government publications, geographical and statistical sources (among others), and how to use them. Perusing a good guide will provide insights into resources vital to support any project. After browsing a guide, beginning historians should poke around in the reference section of their local library to become familiar with its organization and to locate its specific types of holdings. Even a basic knowledge of the library's reference section will later save time and can facilitate research.

Review basic guides to reference books and bibliographies of bibliography
Armed with this introductory information, historians are ready to begin a close examination of three important reference sets available in many college libraries:

- Robert Balay, ed., *Guide to Reference Books.*
- Theodore Besterman, *A World Bibliography of Bibliographies and of Bibliographical Catalogues, Calendars, Abstracts, Digests, Indexes, and the Like.*
- *Bibliographic Index: A Cumulative Bibliography of Bibliographies.*[4]

While there are certainly others that might be used fruitfully, these three are the most comprehensive. All beginning researchers should work through each reference for their specific subject areas. After becoming familiar with their organization and contents, researchers may later employ shortcuts for subsequent reasearch projects; however, the first review should be meticulous, with careful, detailed notes recorded.

Balay's *Guide,* the 11th edition of a volume first published by the American Library Association in 1907, is the basic reference for libraries and librarians. It covers works and collections throughout North America. Among its more than 15,000 **annotated** entries, the largest single group, under classification (D), is for history and area studies. (An annotation is a brief description of the contents and nature of a particular work and provides researchers with very basic information.)

Although dated, Besterman's five volumes should also be studied. Global in scope and coverage, this monumental work—the fullest bibliography of bibliographies ever printed—lists more than 117,000 titles by subject and by country, and includes works in all languages.

The *Bibliographic Index* complements Balay and Besterman by listing titles that have appeared since they were last published. By using these resources together and reading them intelligently, the beginning student will likely identify all of the possible bibliographies and references that potentially include information about a given topic. As researchers become more familiar with a particular area of scholarship,

---

[4]Robert Balay, ed., *Guide to Reference Books,* 11th edition (Chicago and London: American Library Association, 1996). Theodore Besterman, *A World Bibliography of Bibliographies and of Bibliographical Catalogues, Calendars, Abstracts, Digests, Indexes, and the Like,* 4th edition (Lausanne, Switzerland: Societas Bibliographica, 1965–1966), 5 vols. *Bibliographic Index: A Cumulative Bibliography of Bibliographies* (New York: H. W. Wilson, 1937–). A WorldCat search indicates 2,260 libraries include Balay in their collection, while Besterman is held by 666 and the *Bibliographic Index* by 1,134. Thus, most students should have access to some of these standard works.

they will learn which bibliographies to consult first; but, newcomers must know where these volumes are located in their library and examine each systematically.

The researcher's paper found in Appendix B began with a review of the three standard bibliographies. This first step in the research trail identified the following: Mary Frear Keeler's updated edition of Godfrey Davies's *Bibliography of British History: Stuart Period, 1603–1714,* William Sachse's *Restoration England, 1660–1689,* and Geoffrey R. Elton's *Annual Bibliography of British and Irish History* (online since 1998, The Royal Historical Society Bibliography, http://www.rhs.ac.uk/bibl/).[5] These bibliographies led the researcher to basic primary and secondary sources on the topic. Individual searches will yield different results; however, each will reward the researcher by identifying the best resources to advance a particular piece of research.

Search standard subject bibliographies and databases   Having reviewed the three Bs (Balay, Besterman, and the *Bibliographic Index*) help the historian to locate bibliographies that relate more directly to the topic. These more specific subject bibliographies and databases should also be systematically examined. The number of subject bibliographies in history is daunting; researchers must avoid becoming overwhelmed or discouraged by the sheer quantity.

One of the most important subject bibliographies is the American Historical Association's *Guide to Historical Literature;* it should be reviewed closely early in the search of the literature for most projects.[6] The third edition (1995) of this richly annotated survey of the most important modern secondary scholarship covers all periods and all countries. The two volumes are divided into topical and chronological sections; each opens with a brief and useful essay outlining recent scholarly interests, issues, and questions. For many topics, particularly in political, diplomatic, or military histories, it may also be helpful to consult the earlier editions (1931, 1961). Researchers should continue conversations similar to those noted earlier in this chapter about the kinds of sources that will be most useful in light of the themes or questions they plan to pursue. These conversations should evolve throughout the

---

[5]Godfrey Davies, ed., *Bibliography of British History, Stuart Period, 1603–1714,* issued under the direction of the American Historical Association and the Royal Historical Society of Great Britain (Oxford: Clarendon Press, 1928); Mary Frear Keeler, ed., 2nd ed. (Oxford: Clarendon Press, 1970); William L. Sachse, ed., *Restoration England, 1660–1689* (Cambridge: Published for the Conference on British Studies at the University Press, 1971); Geoffrey R. Elton, ed., *Annual Bibliography of British and Irish History,* printed for the Royal Historical Society in association with the Institute of Historical Research (Brighton, Sussex: Harvester Press; Atlantic Highlands, NJ: Humanities Press, 1976–). Volumes for 1975–84, edited by G. R. Elton; 1985–87, edited by D. M. Palliser; 1988–92, edited by Barbara English and J. J. N. Palmer; 1993, edited by Katharine F. Bedham, Barbara English and J. J. N. Palmer; 1994, edited by Barbara English and J. J. N. Palmer; 1995–98, edited by Austin Gee. Since 1998, the *RHS Bibliography of British and Irish History* has been available online at http://www.rhs.ac.uk/bibl/.

[6]Mary Beth Norton, ed., *Guide to Historical Literature,* 3rd ed. (New York and Oxford: Oxford University Press, 1995). 2 vols. Students should also consult the earlier editions for many topics. George Matthew Dutcher, ed., *A Guide to Historical Literature, prepared by the Committee on Bibliography of the American Historical Association* (New York: The Macmillan Company, 1931); George Frederick Howe, ed., *A Guide to Historical Literature,* 2nd ed. (New York: Macmillan, 1961). The 3rd edition is found in more than 1,700 college and university libraries in North America.

literature search, becoming gradually more detailed and more substantive. During the close examination of subject bibliographies, researchers begin to recognize specific authors of secondary studies whose publications tend to appear more frequently than others.

The next choice of subject bibliography depends upon the particular area or topic under study. Some bibliographies are regional or national in coverage; others focus on specific topics, themes, or source types. In more recent years, some of the very best subject bibliographies may be accessed online. To increase the probability of locating the fullest number of potential sources, more than one subject bibliography should be consulted. Some examples of standard print and online subject bibliographies for various geographical regions include the following:

Africa

> Asamani, J. O. *Index Africanus.* Stanford, California: Hoover Institution, 1975.

> Blackhurst, Hector, comp. *Africa Bibliography.* London, England, Dover, NH: Manchester University Press, 1985– .

> *Africa Since 1914: A Historical Bibliography.* Santa Barbara, CA: ABC-Clio Information Services, 1985.

Asia

> *Bibliography of Asian Studies.* Ann Arbor, MI: Association of Asian Studies, 1946– .

> *Cumulative Bibliography of Asian Studies, 1941–1965.* Boston: G. K. Hall, 1970.

> *Bibliography of Asian Studies.* http://bas.umdl.umich.edu/b/bas/. Ann Arbor, MI: Association for Asian Studies, 1900s– .

Europe

> Modern European History: A Research Guide. http://www.nypl.org/research/chss/grd/resguides/eurhist.html. New York: New York Public Library, 1996.

> *International Bibliography of the Historical Sciences. Internationale Bibliographie der Geschichtswissenschaften.* Paris: Librarie Armand Colin, 1926– .

> Roach, John, ed. *Bibliography of Modern History.* Cambridge: Cambridge University Press, 1968.

Latin America

> *Handbook of Latin American Studies.* Gainesville: University of Florida Press, 1935– .

> *HAPI, Hispanic American Periodicals Index.* Los Angeles: Latin American Center, University of California. 1970– .

Modern Middle East

> Selected Middle East Reference Works at Columbia University Libraries, prepared by Frank H. Unlandher, Middle East Studies Librarian. http://www.columbia.edu/cu/lweb/indiv/mideast/cuvlm/CulBib.html.

Islam and Islamic Middle East, Reference Works at Stanford University Library. http://www-sul.stanford.edu/depts/ssrg/mideast/guides.html

United States

Writings on American History. Millwood, N.Y., KTO Press, 1902–1990. Some volumes published by the American Historical Association; others by the Library of Congress; annual, irregular.

Merriam, Louise A. and James Warren Oberly, eds. *United States History: A Bibliography of New Writings on American History.* Manchester, England and New York: Manchester University Press, 1995.

The AHA's *Guide* and other subject bibliographies will thus provide a reliable preliminary list of secondary works on most topics. Many also include primary sources. Numerous online search engines allow access to websites that include subject bibliographies to supplement what is available and appropriate in print.

Online searches generally complement or supplement the review of standard printed bibliographies of bibliography and subject bibliographies. They are not intended to replace them. These print bibliographies contain a wealth of information regarding the primary and secondary sources necessary to complete any research project. Once they have been consulted, the beginning researcher should review the list assembled and check the local library holdings to determine which are available. It is wise at this stage to handle them to gain some idea of their value. Next, turn to online searches. Using such broad search engines must be done with the greatest of caution since anyone can create a website and there is no professional review process for them. One of the better online bibliographies is **The Witchcraft Bibliography Project** (http://www.hist.unt.edu/witch.htm) housed at the University of North Texas Department of History website. It is a treasure of primary and secondary sources in multiple languages for witchcraft in early modern Europe. Beginning researchers may profitably consult this site as a model.

Search WorldCat, EBSCO, LibDex, other research databases and online catalogs   A review of the subject bibliographies is followed by a search of important online catalogs: the researcher's institutional library, the catalog of the nearest major research library, WorldCat, EBSCO (particularly Academic Search Premier, ASP), and, if appropriate, LibDex and other online catalogs. An examination of such online resources fills in missing titles and indicates likely libraries that own specific sources.

Each online library catalog has its own idiosyncrasies; however, there are some general guidelines for searching them to produce satisfactory results. It is important to become familiar with the guidelines of a particular library's search engine before conducting a search for sources. Most library catalogs can be searched by keyword, subject, author, and title. Researchers should examine the various online search engines and seek to identify the broadest number of sources. Both beginning and experienced historians may fruitfully begin their searches with **keyword** queries. Such keywords result from the earlier readings on the subject. Many libraries allow for the combination of keywords with

AND, OR, IN, or NOT (a Boolean search) to help identify potential materials. In the beginning researcher's prospectus introduced earlier in this chapter, the proposed topic centered on English towns and cities in the seventeenth century. Some possible Boolean combinations include the following: History London AND social history, English towns OR English urban centers, or English cities NOT London.[7] More varied and creative keyword mixtures will result in a more fruitful search. Some library catalogs also include a browsing function that enables the researcher to highlight the call number for a particular work, and then search for those items that appear on the same or adjacent shelves. If initial combinations fail to produce the desired result, vary the terms or try other keywords. If the resulting combinations are not especially fruitful, then consult a reference librarian and specify what searches have been conducted, what keywords were used, and what the results were.

As the systematic search of subject bibliographies and the local library catalog takes shape, the researcher's conversations and questions should begin to relate more specifically to the viability of the projected topic. Do there appear to be enough secondary source materials on the topic to write this paper? Are the available monographs and journal articles sufficient to support further inquiry into this subject? Did the same author write most of the books and articles on a given topic? These questions and others like them help determine whether or not the original topic idea needs to be modified or changed.

The remaining vital online catalog searches include those of the best research library in the region and WorldCat or other appropriate online catalogs. The former should be searched with an eye to what volumes are not available in the researcher's own library and might reasonably be obtained either through interlibrary loan or by a visit to the research library itself. While conducting this search, historians should also learn how to use their own library's interlibrary loan services. This service provides access to books, articles, and other materials not found in the local library.

WorldCat includes the catalogs of libraries primarily from the United States, Canada, and the United Kingdom, offering scholars access to millions of book titles from more than 9,000 participating libraries and institutions. It is linked to a variety of online resources, including full text and electronic journals, web resources, and computer files. It may be examined using the same types of searches used to identify records in a local library. Another useful feature of WorldCat is that it lists the libraries that hold particular volumes in their collections. This information facilitates ordering titles through interlibrary loan and thereby accelerates research. In addition, individual WorldCat records include a wealth of critical information to assist both beginning and experienced researchers. Individual records may be tagged to simplify identifying only those items the searcher wishes to save, download, or copy. An e-mail button at the bottom of each record allows users to e-mail themselves a copy. Finally, WorldCat is a useful

---

[7]Using the first combination at James Madison University's Carrier Library, for instance, yielded about 150 entries; the second combination yielded about 75; the third about 50. Totals, of course, will vary significantly among libraries.

source to identify the most recently published materials on a topic. LibDex is more international in scope with links to libraries in most countries.

The searches done to this point should identify most books and some articles necessary to complete any research project. The source type most commonly ignored by beginning historians—scholarly journal articles—must however, receive the same careful scrutiny. Journal articles provide ready access to a rich variety of interpretations about a topic and often represent a scholar's initial public discussion of a new idea. Beginning historians would be well served to have a strong grasp of journal articles, which can provide a better understanding of major interpretations than books. At the same time, searching online journal article databases helps familiarize beginning researchers with the most important scholarly journals for the various history sub fields.

There are five principal online databases historians use to locate scholarly journal articles: *PIO (Periodic Index Online), Humanities Index, Social Sciences Index, America: History and Life,* and *Historical Abstracts.* All appear in both print and online versions. The principal advantages of the online versions, if available, is ease of searching. The advantage of the bound volumes, if available, is coverage, since most include access to the most recently published items before they are accessible in online form.

- *PIO (Periodic Index Online)* is probably the fullest electronic index to scholarly periodicals for the study of history currently available. The database includes more than 4,000 periodicals in the humanities and social sciences, and indexes full runs of periodicals published continuously since the eighteenth century. It also covers all chronological periods and includes journals published in about 40 languages. *PIO* is also an essential resource for researchers seeking scholarly book reviews of works published before 1960. Like most online databases, *PIO* is searchable by keyword, title, subject, or author. Some libraries provide direct access to full text versions of these articles through *Periodical Archive Online (PAO)*; others only subscribe to the index. Because of its lengthy chronological coverage and the rich variety of scholarly periodicals included, *PAO* is particularly helpful in identifying journal articles not found in a researcher's local library, thereby facilitating the processing of interlibrary loan requests.

- *Humanities Index* and *Social Sciences Index* include articles from many disciplines. *Humanities Index* provides citation access to about 500 English-language periodicals and is searchable by author, title, or keyword. Updated monthly, it also includes scholarly book reviews. Each record indicates, in addition to the standard bibliographical information, whether or not the journal is **peer reviewed.** (Peer-reviewed journals are more scholarly, because recognized specialists in the discipline have evaluated all articles prior to their publication to determine their value and contribution to knowledge.) *Social Sciences Index* functions in the same manner as *Humanities Index.* These databases include articles and reviews from several disciplines and from all chronological periods. All researchers should become familiar with both of these databases and use them on a regular basis to locate scholarly articles and reviews on any subject. The student researcher, whose paper is referenced throughout the text, examined *Humanities Index* and *Social Sciences Index* to identify several periodical articles used in the paper to enhance the context of the discussion and provide crucial evidence supporting the conclusions. Scholarly articles led to materials not found in the books cited, and helped define the topic in new ways. They provided the student researcher with good information about specific issues relating to the design of London and areas addressed less effectively in the remaining secondary sources used to complete the paper.

■ *America: History and Life* and *Historical Abstracts,* although narrower in scope, are equally valuable. The former includes journal articles and reviews for United States and Canadian history, while the latter does the same for world history since 1453; thus, both are restricted geographically and chronologically. Both, however, provide researchers with abstracts of articles and reviews to help make choices among potential secondary sources. Like most other online databases, records located in *America: History and Life* or *Historical Abstracts* may be saved to a researcher's disk, downloaded directly to a laptop or other computer, or emailed.[8]

Scholarly journal articles identified in any of these five online databases may sometimes be read in full text online through one of three major databases. That is, once the title, author, and other bibliographical information are known, it is possible to find the actual article online as well as in a bound periodical on library shelves. There are three major online full text journal databases for history: *PAO* (which has already been described), *Journal Storage Project (JSTOR),* and *Project Muse.*[9] If a researcher finds a particular title in *America: History and Life,* for instance, it is possible to click and be directly linked to the actual article in full text from one of these databases. If there is no direct link to any of these or other services, the researcher records the citation and locates the journal among the library holdings in hard copy or secures it through interlibrary loan. *PAO, JSTOR,* and *Project Muse* are also searchable using the online search strategies outlined earlier. They provide researchers with ready access to a wealth of scholarly articles and book reviews. Researchers should check with their library homepage or its electronic text listing to determine whether or not periodical articles are available online.

Search and evaluate relevant websites and digitized databases for primary and secondary sources   The examination of printed subject bibliographies and the online search of printed materials are fundamental in identifying appropriate primary and secondary sources. This ever-growing list must be augmented by a

---

[8]Online book reviews, especially of more recent publications may also be accessed through H-NET online. H-NET is an international interdisciplinary organization of scholars and teachers. There is a direct link to reviews from its homepage.

[9]*JSTOR* (Journal Storage Project) began in 1995 with assistance from the Andrew W. Mellon Foundation. It has digitized runs of select scholarly periodicals and made them available online in full text versions. *Project Muse* offers similar networked access to full texts.

search for online materials, the availability of which has increased exponentially with the Internet. Beginning historians now more easily link to manuscripts and documents once only accessible in archives, other repositories, or in microform. The holdings of many national and international archives may be searched via the Internet. Online primary sources are now so voluminous that no discussion can reasonably identify them all; what follows is merely a sampling to suggest some possibilities. The ability to search and locate these collections has already transformed research, and the future is even more promising.

For historians of the United States, the major online resource to locate and identify primary sources is the Library of Congress American Memory website: http://memory.loc.gov/ammem/amhome.html. It offers direct access to millions of digitized records. Its homepage is clearly marked with links to the collections and explanations of how to use them most effectively. The Library of Congress American Memory collection includes written materials, photographic records, motion pictures, and sound recordings. The holdings may be searched by keyword and the system is simple enough for beginners to navigate comfortably. For any topic in United States history requiring primary sources, a virtual visit to the American Memory website is mandatory. Its holdings are regularly supplemented and researchers should check periodically to see what new resources have been added to existing files.

Complementing the holdings of the Library of Congress are the collections of the National Archives and Records Administration at http://www.archives.gov/. NARA's homepage is also easy to navigate, and has many direct links to online documentary records. NARA also links directly to the various presidential libraries, which contain a wealth of digitized information. Although the volume of online records is less than the number digitized by the Library of Congress, the site allows sophisticated searches for manuscripts and other records found among its holdings.

National archives outside the United States may be similarly searched. Many nations and institutions around the globe have established online catalogs or homepages that link to indexes of documents or digitized images. They sometimes include information about ordering hard copies of their holdings or ordering materials through interlibrary loan, though some actually have hypertext records online. For instance, the National Archives of Canada/Archives nationales du Canada at http://www.collectionscanada.ca/, with links in English and French, explains how to order copies or request microfilm items from its collections through interlibrary loan. Such materials may even be borrowed through libraries and institutions outside Canada. Like many others, the Canadian National Archives offers information for beginning researchers explaining how to consult its holdings. Some document categories may be accessed and consulted online. For example, the diaries of former Prime Minister William Lyon Mackenzie King may be searched by date, word, or phrase. The *Colonial Archives* database offers online access to more than 500,000 documents found in the Canadian National Archives. These materials document the British and French colonial periods in Canada, as well as the Catholic Church.

In addition to state archives worldwide, researchers should consult online library holdings. Many universities, colleges, departments, and individuals have pioneered efforts to digitize primary sources (most often, though not exclusively, those found in their own special collections). Beginners should be aware that most require a user ID and password, and are therefore closed to outsiders; however, many resources are open and available. Copyright laws, however, govern all such digitized sources and researchers should make certain they understand and follow all regulations. The proper citation of these and all other records will be discussed in Chapter 6.

Five examples illustrate the range of source possibilities currently available:

- *History Matters,* http://historymatters.gmu.edu/, is an excellent site for various materials on United States history. Maintained by George Mason University, it includes numerous primary sources, guides to analyzing various kinds of primary sources, as well as reviewed and annotated links to other websites pertaining to United States history.

- The *Internet History Sourcebooks Project,* http://www.fordham.edu/halsall, is another collection of public domain historical texts intended for educational use. The sourcebooks include materials for ancient, medieval, and modern histories and the collection for medieval and Byzantine studies is especially rich. The site also includes Asian and African resources and is easy to navigate.

- *Documenting the American South,* found at the Academic Affairs Library of the University of North Carolina at Chapel Hill, http://docsouth.unc.edu/, is a comprehensive digital archive. It is an outstanding collection of materials relating to Southern history from colonial times through the first decades of the twentieth century. There are more than 1,000 books and manuscripts in the collection and it continues to grow.

- *The Records of Earls Colne,* http://linux02.lib.cam.ac.uk/earlscolne/intro/project.htm, is a comprehensive compilation of materials on an English village spanning from the late medieval period to the mid-nineteenth century. It includes all estate, ecclesiastical, and state records for the village.

- *The Valley of the Shadow: Two Communities in the American Civil War,* http://www.iath.virginia.edu/vshadow2/, contains a variety of public and private sources on Chambersburg, Pennsylvania and Staunton, Virginia.

The research topic certainly determines the primary sources that should be consulted, and historians should now consider the types available through the Internet when completing a research trail. Student Jack Sheehan located many printed primary sources through his research trail; however, he lacked an official contemporary account that described the actual fire of London to corroborate information contained in diaries, letters, and other sources. His online searches led him to the newspaper the *London Gazette* for early September 1666, http://www.adelpha.com/~davidco/History/fire1.htm. The online source was not essential to his research project, but it did verify other evidence and enhanced the final product.

In the search for primary sources, researchers also make extensive use of **microform** collections. Microform is the filming on reel or card of large sets of materials. These materials can be read using a special microform reader found in most libraries. Most libraries list their microform holdings in the online catalog. These collections allow researchers direct access to vast quantities of material and many libraries now provide either photocopying or digitizing services. Perhaps the clearest examples of microforms are newspapers, printed books, and popular magazines. In recent years, many of these sources have been digitized and placed on the Internet to provide easier access.

Identify available reference sources for use throughout the research project   After locating and recording the most useful primary and secondary sources that will be used to construct a body of historical research, beginning researchers should next identify a group of reference tools that can be used to answer questions that emerge from the reading and analysis of individual sources. While the permutations are limitless, these questions are often about people, places, events, even terminology, and they require clarification if the research is to proceed smoothly. All researchers should become familiar with the reference works essential to successful scholarship in their subfields of inquiry. Knowing which are the best dictionaries for terms, biographical sketches, or background information, and having them readily available will save hours, avoid embarrassing mistakes, and help keep research focused on more significant issues. Some of these reference materials may apply to issues of writing and scholarly citation. Having a copy of Turabian or *The Chicago Manual of Style* will allow citation and other questions to be answered promptly and correctly.[10] A guide to writing can help with issues of grammar, organization, and style. In addition, every historian should own a dictionary and thesaurus. Among the best dictionaries is the *Oxford English Dictionary (OED),* which is available online, in CD format, and in print. An etymological dictionary, the OED provides definitions for many different time periods with examples of how a word was used in the past. If it is not possible to gain access to this dictionary, researchers should consult basic guides to reference works or reference sections of the local library to find the best substitute. The same process should be followed for encyclopedias and atlases.

If the topic under examination requires knowledge of a different calendar or the cost and value of specific items, the researcher should anticipate these kinds of needs as early as possible and identify necessary references in print or online. Understanding the distinctions between the Gregorian, Julian, or other calendars may be important and those students considering global topics must make certain they know the calendar used in a particular region or how to quickly find such information. Similarly, researchers often need to know the modern value of goods, services, or monies found in the historical evidence. A useful website for comparing the value of American and British money since the seventeenth

---

[10]Kate L. Turabian, *A Manual for Writers of Term Papers, Theses, and Dissertations,* 6th ed. (Chicago: University of Chicago Press, 1996); *The Chicago Manual of Style,* 15th ed. (Chicago: University of Chicago Press, 2003). A full discussion of citation form can be found in Chapter 6.

century is http://www.eh.net/ehresources/howmuch/sourcenote. As new questions occur during the process of assembling and interpreting evidence, compiling a list of reference sources will help resolve these potentially thorny matters.

Know the scholarly journals that print articles in the area of the research   Finally, as part of the search for journal articles, historians should become familiar with journals that include articles on their research topic. One purpose is to have an idea of the most logical journals to search for book reviews once the actual process of examining the secondary sources begins. In examining these journals, keep in mind how long it takes after a book is published for a review to appear. This is particularly important if the researcher lacks access to online book review services. Those with Internet access should consult H-Net Online Reviews, http://www2.h-net.msu.edu/reviews/, which is a part of H-Net, a collaborative organization of scholars. H-Net Online Reviews also include listservs in many subfields that can help beginning researchers better understand current debates and discussions among scholars.

A more significant reason to become familiar with the journals in a historical field is to readily know the most important ones and to read their contents regularly. Even if the research topic is a classroom assignment, knowing the basic journal sources is a good idea because it helps beginning researchers learn from good scholarly models and improves their understanding of a basic disciplinary tool.

The comprehensive search for primary, secondary, and reference materials is now concluded and research turns to examining the sources identified. If each step has been followed systematically and all the sources discussed have been exploited fully, researchers can be confident that they have not overlooked anything major and are now ready to initiate conversations to decide which of the many works they have found are essential and which are less important. Although the process of locating resources is labor intensive and there may be a temptation to omit several steps or ignore certain guides, bibliographies, or other potential resources, the consequences of such an approach may create problems, especially for the beginning researcher. Being aware of all the major secondary and primary sources on a topic, especially if the references have been annotated in the work consulted, allows researchers to make informed decisions as they decide which sources are most important to their study. Having identified the secondary and primary sources through the research trail, the researcher begins the process of critical reading and analysis.

3

Tools for Analysis—
Secondary Sources

The identification and selection of evidence described in the research trail is only the first step in the process of writing history. After locating the sources, historians review and evaluate the secondary literature on a topic. For beginning historians in particular, it is wise to begin scholarly analysis with the secondary sources. This examination offers researchers a basic vocabulary about the topic, a good sense of historical context, and an appreciation of the contributions of earlier historians. The questions posed by these historians, their interpretations of the sources, and the ways in which they supported their arguments provide a framework for approaching a topic. Once this information is examined, the researcher is better equipped to add to the body of historical knowledge with new analyses and interpretations.

Reading the secondary sources begins the exciting chase for historical knowledge. A generation ago, immersion in the secondary literature required a trip to one or more libraries to locate books, journal articles, dissertations, reviews, and other materials that offered scholarly interpretations of a past event, as well as a visit to the interlibrary loan desk to request those materials not readily available. The advent of the Internet has made a wide and growing array of secondary sources available at the click of the mouse. Historians still must visit libraries and use the resources of interlibrary loan to find the necessary secondary materials, but only after searching the vast quantities of secondary literature available online.

A careful review of the secondary literature is essential to historical research and writing on several levels. As the first part of the research process, it will shape how a historian begins to think about a topic and the historical context. More subtle and perhaps more important, the final result of the historian's efforts is a contribution to the existing secondary literature. Historians must therefore approach secondary works critically from the outset, questioning what they read through a conversation with the secondary literature and, by extension, with the historians who wrote them. This chapter will examine the critical reading of secondary sources.

WHAT IS A SECONDARY SOURCE?

Often, a textbook, or a section of a textbook, piques the researcher's interest. This can lead to consulting a historical dictionary or encyclopedia to learn more about the topic. If the subject proves interesting enough, it may become a topic for research. Most historians proceed from this point, beginning with a careful collection of the secondary literature discovered on the research trail. **Secondary sources** are interpretations of the past written by historians relying on **primary evidence,** which are contemporary accounts of an event. Unlike a novel, secondary historical works are nonfiction. Secondary works include **monographs,**[1] **biographies,** and **scholarly articles,** which offer scholarly interpretations of cause, effect, implication, and meaning. Researchers should also be familiar with scholarly reference materials and read them when necessary. They may include **textbooks, historical dictionaries, encyclopedias,** and **other printed online materials.**

Reading secondary sources should be an active process that involves critical review of all the material. Initially, historians may seek answers to the basic questions of who, what, where, when, and why. Eventually the inquiry should become more sophisticated. A review of the secondary works has three important purposes:

- To provide background material on a topic
- To provide historical context
- To provide historiographical context, including the theoretical and methodological approaches employed by historians

The concepts of historical context and historiographical context need some explanation.

HISTORICAL CONTEXT

One of the most important intellectual contributions historians make is their ability to place people, ideas, and events in a **historical context.** Historical context can be described as the forces that shaped people's lives, or the beliefs and mindset people possessed during a particular time. For example, it would be difficult to understand 1950s America without knowing about the Cold War, challenges to existing racial relations, or the impact of television and the automobile. Such

---

[1] A thesis-centered extended essay that nonhistorians simply call a book.

context yields valuable perspective by conveying a sense of what has changed and what has persisted over time. The old adages that "people never change" and that "history repeats itself" could not be further from the truth. Historians recognize that technology, wealth, values, religious beliefs, language, and a host of other factors can vary greatly even within a generation. Such changes render much of the past a foreign country. In much the same way that one must learn a foreign language to begin to communicate and understand that culture, so too must the historian understand the historical context of a particular time and place.

Secondary sources provide excellent access to these different worlds by providing the historian with an examination of a particular event, issue, or trend during a time period, or a description of everyday life in a particular historical era. An understanding of historical context enables the historian to better understand a period on its terms, rather than impose present values and points of view on the past. Without an understanding of historical context, it is impossible to understand and appreciate the differences between past and present, as well as to discern that which has changed little or not at all.

HISTORIOGRAPHICAL CONTEXT

Secondary sources are also invaluable in helping one understand the **historiography** of a period or theme. Historiography is the history of how historians' interpretations and methodologies have changed regarding a specific topic. Some of this change is generational; historians often reflect many of the same values, biases, and perspectives of their own time.

The discoveries of new primary sources, as well as new approaches to the use of existing primary sources, also influence historiographic trends. For example, the opening of Soviet archives following the collapse of communism shed new light on many important events in twentieth-century global history. It is more difficult to ascertain historiographical context than historical context. But a familiarity with the types of questions historians have asked about a topic, their approach to a subject, their use of sources and, in particular, the dominant interpretations of a historical period or theme provide all historians with a sense of how to frame and approach their own questions. A close search through the standard bibliographies and other reference sources provides access to the historiographical context of a subject.

WHICH SECONDARY SOURCES ARE BEST?

Historians must be able to determine which of their secondary sources are most useful. The research trail, discussed in Chapter 2, serves two purposes when considering secondary sources:

- To familiarize students with the most useful guides and bibliographies
- To enable researchers to locate and conduct a preliminary evaluation of specific sources

By reading guides, bibliographies, abstracts, and book reviews, researchers can save time in determining which secondary sources are best. In a perfect world where time is not a problem and where deadlines do not exist, researchers could take the time to review all of the extant secondary literature turned up by the research trail. However, such a world does not exist.

The research trail enables the historian to identify the most important sources for consultation. Most beginning researchers will have examined the American Historical Association's *Guide to Historical Literature,* as well as located subject bibliographies as part of the research trail. In addition, **abstracts** of books and articles, annotated bibliographies, and bibliographic essays are useful for this purpose. These reference works often identify the best scholarship on a particular topic. Abstracts and annotations offer fairly simple synopses of a book or article, providing a brief summary and little else.

Beginning historians are well-advised to consult comprehensive abstracts. The best collections of abstracts are described in Chapter 2. For North American (U.S. and Canadian) history since 1492, researchers begin with *America: History and Life.* This database provides brief abstracts of scholarly journal articles and bibliographic entries for doctoral dissertations and book reviews. The non–North American equivalent is *Historical Abstracts,* which includes journal article and book review abstracts on world history subjects since 1453, as well as bibliographic information on monographs and doctoral dissertations. For earlier periods and more global areas, *WilsonWeb OmniFile* includes similar materials.

One of the most useful sources of information on scholarship is the **book review.** They differ from abstracts and book reports by going beyond a summary to offer analysis of a book's strengths, weaknesses, approach, use of sources, and appropriate audience. Scholars frequently make use of reviews to better understand a monograph's content and place in the literature. Historians of the United States and Canada can locate relatively recent reviews by using such resources as *America: History and Life;* non–North American historians must examine *Historical Abstracts. Book Review Digest* also provides access to book reviews. A fuller resource for earlier scholarship is the *Combined Retrospective Index to Journals in History, 1838–1974.* The first three are available as online databases. The fourth, printed in 11 volumes, is found in many libraries.

Beginning scholars should avoid relying solely on abstracts and book reviews when making final selections about which journal articles, monographs, and dissertations to consult, but they can use these guides effectively to eliminate sources.

THE PRELIMINARY REVIEW

Despite the usefulness of bibliographies, guides, abstracts, and book reviews, students will ultimately have to make choices about secondary sources on their own. Some monographs and articles may be too recent to appear in the reference works listed above. It is not always possible to determine if a book, article, or website is worthwhile; therefore, it is helpful to understand how to conduct a preliminary review of a secondary source. The beginning historian should ask several questions of a secondary source before determining its usefulness.

Who Is the Author?   Many monographs offer brief biographical information about the author, and some journal articles and websites do as well. A quick consultation of the Internet or the *Directory of American Scholars* or *Contemporary Authors* (now the *Literary Resource Center*). In the library reference section can generally provide more information. Focus on the author's qualifications. For example, does he or she possess professional training, such as a PhD? While one need not be a professionally trained historian, such qualifications generally mean a more scholarly approach to a topic. Regardless of the author's qualifications, one should determine if the author has written works on this topic previously. If not, has the author written other reputable historical works on the time period or the theme?

Who Is the Audience for This Work?   Knowing the audience can often tell much about the work itself. The inclusion of footnotes and a bibliography suggests a scholarly audience. Is it written for a popular audience? For children? Often, the publisher indicates the anticipated audience. In addition, the tone of a secondary source may yield clues about the audience. For example, essays aimed at a popular audience are likely to be well written, but may lack depth of analysis.

When Was the Source Written?   Although some might insist that only the most recent scholarship is worthwhile, knowledgeable historians understand that a number of fine monographs, articles, and lectures appeared in years past. The most recent scholarship offers the advantage of being able to reflect upon and incorporate earlier interpretations. In addition, the values and beliefs of a particular time may influence the historian's interpretation, but older scholarship is often of great use.

Who Published the Secondary Work?   Knowing who published a monograph or scholarly article is also important. Quality scholarship is generally produced by university presses and scholarly journals (which produce monographs and articles for academic audiences), and trade presses with a background in academic publishing. Such works undergo a **peer review process.** This process begins with an editor, or members of an editorial staff, reviewing an essay to see if it meets scholarly standards. If the internal review is positive, the essay is sent to two or three leading academic experts in the field, who offer a critique of the work, recommendations for revision, as well as a final recommendation of whether the work should be published by the press or journal.

Some scholarly presses and journals carry more prestige than others, although one should not assume a rigid hierarchy of publishers. Many excellent works have been produced in unusual venues, so it is important to examine a book or article carefully on its own merits. Regardless of where they are published, most of the best monographs and articles have gone through a lengthy peer review process and may be accepted as reliable.

Does the Secondary Source Include Footnotes and a Bibliography?   If so, how complete are the footnotes? Footnotes indicate that the author can substantiate the claims made in a book or article. Conversely, a lack of footnotes might mean that the book has been produced for a less-than-scholarly audience, or that the author's reputation is so great that footnotes are deemed unnecessary by the publisher.

Bibliographies are especially useful if they are annotated or appear as a bibliographical essay. A researcher should examine the sources in the bibliography. Are primary sources included? Is the collection diverse? Do most of the sources that appear in the bibliography also appear in the footnotes? Inexperienced scholars might cite a number of sources in their bibliography, but if few actually appear in the footnotes, this is likely a disingenuous attempt to "pad" the bibliography.

THE INTERNET—OPPORTUNITY AND PROBLEM

The selection of secondary sources has become more problematic with the emergence of the Internet and the proliferation of websites. Although the Internet has democratized publication by providing an unprecedented number of venues for publishing one's ideas, and has made an abundance of information available with a few clicks of the mouse, it has also introduced a number of problems for the researcher. The egalitarianism of the Internet, one of its great strengths, can also be a weakness because there is no peer review process. On the web, all authors may appear equal. So how does the researcher know what is reliable and what is not? While many sites are reputable and offer easy access to useful information, the web is full of sites containing half truths, lies, conspiracy theories, and distortions conjured by individuals and groups who possess little more than an agenda and an active imagination. Most of these sites might be useful for conducting a study of modern psychopathologies, but are of little use to the historian. With monographs and scholarly articles, a well-established peer-review process enables scholars to know with reasonable certainty that a secondary source is reputable. When reviewing literature on the Internet, the researcher **must** make use of a review process similar to that for other secondary sources.

Who Is the Author of the Website?

Sites run by scholars, scholarly organizations, universities, libraries, and archives are likely to be reputable. Since Internet sites generally indicate who maintains, produces, or edits the site, discerning this information should be relatively easy. Many of these have the added benefit of providing hot links to other websites. In many ways, these online guides provide a preliminary version of the more traditional guides available in print. An example of a first-rate website is the American Council of Learned Societies History E-Book Project, located at http://historyebook.org/titlelist.html. Information made available through hot links at the site clearly demonstrate its reliability. Another highly regarded website is the American Memory website, http://memory.loc.gov/, maintained by the Library of Congress.

Conversely, sites run by individuals or groups with an avowed agenda will have little regard for anything other than advancing their own agenda. A keyword search of "Holocaust" will turn up over one million "hits," a small percentage of which will deny the Nazis' well-documented extermination of European Jews. For example, the Committee for Open Debate on the Holocaust (CODOH) archive of Historical Revisionism maintains a website at http://www.codoh.com/. A perusal of the website will reveal that its author does not believe that the Nazis engaged in the systematic extermination of the Jews during World War II. While the title might convey a sense of legitimacy, the site does not allow researchers to test the credentials of those who maintain the website. Perhaps a more important way to check a website is to compare known facts with information contained within the website. Where significant discrepancies exist, beware.

A second, and perhaps more common problem with websites, is their seductiveness. It requires less effort to sit at home in front of a computer at any convenient time rather than to make the trip to a library or archive. Despite the vast and growing quantity of material available on the web, numerous sources cannot be found online.

READING THE SECONDARY SOURCE

Historians review secondary sources on a variety of levels. They begin by trying to learn more about the specific topic they are studying, but they are also interested in understanding historical context, and are eager to discern historiographical nuance and scholarly approach. The reading that often begins a research process is basic and informational. In some cases, a researcher will discover that much has been written on a topic. For example, a student interested in writing a paper on the rise of Nazism in Germany would quickly discover that a mountain of information exists. However, the existing scholarship might provide suitable context for the exploration of a more limited topic, which might still address the larger question.

Another aspect of reading secondary sources is to determine the historiographical landscape. There are two major ways to do this. First, a researcher may read several works that interpret the same topic in different ways. From this reading, the beginning researcher develops an appreciation of the various interpretations of the topic and the evidence used to construct and support the arguments. Second, a researcher can read a historiographical essay that outlines the various scholarly interpretations.[2] Secondary sources may also demonstrate what historians have not yet discovered.

READING CRITICALLY

Historical reading must go beyond gaining a general understanding of a topic. One of the most important historical skills is reading critically. This is different from simply knowing how to read. Many beginning historians complain that

---

[2]There is a fuller discussion of historiography later in this chapter.

they cannot remember what they read. This is not surprising, as the investigation of a new topic often presents a profusion of new and unfamiliar information. One of the best approaches to reading is **not** to simply open to page 1 and begin reading. If the researcher wants to retain background and contextual material and understand the author's argument, other approaches must be employed. The initial examination of a topic might begin with some general reading about an event of interest. By doing so, the historian can begin to learn the who, what, and where of the event in question. The beginning researcher should also consider taking cursory notes about these questions. Early selective reading should also include a perusal of the index, table of contents, footnotes, and bibliography. But to understand the process more deeply, it is essential to go beyond an understanding of the basic events and to interpret what is significant about them. This requires a more critical read of the material.

One of the most important attributes for reviewing secondary sources is knowing how to read them. Many inexperienced historians need to learn how to read critically. To fully grasp the argument offered in a several-hundred-page monograph, or even in a 30-page journal article, a careful reading of the prefatory and introductory materials is mandatory. While those uninitiated to the standards of critical reading often skip these sections as extraneous, the preface and introduction are chock-full of important information. Most modern secondary sources will offer the reader a fairly clear statement of their **thesis** early in the essay, or in the preface of the monograph. The thesis is the central argument around which the monograph, journal article, or lecture is developed. Knowing the thesis of a secondary source is requisite to understanding the reading, as most authors use the central argument as a "spine" that holds together the body of their narrative.

An examination of Jack Sheehan's paper provides the reader with a clear statement of his argument at the bottom of his first page:

> Many architects and city planners worked on the rebuilding of the city over the years that followed. However, a plan to build a unified city of grandeur fell greatly short. Due to the elaborate plans, property laws, general disagreement, and the inability to coalesce the plans into reality, London soon became the ideal city that was never realized.

Like many journal article length studies, Mr. Sheehan uses his introductory paragraph to set the stage for the paper and state his argument.

Reading the **conclusion** can further enhance the understanding of a scholarly work. The conclusion does more than summarize the contents of a monograph or scholarly article. Most recent historical scholarship contains an elaborate restatement of the thesis as well as drawing subsidiary and related conclusions from the study. Again, refer to Jack Sheehan's conclusion:

> Even though none of the plans were undertaken, London was still rebuilt to a better standard than it had held previously. The roads were now wider, the houses safer, and the streets cleaner. The social impacts of the fire and fear of what was to happen to the city had driven the people to

their breaking points. The people did not seek a magnificent work for themselves; instead they sought a functioning economic area that was safe from any more tragedy. It is this mindset that forced Parliament, the King, and city officials to rebuild the area in a manner that incorporated safety precautions and also speediness. Although fires still struck the city on a regular basis, no significant damage was done to London until the mid-twentieth century. What is more important than the actual design of London as it stands today, are the thoughts and ideas that the committee of men in the latter half of the seventeenth century dreamed the city would look like. So, whether the city was built according to the ideal plans or not, the seeds of the progressive city planning had been planted, and it would not be long before others noticed, but the dream of an ideal city of London died within a year of the fire.

The concluding paragraph offers a restatement and brief elaboration of Jack Sheehan's central argument, while tying up some additional loose ends about the legacy of the fire and the reconstruction of the city.

Knowing the thesis and conclusion of a monograph, biography, dissertation, or scholarly article can provide important clues about the main points of a work. In addition, a review of citation materials, and, if available, a table of contents and index can provide additional clues about a work.

THE PAST IS A FOREIGN COUNTRY—READING FOR HISTORICAL CONTEXT

"The past is a foreign country"[3] and one cannot make accurate historical assertions without an understanding of historical context. Because of the unique nature of the historical past, historians must read beyond the narrow confines of their chosen topic to develop a better understanding of a time period. Only by understanding this broader setting can one begin to understand and interpret an event or trend.

Reading for historical context involves looking at an event from a number of vantage points; some close to the event in question, others more distant. A historian who sets out to write a story about a figure in the Mexican Revolution might provide an exciting narrative of events, but without some understanding of conditions during the period of the *Porfiriato* before the Revolution, the impact of global capitalism in late nineteenth-century Mexico, the concerns of traditional Indian communities, and the relationship between the United States and Mexico, the historian could not begin to provide a satisfactory interpretation of what transpired in early twentieth-century Mexico or comment effectively on its significance.

---

[3]English writer L. P. Hartley used this phrase to open his award-winning novel, *The Go-Between* (London: H. Hamilton, 1953).

A list of questions that beginning researchers should keep in mind while reading for historical context might include the following:

- Who are the important participants in a particular event? How did they respond to events?

- What factors seemed to condition this response?

- What are their values? Beliefs? Are they at odds with others of the time period? In what ways?

- What is the economic system like? Political system? Social structure? Culture? How do these function? To what extent are issues such as ethnicity, class, and gender important? Are these changing?

- What seem to be the major historical forces at work during the time? How do these effect different groups?

Without such grounding in context, the uninitiated are likely to make judgments that are **ahistorical**—that is, without historical basis. Often, this comes in the guise of **presentism,** where an individual with little regard for historical context either reads the present into past events or more commonly assumes that present points of view, assumptions, and even word usage were the same as in past generations. Writers employing such methods often grotesquely distort the past, sometimes out of ignorance, but often to advance some sort of present political agenda. For example, many partisan writers have credited President Ronald Reagan with single-handedly "winning" the Cold War. Although President Reagan played an important role in the demise of Soviet-style communism, to argue that the achievement was his alone would ignore the significant contributions of many others—two generations of American presidents, whose policies he followed; Pope John Paul II, Mikhail Gorbachev, and Lech Walesa in challenging communist orthodoxy; as well as the millions of people living in communist countries who ultimately had to face down these regimes. A usable past is important to understand the present and how it came to be; it is absolutely essential that the reconstruction and interpretation of past events take place within the discipline of historical context. Anything less is ahistorical, and, indeed, intellectually dishonest.

READING FOR HISTORIOGRAPHICAL CONTEXT

Historians read secondary sources to develop a sense of background, historical context, historiographical context, and to understand the author's central argument and use of sources. Beginning researchers may have little trouble grasping background material or the concept of historical context, but have less familiarity with historiographical context or even how to identify the central argument of an essay. Having a sense of historiography can help the reader understand why interpretations, methodology, and scholarly approaches have evolved. Although the uninitiated may believe that history is simply an arranging of facts into a narrative, history is really an interpretation based on the weight of available evidence. This allows historians wide, but not unlimited, latitude in interpreting the past. In addition, the questions asked by historians and the approaches—both theoretical and methodological—employed by historians have varied greatly over time. It is necessary that the researcher have some sense of the types of theory and methodology historians have employed in the past, and which of those have held up over time and which have not.

Some historiographical change is quite stark. For example, historians of the American frontier traditionally followed Frederick Jackson Turner's thesis as a key to understanding the significance of the frontier in U.S. history. Writing during the 1890s at the end of the Indian Wars and following the Census Bureau's announcement that the unbroken line of frontier in the West no longer existed, Turner sought to explain what the end of this era meant to Americans. According to Turner, the frontier process could be explained as the unfolding of "superior" Western culture across the continent where it displaced more "backward" peoples, plants, animals, and landscapes. Turner believed that the frontier experience gave America its unique character, including democracy, and helped to explain America's exceptional nature. Writing in the late nineteenth and early twentieth centuries deeply affected Turner's perspective, giving him strongly nationalist views and stridently ethnocentric beliefs that led him to laud the westward movement of American culture as a sign of progress. Today, most historians describe the process as one of conquest, dispossession, and genocide. Patricia Nelson Limerick, writing in the more multiculturally spirited milieu of the late twentieth century, argues in her work, *Legacy of Conquest: The Unbroken Past of the American West,* that the conquest of the West was incomplete and that the so-called conquered were beginning to reassert their cultures.[4]

Often, historiographical fashions are not such binary opposites. The scholarship of the American Revolution has evolved over time, but for the past 100 years, two major approaches have dominated with only a few interruptions: A Whig (and later neo-Whig) thesis has argued that the Revolution was ideological in nature, while Progressives (and more recently neo-Progressives) believe that social conflict is the main cause of the Revolution. Here, each side has subsumed some of the other's argument while relying on increasingly sophisticated methodologies to make their case. Only through understanding the historiographical context can a student test a prevailing thesis against the evidence and argue, pro or con, with the existing interpretations.[5]

---

[4]Frederick Jackson Turner, "The Significance of the Frontier in American History," *The Frontier in American History* (New York: Henry Holt and Co., 1920); Patricia Nelson Limerick, *The Legacy of Conquest: The Unbroken Past of the American West* (New York: W. W. Norton, 1987).

[5]An excellent and brief introduction to the major schools of thought on the American Revolution can be found in Richard D. Brown's introduction to "Chapter 1: Interpreting the American Revolution," in *Major Problems in the Era of the American Revolution, 1760–1791: Documents and Essays*, 2nd ed., ed. Richard D. Brown (Boston: Houghton Mifflin, 2000). Alfred F. Young offers a more detailed discussion with a decidedly neo-Progressive slant in his introduction to *Beyond the American Revolution: Explorations in the History of American Radicalism*, ed. Alfred F. Young (DeKalb: Northern Illinois University Press, 1993). A detailed, but slightly dated bibliographic essay, see: Edward Countryman, *The American Revolution* (New York: Hill and Wang, 1985), pp. 246–274.

But how do historians read for historiographical context? How do they confidently determine an author's central argument? A careful examination of book reviews appearing in scholarly journals offers an excellent means to quickly discover much about a monograph's historiographical context. But what if the reviews are less than helpful, or if the monograph is too recent to have been reviewed, or if the beginning researcher is dealing with a journal article or a dissertation, which generally are not reviewed?

Many important clues about a secondary work may be found in the prefatory or introductory materials. Here, historians can find fairly clear assertions of thesis. The preface and introduction provide hints about the author's **point of view, use of sources,** and **theoretical approach.** For scholars who are evaluating a secondary source, it is essential that they understand the author's **point of view.** Often, authors simply state their point of view, but even if they do not, there are numerous clues. Footnotes, historiographical footnotes, and bibliographical essays often include references to favored works, historians, or philosophers, offering clear clues to an author's preferences. But to fully understand the author's point of view, beginning researchers must know who the author is, when he or she lived, what his or her values are, under what conditions the secondary work was written, and the author's relationship to the topic. Researchers can learn much about the author through reviews of his or her works, online searches, and by consulting guides such as *The Literature Resource Center* (formerly *Contemporary Authors*). For example, a search of "Eric J. Hobsbawm," one of the most important historians writing in the English language, would provide a clear hint as to his approach with the following statement:

> "Hobsbawm is important," states *Historian* contributor Ronald Story, "for students of mass and popular culture generally as well as of music and jazz, because his Marxist grounding allows him to see jazz as socially produced and in international perspective."[6]

Working-class issues and revolution are major themes throughout Hobsbawm's work. Here, one can clearly see that Professor Hobsbawm's use of Marxist theory influences his point of view.

One of the most important influences on an author's approach to history is the use of **theory.** Those who acclaim the use of theory argue that it helps historians consider new types of evidence, or consider old types of evidence in new ways. They claim that theory can shape new questions to be tested against the evidence, and provide a structure for understanding an event or trend in a new way. Indeed, many important contributions among historians are informed by the theory, enabling historians to consider the past from a different perspective, thus enhancing the understanding of it. For example, Marxist theory—with its emphasis on economic structures and their impact on society, culture, and ideology—led Marxist and non-Marxist historians to a clearer understanding of the interplay between these factors. The linguistic turn, employed by historians

---

[6]Information on Eric J. Hobsbawm can be found at *The Literature Resource Center*, http://galenet.galegroup.com.

informed by postmodern theory, has carefully analyzed language as a cultural arti-fact that yields important clues about past societies. This development has led his-torians to more carefully examine the nuanced meaning of words and phrases used in the past, since such words and phrases often had different meaning. An etymological dictionary that examines the origin and historical development of words and phrases can be useful, but more often only a thorough knowledge of the historical context will enable the researcher to truly understand the mean-ing. Historians of gender have used theory to illuminate key aspects of how men and women relate to power and to one another. Generally speaking, gender his-torians have examined the past by looking at how the expectations and limits of gender roles during a certain period affected historical actors. These findings have opened up a world of structure, thought, and culture that has greatly enriched historians' understanding of the past.

Despite the effective use of theory, many historians remain bitterly critical of its application to historical study. Arguing that the selection of a particular theory often determines the final conclusion, they see theory as driving the selection of facts to fit a preconceived agenda. Still, a familiarity with theory and its applica-tion can greatly enhance the historian's understanding of monographs and journal articles, and can help to shape his or her own approach to research.

It is important to remember that theories should be tested against the evi-dence, but the evidence should not be made to conform to the theory. Marxist theory might seem the likely key to understanding working-class unrest in a soci-ety, but such an approach might exclude the roles that religion and ethnicity play. Theory can yield great benefits to an understanding of the past, but it should be employed with caution since using evidence to fit a preconceived structure only obscures the understanding of the past, while relieving the author of the difficult burden of thinking for himself or herself.

READING FOR SOURCES

The types of sources employed by a historian can also offer important clues about point of view. For example, a study of France's role in Vietnam that included only primary sources from French officials involved in the war's decision making, clearly shows a possible bias on the part of the author. The **historiographical footnote** offers the best introduction to the most important sources in a mono-graph or journal article. This type of footnote is essential reading, and it generally appears in the same paragraph where the author offers the thesis statement. It offers the author's view of the major sources that have shaped his or her approach to the subject, and is an abbreviated version of the bibliography. The note pro-vides brief descriptions of major sources and comments on their respective use-fulness, but it also should demonstrate that the evidence is multifaceted and represents a variety of perspectives.

Jack Sheehan included his historiographic footnote at the end of the para-graph where he made his thesis statement. The footnote appears in Sheehan's paper, which appears in Appendix B. His historiographic footnote is a model; he organizes sources around major themes in his paper, offering comments on the usefulness of each source. He also includes significant primary sources.

The historiographical footnote provides helpful information concerning the significance of different sources used by an author, but a perusal of all the footnotes in a monograph or scholarly article can provide an even better idea of how sources are used. Finally, reading scholarly reviews of monographs can also provide the reader with a clearer sense of a work's value.

Having read the preface and introduction, conclusion, bibliography (if one exists), historiographical footnote, and footnotes, and having consulted scholarly reviews, the historian should be able to discern the author's argument, conclusions, approach to the subject, methodology, major sources, and to some extent biases and assumptions. Thus equipped, the historian is ready to begin reading the rest of the work with the foreknowledge of what the author is trying to say and why, rather than trying to make sense of a profusion of evidence presented in a sometimes confusing narrative. Such preliminary efforts will actually result in a better understanding of the material read, and should also enable the beginning researcher to complete the reading in a more expeditious manner.

No scholar working with deadlines has time to read every secondary source on a topic. The research trail, discussed in Chapter 2, provides a guide on how to select and choose the most useful sources. After narrowing the list of suitable secondary sources, the historian reads several of the important monographs and essays on a topic. Researchers may not be able to read them all, but should read until they have a strong sense of both the historical and historiographical contexts. Short cuts are available to those with some degree of mastery of these contexts. To reiterate, experienced scholars often rely on book reviews and abstracts to get a sense of the argument in a particular book or article. Relying on others' expert opinions about a work helps narrow choices. Researchers should avoid an over-reliance on others' critiques, but their usefulness should not be underestimated either. As such, book reviews are one of the most important tools available to historians seeking to judge the value of a monograph. Knowing how to read and write such reviews is central to the craft of a historian.

THE REVIEW

One of the best ways that young scholars can learn to evaluate a secondary source is by writing a book review or a review of a scholarly journal article. A book or scholarly article review can be written at a variety of different levels for a number of different audiences, but all reviews should accomplish the following:

- Give the reader a sense of the book or article
- Comment on the quality of the work
- Compare the work with other, similar works

- Assess the contribution to the scholarship
- Discuss the appropriate audience for the monograph or article[7]

It is crucial in every instance to be fair to the book or article as written. Although reviews vary in length, most are usually between 500–1,000 words.

The prospective reviewer begins the review by including a heading that indicates the book's author, title, and publication information. The following heading appeared in a review completed by student Sean Crowley:

> *Flight and Rebellion: Slave Resistance in Eighteenth-Century Virginia.* By Gerald W. Mullin. (New York: Oxford University Press, 1972. Pp. xii, 219.)

The text of the review starts with a statement that simultaneously draws the reader's interest while hinting at the central idea or tension discussed in the book or journal article. After this opening, the reviewer provides the reader with a brief description of the author and a statement of the author's thesis. Knowing who the author is should enable the reviewer to discern something about the quality of the work and the point of view, as well as provide insights into the author's level of expertise on the subject matter. Many monographs contain brief descriptions of the author at either the beginning or end of the book, but few articles contain such information. At any rate, a reviewer should seek more information about the author. One of the most convenient ways to find this information is by searching reference works such as *Biography and Genealogy Master Index, Contemporary Authors* (the *Literature Resource Center),* and the *Directory of American Scholars.* In some cases, simply conducting a Google™ search of the author's name will yield results.

The reviewer must provide a sense of the theses of the monograph or article. While it is important to practice the techniques of critical reading discussed earlier in this chapter, authors often clearly state the thesis in their prefatory or introductory comments. If not, a careful reading of the book or article should make clear the author's central point.

The first two paragraphs of Sean Crowley's review follow. Note how he draws the reader's attention, and then identifies the author and his thesis:

> Late one evening on July 10, 1800, a few miles outside the city of Richmond, Virginia, a black slave named Ben Woolfolk is cutting wood. A man steps out from the surrounding "scrubby, pine woods." "Would you join a free Mason society?" asks the man. Ben replies, "All free Masons would go to hell." Undaunted the man replies, "It [is] not a free Mason society I have in mind [but] a society to fight the white people for [our] freedom." George Smith, himself a slave, stepped out of the woods

---

[7]Several essays address book reviews in detail. Among the most useful are: Robert Blackey, "Words to the Whys: Crafting Critical Book Reviews," *The History Teacher* 27 (February 1994): 159–166; *LEO: Literacy Education Online—Writing Book Reviews* http:// leo.stcloudstate.edu/acadwrite/bookrev.html; John E. Drewry, *Writing Book Reviews* (Westport, CT: Greenwood Press, 1974); Dale R. Steiner, *Historical Journals: A Handbook for Writers and Reviewers* (Santa Barbara, CA: ABC-CLIO, 1981).

that night in search of recruits; recruits for what would become the "most sophisticated and ambitious slave conspiracy" in United States history; recruits . . . for Gabriel's Rebellion.

Although Gabriel's Rebellion (named after its leader, Gabriel Prosser) failed before it began, it nonetheless represented a significant shift in slave behavior toward the institution of slavery. Using this event as the culminating and defining moment in his book *Flight and Rebellion*, California State University Professor of History Gerald W. Mullin looks to explain how slave resistance escalated from individual acts, like running away, to group action in the form of outright rebellion. Examining the patterns of slave resistance in eighteenth century Virginia and the degree to which slaves differed in their reactions to slavery, he offers this central thesis: that the level of slave acculturation (or assimilation) and the type of work performed were the determining factors in the type of resistance that was engaged in and "that as slaves acculturated they became outwardly rebellious and more difficult for whites to control."

At some point in the review, the reviewer must also comment on the author's conclusions and sources. Often, the last chapter of a book or last paragraph of an essay will summarize the main points and offer the author's conclusions. It is more difficult to discern the sources used by an author. While many historians provide a bibliographical essay or an annotated bibliography that provides commentary on sources, it is often best to examine the footnotes to see which sources are consulted most frequently.

The heart of a review is the summary. Summarizing a monograph or journal article is challenging work. An effective summary should not only reflect how the author supported and elaborated on his or her thesis, but it should provide an abstract of the main points and give the reader a sense of the book's organization. This requires reviewers to be selective in what they comment upon. Inexperienced writers who attempt to write a paragraph about every chapter or who provide a sentence on each paragraph in an article will produce incoherent summaries of little use. An effective summary elaborates on how the thesis is supported, citing selected sections that will be explored in greater depth because they more clearly illustrate the author's main point, or because they are simply more interesting.

In the following paragraph, Sean Crowley summarizes the main points of the book while including some commentary on sources:

Mullin analyzed and interpreted the primary sources often known to historians as "witnesses in spite of themselves"; for example, court, county, and plantation records, ledgers, and census returns were used. His primary focus, however, rested upon examination of notices for runaway slaves published in Virginia newspapers. He analyzed approximately 1,500 such ads from 1736 to 1801 and from these exhumed a wealth of insightful information, such as the origin of the slaves who ran away and the type of work they performed; he even gained an understanding of their use of English. He was thus able to develop a good idea of various types of slaves and their behavior toward slavery. The newly arrived African (or "outlandish") slaves often attempted escape, either seeking to return to Africa or establish settlements to "re-create their old life." Those Africans that remained within the plantation system and became what Mullin calls "new Negroes" often engaged in relatively minor forms of "inward-directed" rebellion, such as truancy, thievery, property destruction, "feigned illness," and general laziness. This type of resistance produced only short-lived gains and temporary relief, yet often resulted in more suffering on the part of the slave. Lastly, and most importantly, were the highly acculturated, American-born, skilled/artisan slaves. This group, with its variety of occupational skills, good command of the English language, and useful understanding of the ways of the whites—all elements of a high degree of acculturation—included men like Ben Woolfolk and George Smith. It was these slaves, the "artisans and waitingmen," who had the means, the understanding, and the desire to organize and fight for their freedom. As individuals, these skilled artisan-slaves initially exhibited "outward-directed" resistance by becoming fugitives and often attempted to pass themselves off as free men. By 1800, however, partially influenced by the ideals of the American Revolution, many of these individuals had begun to view resistance as a collective effort. It was they who would become the motivators and leaders of America's first large-scale slave insurrection.

If the heart of a review is the summary, the brain of the review is the analysis. Indeed, it is analysis that makes a review different, and much more useful than a book report. Analysis may be of many different types. For example, a review in a professional journal includes commentary on where the work fits into the existing scholarship, as well as what, if any, scholarly contribution has been made to a field. Professional reviews might also discuss the use of sources and whether their use was appropriate, and if other extant sources were ignored. Beginning researchers often lack the experience and knowledge of the field to make such judgments. But a careful review of the book should enable them to comment on many aspects of a scholarly work. For example, they can determine if the thesis is clear and supported by the evidence. Are the author's main conclusions consistent with the thesis? Might other conclusions be drawn from the evidence presented?

A review needs to comment on the sources. Historians ask: What types of primary sources are used? Who wrote them? Do these primary sources seem appropriate to the topic? Have sources that might have been used been neglected? What secondary sources does the author use? What do these works focus on? Who wrote them? When? Is there some significance to the works selected by the author?

Reviews should also comment on additional features within the book. These frequently include maps, illustrations, charts and graphs. All reviewers should answer questions about a book or article's readability, clarity, and organization. Although many inexperienced reviewers may find some words outside of their existing vocabularies, writing about history does not involve the same type of vocabulary and technical knowledge as writing about nuclear physics. Historians write about people, and the cultures and institutions they create. Beginning researchers do not need a special vocabulary to decipher an author's meaning.

Reviews should include a brief commentary on the appropriate audience for such a work. Remember, a review should provide scholars with a sense of the book's value. Identifying the appropriate audience for an essay or monograph is not easy, but a few guidelines might be helpful. A heavily footnoted essay written on a relatively narrow topic is likely meant for specialists; a book or article that contains no or few citations written about an event that has been covered in detail by other historians might be intended for a popular audience. But a reviewer should not automatically jump to such a conclusion if footnotes are not present; some scholars' reputations are so great that their expertise is taken for granted. The publisher might also indicate audience. Books produced by university presses and essays published by refereed professional journals are intended for a scholarly audience. Books produced by trade presses or in popular magazines, such as *American Heritage* or *History Today,* are meant for a broader readership. The tone of an essay might also indicate its potential audience. Is the writing scholarly? Are the author's findings and interpretations dispassionately presented? The depth of an essay might also be a clue to audience. For example, does it provide an overview or introduction to a topic, or does it examine a more esoteric point in careful detail?

Reviewers conclude by commenting on the quality of the work. Suggesting that a piece of historical scholarship is too long or repetitive is more often a sign of a short attention span than an informed commentary on the work. Instead, the reviewer should consider whether the thesis is supported by the evidence, whether the essay is clearly written and easy to understand, and in particular, where the monograph or essay fits into the existing scholarship and what specific contribution it makes to this scholarship. In passing this final judgment, it is essential that the reviewer always remember to review the work as it was written; not as he or she wishes it had been written.

The final paragraphs of Sean Crowley's review analyze the book and offer comments on the appropriate audience. The author's name and institutional affiliation appear on separate lines at the end of the review.

> *Flight and Rebellion* is full of quotes and outtakes from the runaway slave notices and other primary source material. Mullin weaves these excerpts into his prose almost flawlessly; however, they do, at times, slow the pace of the book. That professor Mullin was able to glean so much information from these ads is remarkable, but this reviewer is left wondering if it is enough to make the case beyond contestation. Nonetheless his argument is very persuasive and despite the book's short length (it weighs in at only 163 pages of actual text), it still serves well to bolster his argument. Mullin efficiently packs a lot into a tiny space, presenting his ideas in five chapters, each showing a progressive step in the slave's development towards rebellion. Mullin also provides for his readers a few maps of Virginia

counties and towns as well as some tables showing, among other things, the differing value of slaves, their jobs, and their destinations when they ran away. The maps did not seem to be entirely necessary, but the tables were helpful and easy to use. The most interesting was "Table Two: The Assimilated Slaves' Jobs." This table outlines the type of jobs performed by the slaves whom Mullin studied in the notices, and shows both the number of slaves who held the various jobs and the percentage they represented of the whole. The index is adequate, yet could be more detailed with its entries. Finally, there are also 39 pages of extensive endnotes as well as a bibliography listing the primary materials, but only "selected" secondary sources.

Mullin has produced a book that is inclined toward the academic audience more so than toward the general reader, but as its thesis is so intriguing and the evidence presented appears to solidly back it, anyone interested in slave resistance should read this book. It must be said, though, that it will be helpful if one has a **serious** interest in the subject of slave resistance and also does not mind stopping to think and reflect every few paragraphs. Despite its sometimes dry tone, Mullin does manage to draw the reader into his vision of slavery from the "bottom up" and is ultimately successful in his attempt not only to prove his thesis, but also to provide the reader with a "new perspective on slave behavior."

L. SEAN CROWLEY
James Madison University

THE ANNOTATED BIBLIOGRAPHY

As researchers initiate the process of locating and selecting secondary sources through the research trail, it is essential to start an **annotated bibliography.** Most students are familiar with the format of the standard bibliography, which lists the sources consulted for completing a research paper. But serious researchers generally avoid such a bibliography in favor of one that is annotated. An annotated bibliography not only lists sources consulted, but provides brief descriptions of each source as it relates to the topic. The typical annotation is two or three sentences in length.

BIBLIOGRAPHIC NOTE CARD

The researcher cannot wait until having completed the research to begin the annotated bibliography. Whenever a researcher encounters a new source, he or she should record the necessary bibliographic information on either a separate note card or on a preliminary bibliography that is maintained electronically. For a monograph, this would include the following:

- Author's full name (for example, Kennedy, David M.)

- Complete title of the secondary source (*Freedom from Fear: The American People in Depression and War, 1929–1945*)

- Place of publication, publisher, and year of publication (New York: Oxford University Press, 1999)

For other sources, consult an appropriate style manual such as Kate Turabian's *A Manual for Writers of Term Papers, Theses, and Dissertations* or *The Chicago Manual of Style*.

Kennedy, David M. Freedom From Fear: The American People in Depression and War, 1929-1945

New York: Oxford University Press, 1999

E 173. 094 v.9   James Madison Univ.

Excellent coverage of this period

Manning, William Ray. Diplomatic Correspondence of the United States: Canadian Relations, 1784-1860. 4 vols. Washington, DC: Carnegie Endowment for International Peace, 1940-45.

Vol 2 - 1821-1835 , pubd 1942

E 183. 8. C2   Library of VA
                                          Richmond
Excellent Primary!

Beginning researchers might also include other necessary information in the preliminary entry such as Library of Congress call number, library or archive where the book or article was located, and a brief annotation about the secondary source and its contents. (It would be prudent to use information located in guides and other bibliographies to supplement your own annotation.) This may seem like a lot of work at the outset, but it will actually save time in the long run. Maintaining this information systematically makes it easier to retrieve materials during the research and writing process. While the preliminary annotated bibliography may look different from the finished copy, it will be useful as a working bibliography as well as facilitating the task of compiling the final bibliography.

A working annotated bibliography enables the researcher to ascertain which sources will be most useful to the various sections of the paper. Such a bibliography enables the reader to better understand the ways in which sources were useful and also grasp the limitations of some sources. The final annotated bibliography should be arranged alphabetically with primary sources listed first, followed by secondary sources. Appendix B contains an outstanding example of an annotated bibliography. Note how Jack Sheehan limits his comments to two to three sentences, and not only provides a clue as to what information appears in the book, but also notes its usefulness.

Many scholars, operating in the spirit of an annotated bibliography, will produce a **bibliographic essay.** A bibliographic essay is simply an annotated bibliography written in a narrative format, and organized by topic or subject rather than alphabetically. Bibliographic essays often provide more insight into a source than an annotated bibliography, but writing a bibliographic essay is much more difficult than simply compiling a bibliography with annotation. An example of such a bibliography can be found in Chapter 6.

TAKING NOTES

After a preliminary reading of the key secondary sources, a researcher must begin to take notes. Most scholars who have not shifted to electronic formats use note cards. After creating a bibliographic note card, the beginning researcher should develop a system for subsequent informational note cards. All notes—whether written the old-fashioned way with pen or pencil on a note card, or typed into a digital note card format—should be systematically recorded to show where information is from and to indicate the topic of the note card. Each note card should contain the author's last name and a shortened version of the title on the first line of the card. When recording notes on a card, leave a blank line between the author and title information, then indicate the page number of the book or article from which notes are taken. After taking notes from one page, skip to the next line on the card, write down the next page number, and continue taking notes. Once one side of the card is full, quickly read it and provide a few keywords on the top line. This will enable easy retrieval of information once the writing process begins. Be sure to write notes on one side only! Remember, while most writing comes from primary sources, secondary sources provide information that is essential to understanding time and place, and can be very useful in filling in any holes in one's primary evidence.

Below are two examples of note cards. The first indicates notes taken from diplomatic correspondence. Notice how the note taker used << . . . >> to highlight the direct quote of Enoch Lincoln's letter to Henry Clay.

Manning, Diplo. Corr, Can-Am vol 2 ①
    Gov Lincoln's on Maine Bndy

    E Lincoln (Gov of Maine) to Henry Clay
(Sec of State), Portland, Me, 3 Sep 27′
    P36- Maine will << . . . never
assent to the results of an
    P37- arbitration unfavorable to
her interests . . . >> Maine must
have boundary settled.

The note card below is paraphrased from a secondary source.

Kennedy, Freedom From Fear   ①
    Yamamoto/Japan's Plan - Dec 1941

    516- Japanese Admiral Isoroku
Yamamoto, comm-in-chief of Japanese
Fleet, had concerns about upcoming
Pearl Harbor attack. Pearl Harbor
was part of a larger strategy to
attack Philippines, Malaya and Dutch
East Indies.

The notes taken from secondary sources reflect the different types of reading described earlier in this chapter. Initial notes may simply provide narrative description of the event or process being analyzed. The first notes of this type tend to be lengthy, but as the researcher sees different secondary sources repeating similar points, the researcher will take briefer notes. In examining more secondary sources, the beginning researcher will become aware of historical context as well as some historiographical nuances. This process of taking notes should be active; it is a written conversation between the young scholars and the scholarship.

In recent years, note-taking software intended for scholarly use has appeared in many forms. One of the better programs is Scribe, available through the Center for History and New Media at George Mason University. This program permits extensive notes, allows for document storage, and is easily searchable. Scholars may search their notes by keywords and may connect directly to online resources. Scribe is both flexible and easy to use.[8]

Experienced historians can offer advice on taking notes for beginning researchers. Never take notes on notebook-sized paper; too much information appears in one place, and it is difficult to organize and retrieve. Even when conducting the most preliminary research, recording notes straight from the book should be avoided since it is likely to lead to hundreds of note cards on any given source and, furthermore, increases the chances of inadvertent **plagiarism.** Plagiarism, the appropriation of another's material—intended or unintended—for one's own use, is one of the cardinal sins in academia. Those found guilty of such an offense are generally drummed out of the profession. In order to avoid plagiarism, read the source material and paraphrase what is written. If historians quote directly in their notes, they must make absolutely certain the quote is enclosed in quotation marks and appropriately labeled.

CONCLUSION

Secondary sources do more than enhance our knowledge of a specific event and provide a sense of the time and place. Scholarly interpretations also offer the reader an introduction to the historiographical context. A careful reading of the important scholarship should provide the reader with a sense of the state of the scholarship, such as the perspective of those scholars working the field, what questions they consider important, the differing interpretations of an event, and the methodologies employed to make sense of the evidence. Since any history paper is also a secondary source, good papers will engage the lines of argument in a field, or test some of the theses offered on a topic.

---

[8]Center for History and New Media, George Mason University, Scribe http://chnm.gmu.edu/tools/scribe/.

4

Primary Evidence

Once relevant secondary literature has been examined to provide background, historical context, and historiographical context, beginning historians start interpreting the primary sources identified in the research trail. Researchers should identify additional primary sources from their reading of the secondary sources—in particular, examining footnotes and bibliographies. The analytical process associated with primary sources is the most satisfying aspect of research because the researcher ultimately reaches independent conclusions about the evidence that goes beyond a simple summary of the documents.

The opportunities for beginning researchers to access primary sources used to be more limited. College libraries or local archives might contain scattered manuscript holdings, sources on microform, government documents, or newspapers; however, except at major research libraries, such collections tended to be limited and were normally reserved for scholars. Beginning researchers usually gleaned what primary evidence they could from edited collections in print or from selected document readers; thus, access to primary sources remained restricted. Such constraints often determined the kinds of topics explored and the questions that could be reasonably posed.

The availability of materials on the Internet has transformed access to historical evidence and brought entire collections of primary sources within reach of historians almost anywhere on the planet. The possibilities for researching topics have increased exponentially as a result. In addition, many Internet websites include effective search engines that permit researchers to sift through larger quantities of evidence more efficiently than historians in past generations. While digitized technology has made an infinite variety of rich source material potentially accessible to all historians, the very volume of evidence creates the necessity for a more systematic understanding of how to evaluate and use it.

This chapter will first define primary evidence, then examine ways to read, analyze, and interpret it. The focus will be on the kinds of questions to ask as part of the ongoing conversation with the sources. Once students are familiar with the techniques of analysis, they are better prepared to interpret various primary sources. Finally, the chapter concludes with a discussion of how student author Jack Sheehan has interpreted primary evidence to construct his argument.

WHAT IS A PRIMARY SOURCE?

A **primary source** is any record contemporary to an event or time period. Primary sources may be written, oral, visual, or physical. Some of these sources were produced with the intent of being preserved for the future. Such **intentional sources** include government documents, church records, autobiographies, or memoirs. On the other hand, many primary sources were produced without any intent of future use. Such **unintentional sources** may include private correspondence not originally meant for posterity but which later are deposited in archives and libraries. Physical evidence such as buildings, clothing, tools, and landscapes may also be labeled as unintentional sources.

Identifying a primary source is far simpler than analyzing such sources effectively. The most common sources used in historical research are written; any discussion of primary evidence must begin with them. Before the analytical process can begin, however, researchers must read the source closely to make absolutely certain they understand its content, language, meaning, and thesis—if it has one. Only then is it possible to begin to analyze. Beginning historians must learn to adopt a critical or skeptical approach to thinking about evidence and go beyond basic issues of factual content (who, what, when, where). Such an approach helps begin an active dialogue with the evidence. All researchers initiate their analyses of primary written evidence with questions to help them understand particular documents and how groups of these fit together within the context of other primary sources.

When analyzing primary evidence, certain questions are standard. Who authored the source? How long after the event is it being described? Is the author an eyewitness? Who was the intended audience? What is the audience's relationship to the author? What is the purpose of the source? What is the tone of the language used? Does an obvious point of view color the evidence? How reliable is the evidence? How does the source fit into the historical context established by other primary sources and secondary accounts? What new information does it provide? Does the source help explain causal or other relationships? Is the source significant? How can the source be used to advance the research project?

EVALUATING WRITTEN EVIDENCE

Author

In examining any written source, it is helpful to have some information about the author. A biographical dictionary or other resource may provide the necessary information, but, in some cases, information about the author must be gleaned from the source itself. This is the case when the author is either not identified or unknown. The historian should attempt to ascertain the author's relationship to the event described.

- Was the author an eyewitness to what is described or only a contemporary to the event? A scientist who observed Yuri Gagarin's successful orbit in 1961 aboard *Vostok I* provides different information from someone who happened to be alive at the time but only read about it in the newspaper or was unaware it had taken place.

- How long after the event was the document produced? Fresh memories tend to be clearer and capture the moment more accurately.

- What authority does the author have to describe the event? How much does he or she know about what is occurring? How able is the author to understand what he or she is witnessing? For example, the frame of vision of an Anzac infantry soldier on the beach at Gallipoli in April 1915 was necessarily limited. While that individual may well provide excellent primary documentation for the part of the battlefield he witnessed, he would be less valuable as a source for understanding the broader mission that day. A child who witnessed the same event might describe the event very differently.

Point of View

All authors have biases, prejudices, and assumptions that influence their perspective or **point of view.** Some of the most important factors that influence point of view are family background, religious views, value system, personal experiences, age, time period, place, ethnicity, gender, education, and social class.

- What background factors might influence the author's point of view? Was there any reason for the author to misrepresent or exaggerate the account? For example, a worker's newspaper editorial would likely depict a strike differently than a speech delivered by a company manager. Despite these varying accounts, both may be credible.

- Is the author trustworthy? How do we know? Are there other primary sources that can help to corroborate the account?

Audience

Any source is written with an audience or audiences in mind. The audience may significantly influence what or how the author writes. The audience needs to be differentiated between an **intended audience**—the audience for whom the author primarily crafts his or her message—and the **unintended audience(s)** which may also be of less importance. Knowledge of the audience is nearly as important as knowledge of the author.

- Who was the intended audience for this document? For example, most diaries are composed with the author alone as the intended audience. The famous English diarist Samuel Pepys even composed his diary in shorthand to guard against others reading it. While he wrote out all names, he developed a particular way of recording everything else. Thus, his diary was clearly intended to be private and personal. However, Pepys's diary has been decoded and become widely available to historians, demonstrating that many primary sources have unintended audiences, and, in this case, Pepys's diary provides a unique window into his life and times. Correspondence, like some diaries, is also intended for a limited, private audience. The intended audience may well influence the degree of candor expressed, the familiarity or formality of language used, and the assumptions made by the author. Knowing something about the intended audience is thus a significant part of understanding the source and using it to support a historical argument.

- If a document is produced for private or individual consumption, can the reader assume greater candor by the author? Are there reasons to stretch the truth in a personal diary or private letter? By contrast, if the document has been produced for the public, can the reader conclude its language is more guarded and its content less revealing or honest? The answers to these and other questions require a careful reading of the document, meticulous thinking about what it says, and close corroboration with other primary and secondary sources before reaching a conclusion.

- What cultural assumptions must the reader of a private document guard against? In some cultures, formal language is more standard. In Early Modern Europe, husbands and wives addressed one another differently. John Paston III's salutation to his father in March 1464 illustrates the point: "Right reverend and worshipful father, I recommend me unto you, beseeching you lowly of your blessing, desiring to hear of your welfare and prosperity, the which I pray God preserve unto his pleasure . . ."[1] When studying evidence from other cultures, it is especially crucial to be aware of such distinctions and to evaluate all evidence thoughtfully and critically.

Once researchers have a clearer understanding of the intended audience, or have concluded that such information cannot be known with any certainty, they turn next to the author's purpose in examining the source.

Purpose

When analyzing any written document it is vital to comprehend the author's purpose. Why was the document produced and why has it survived? Some records, such as those produced by government agencies or other organizations or institutions, are intended to survive. Statutes, tax records, annual reports, and the like are recorded with the understanding that they will endure indefinitely. These

---

[1]John Paston III to John Paston I, 1 March 1464, *The Paston Letters: A Selection in Modern Spelling,* ed. Norman Davis (Oxford and New York: Oxford University Press,1983), 103–104.

documents may be more formulaic in their language, neutral in their tone, and precise in the kinds of information they provide. By contrast, private letters, diaries, memoirs, notes, and other such sources are less likely to be written with any intention they will survive to become historical documents. Writers of such documents may be more inclined to be spontaneous and open and, therefore, may be more revealing. The historian must try to classify whether a document is categorized as public or private and whether it was intended to last or survived by accident.

The next step is to determine what the author was trying to achieve with this document. Often, the author's point of view influences the purpose:

- Is the author simply providing information or trying to lead the audience to a particular conclusion? Is the information accurate? That is, can it be corroborated by other primary evidence? If the source includes errors, are they intentional? Are they significant?

- What other kinds of evidence does the author introduce to support a thesis or claim in the source? Why was it chosen?

- Is the coverage balanced? These questions relate to what is called the author's bias.

Tone and Language

The scholar should now consider issues of tone and language within the evidence. For many beginning researchers, these considerations are complex and require attentive reading:

- What is the tone of the source? That is, what is the author's attitude toward the subject? It is sometimes helpful to read the document aloud to get a clearer sense of its tone. Does the author appear to be angry? Argumentative? Sarcastic? Authoritative? Judgmental? Even-tempered? Omniscient? Conversational? Consider, for example, Mohandas K. Gandhi's bitter condemnation of Western "civilization" in his 1908 pamphlet *Hind Swaraj* (Indian Home Rule), or the eloquence of Abraham Lincoln in the 1863 *Gettysburg Address.*

- Is there a single tone employed throughout the document or does it vary from part to part? How does the tone in one document by a particular author contrast with the tone in another, especially one written at a different time? How does a particular source's tone differ from other sources describing the same event or issue, especially when they share the same or similar positions? Obviously, an understanding of historical context obtained through a careful reading of primary sources will help the researcher to understand the tone of a particular document.

The language of a document takes many forms and reveals much about the author, the source, and the purpose. If the language is informal or conversational, the source may have been written in haste, written to a friend or someone close, or not intended to be permanent. In Early Modern England, for instance, approximately two-thirds of all wills were written within two weeks of an individual's death.[2] Such documents, including oral wills, were often dictated quickly and contain repetitions and language that suggest the individual was struggling to record his or her last wishes. Other documents may be more rigid in structure, form, and language. As noted above, salutations and closings in past correspondence were far more formal than in modern times, and researchers must understand these conventions if they are to draw appropriate conclusions from the information.

Finally, language is often period-specific and researchers must be extremely cautious not to read modern definitions into past times and thereby corrupt meaning. Words may have had a specific meaning or use in the past that is far different from current usage. Further, just as modern English has its own jargon and idioms, they were also present in the past. For example, the past use of the word "icon" would have religious connotations, while in the twenty-first century the word would often be associated with a clickable image on a computer's desktop. Having the *Oxford English Dictionary* or another etymological dictionary close at hand for reference will help researchers avoid this form of potential misinterpretation. This is especially important because of the instability and sometimes open-ended meaning which words may convey. In order for historians to extract precise meaning from language effectively, it is essential that they have a clear idea of how these words functioned in the context of their time.

Significance

One of the most difficult elements for beginning historians and seasoned scholars is determining the significance of a written source. Not every primary source is equal in significance to every other. In examining written sources, a scholar should consider the following:

1. What are the elements that make a particular document important? A useful convention in answering this question is to think about how the document relates to an understanding of the topic.
    - First, how does the source help explain the event or topic being explored? Could the event or issue be explained as fully without the document?
    - Second, does the source offer unique insights or alternative information about the topic?
    - Finally, is the explanation or interpretation in this document different from others?

To this point, the discussion has focused on some of the key questions necessary to analyze primary, written evidence. While such sources are certainly the most commonly used by historical researchers, they are by no means the only kinds of

---

[2]Colin D. Rogers and John H. Smith, *Local Family History in England, 1538–1914* (Manchester and New York: Manchester University Press, 1991), 153.

evidence available. Depending upon the nature of the research project, oral, visual, or physical evidence may offer insights and information, and attention must next turn to these forms.

EVALUATING ORAL EVIDENCE

Oral evidence takes several forms in today's digital environment. Recorded interviews with individuals, following guidelines and standards of the Oral History Association or other professional groups in the United States and their counterparts abroad, emerged by the mid-twentieth century as an important new source for historical research. These interviews have traditionally been either biographical or focused on specific issues. Many personal interviews have been transcribed and survive as written documents while others are available only on tape. Transcribed interviews generally must be evaluated as all other written primary sources. Television and video recordings added another dimension and digitization has extended the availability of oral evidence. Students of contemporary history now have access through their computer terminals to speeches, films, and other examples of oral evidence.

Although the format may be different, the same evaluation criteria are applied to all forms of oral evidence. Thus, the researcher asks essentially the same series of questions about **author, point of view, audience, purpose, language, and significance** as for any other primary source. If the source under study is transcribed, the process is relatively simple because the format of the evidence is written. When working with oral histories that have been transcribed, researchers must seek to discern whether the transcription is complete or edited. Fuller, unedited transcriptions tend to be more valuable as sources since they give the researcher complete access to the testimony. If it is not transcribed, however, the process of analysis is more complex, as the material is heard, not read, and may have to be replayed several times in order to understand its content fully.

The historian asks some critical questions of any oral source:

- Why was the oral source produced and why has it survived? Is it part of a larger collection? Some collections may focus on coal miners, steel workers, or infantrymen, for example, and the historian needs to be aware of this situation. Why was the collection gathered? Speeches and television files may be preserved as part of a station or university archive.

- What is the role of the interviewer? Oral interviewers play a powerful role in the production of oral histories. The questions they pose in conducting an interview frame the discussion and may direct the person being interviewed to specific topics or themes. Thus, in evaluating oral interviews, it is important to determine the degree to which the interviewer is in control. In better oral interviews, the interviewer is less intrusive, tends to ask broader, more open-ended questions, and does not try to direct the individual to particular conclusions. When reviewing speeches or media outtakes, researchers should also be conscious of the underlying assumptions of a source. Certain idioms and allusions to places or persons may not have required explanation in the original; however, as part of the analysis of a historical source, they become more important.

Oral evidence has become more widely used in recent decades and may add significant sources to any project when evaluated critically.

EVALUATING VISUAL EVIDENCE

Paintings, photographs, cartoons, and films comprise the principal categories of visual evidence most widely used by historians. Each variety yields unique insights and each poses specific analytical questions for researchers. When evaluating a portrait, for instance, it is useful to know whether the artist intended a flattering or accurate rendition of the individual. Charles I of England preferred portraits of himself either standing or riding to emphasize strength and manliness. Soviet realist art of the 1930s portrayed Joseph Stalin as a benevolent and caring leader. A Diego Rivera mural would likely champion the common people and the working class. When evaluating such evidence, historians must ask questions such as these:

- Who was the artist? Why was the portrait painted? Who commissioned the painting?
- What is the context of the painting? For example, a painting of Napoleon while a young man would be different from one done after he was crowned emperor of France.
- What does the painting depict, both in terms of its primary subject as well as subjects in the background?

In assessing works of art, it is essential to know something about the artist, as well as the motivation and purpose for the work. It is equally important to think about how portraits and paintings are to be used in the research being conducted. In Jack Sheehan's paper, a painting and a map are used for illustrative purposes only and are not an integral part of the analysis. A comparison of contemporary paintings could add a useful dimension to the work.

Photographs may offer a more accurate visual image than paintings. They may also be staged, with the photography ultimately controlling the picture that is taken. Once again, the beginning historian must ask specific questions about the primary source:

- What did the photographer choose to record? What was the purpose of the photograph? What assumptions does the photographer make about the subject and the audience? Has the photograph been altered? Personal photographs taken by German soldiers in the Eastern Theatre of World War II can reveal much about the average German soldier's view of the Polish and Russian people. A picture may indeed be worth a "thousand words" but it is the interpretation and analysis provided by the researcher that brings meaning to the photograph.

Analysis of cartoons raises other issues because they reflect the times in which they were produced in such different ways. In the original meaning, a cartoon was a drawing on more or less permanent paper intended as a prelude to a painting of the same subject. Leonardo Da Vinci's sketchbooks provide insight into the evolution of the artist's thought about a subject and may illustrate significant changes over time. In a sense, they are comparable to early drafts of correspondence or other written materials. A second meaning of the term is more familiar: a drawing, usually in a newspaper, that may be satirical or humorous. In this sense, cartoons provide rich insights into both the artist's perceptions and how individuals or events were understood by contemporaries. These sources assume certain knowledge by the viewer and must be used carefully. Gilded Age cartoonist Thomas Nast's encapsulation of the infamous Tweed Ring, portrayed here as vultures, revealed corruption in New York City to his many readers.[3]

Library of Congress, LC-DIG-ppmsc-05890

Film is a final example of a visual source type used for historical analysis. This source is potentially the most enticing, especially for beginning researchers.

---

[3]Thomas Nast, "A Group of Vultures Waiting for the Storm to 'Blow Over'—'Let Us Prey,'" *Harper's Weekly*, 23 September 1871, 889. http://app.harpweek.com/. Access to site is through individual or institutional subscription.

Videotape would appear to capture the reality of the moment, but must be scrutinized much like a photograph. On the other hand, motion pictures must be approached with extreme caution. Docudramas, feature films, and the like are produced with many different purposes, and while they may illuminate aspects of the past, they are the creation of the film artist and should not be used in the same way as written, oral, or other visual sources. They may be valuable to help achieve an understanding of the culture and times in which the film was produced, or to provide insights into what it valued, or found humorous, but films differ profoundly from other visual resources. For example, the movie *The Patriot* reputedly depicts events that took place in South Carolina during the American Revolution. Although there is some factual basis for the story, the film is one-sided, it distorts British behavior, and misrepresents race relations in eighteenth-century South Carolina.

EVALUATING PHYSICAL EVIDENCE

Historians only occasionally use physical evidence. Weapons, tools, and other artifacts may provide valuable insights to a period and should not be ignored. Physical evidence from archaeological excavations or other sites can reveal much that is not readily found in other sources. Artifacts help scholars understand individuals and their communities. They enable historians to gain deeper and richer insights into a period and its people. Examining whalebone corsets, crinolines, and other nineteenth-century women's clothing, for example, clearly demonstrated the restrictive nature of women's wear at the time, which underscored their subservience and reinforced societal perceptions. Of course the historian must determine whether or not these artifacts are typical or representative. Such physical evidence provides a better sense of the situation than simply reading accounts of clothing in wills or viewing pictures of them in advertisements. Students of agricultural history who examine field implements and understand their use will empathize more with written accounts of farming realities. Historians may also consider physical evidence such as landscapes, buildings, gardens, and transportation grids. All are simply other forms of text and should be critiqued in similar ways.

FINAL THOUGHTS ON ELEMENTS OF ANALYSIS

The careful researcher approaches all evidence in any format armed with a framework for analyzing it. Each document or primary source must be scrutinized critically in order to understand it and evaluate its worth as potential evidence. The questions posed in the sections above focus on understanding the nature and value of a source and knowing with some certainty whether or not the account or interpretation it offers can be verified and corroborated, preferably by other primary evidence. Beginning historians should scrutinize individual sources of evidence, constantly comparing a particular document or artifact with others they have already studied to determine how they are similar and how they differ. This analytical approach underlines the ongoing conversations necessary with each piece of evidence.

The first sections of this chapter have focused on matters of definition and the standard elements of historical analysis. Equipped with the techniques and terms of analysis, it is now possible to examine different types of primary sources.

SOURCE TYPES AND THEIR APPLICATIONS

Primary sources are often categorized in several ways. The first group comprises those sources that are **unpublished.** Such sources can only be found in one particular location, such as an archive, or the special collections section of a research library, or a particular local library or historical society. These materials do not circulate; thus the historian must visit the facilities to view these documents.[4]

The second group is **published.** These primary sources include presidential papers, government documents, memoirs, autobiographies, and newspapers that are widely available at archives, research libraries, public libraries, and websites.

A third group is **edited** or **selected.** These sources are similar to those previously mentioned; however, edited or selected collections of the writings of Mao Zedong would include very different documents from the complete works of the same individual. In these instances, an editor has culled most of the writings and organized them in a special way (around a theme or chronologically, for example). The active researcher should know the nature of the collection being examined and the role played by an editor, compiler, or even the group digitizing.

Correspondence

Personal correspondence has traditionally been one of the most widely used primary sources. Because such correspondence was between individuals and not intended for public examination, it frequently provides a clearer understanding of the mind of the author and sometimes the recipient of the letter. Correspondence often includes the date when they were written; they are often specifically focused, and sometimes address issues raised in earlier letters. They may offer insights into what a person was thinking or experiencing, what they have observed, and what they have chosen to convey to their reader. They may either inform or persuade and they often offer insights into an individual's point of view. Correspondence may also be official, as letters may be used to convey the wishes of an agency or a government authority. Official letters are more formal in their language and tone and may provide less insight into the individual writer than informal correspondence. While most collections of correspondence remain in archives or special collections, digitized letter collections abound on many topics and are easily accessible in manuscript or typescript formats.

---

[4]Many previously unpublished manuscripts are being digitized and posted to websites.

One especially rich collection for United States history is the American Memory (Library of Congress): http://memory.loc.gov/ammem/. The roughly 27,000 documents found in the Thomas Jefferson Papers include an extensive number of his letters as both a private citizen and public official: http://memory.loc.gov/ammem/collections/jefferson_papers/. A nice feature of this collection is that it provides an image of the original handwritten letter as well as a typewritten transcription. Many digitized letters have been transcribed and, while researchers must be conscious of the potential that mistakes may have occurred in the process, the probability of error is less likely for standard collections in reputable digital archives. One of Thomas Jefferson's letters to John Adams written on 28 October 1813, declared:

> For I agree with you that there is a natural aristocracy among men. The grounds of this are virtue and talents. Formerly, bodily powers gave place among the *aristoi*. But since the invention of gunpowder has armed the weak as well as the strong with missile death, bodily strength, like beauty, good humor, politeness and other accomplishments, has become but an auxiliary ground for distinction. There is also an artificial aristocracy, founded on wealth and birth, without either virtue or talents; for with these it would belong to the first class. The natural aristocracy I consider as the most precious gift of nature, for the instruction, the trusts, and government of society. And indeed, it would have been inconsistent in creation to have formed man for the social state, and not to have provided virtue and wisdom enough to manage the concerns of the society. May we not even say, that that form of government is the best, which provides the most effectually for a pure selection of these natural *aristoi* into the offices of government? The artificial aristocracy is a mischievous ingredient in government, and provision should be made to prevent its ascendency.[5]

This particular letter provides a good example for analysis. First, the author and audience are identified, and the letter is part of an ongoing correspondence between the two former presidents. For a deeper appreciation of the letter's purpose, it would be fruitful to review the full exchange on the topic and take both perspectives into account. This is often a problem when historians rely upon personal correspondence, as one half of an exchange may be missing, although the author may address earlier issues or suggest what was stated in earlier correspondence. One of the critical elements in reviewing this passage and the views of John Adams relates to tone and language. The two men were long retired from politics, though each remained vigorous and active. Jefferson's discussion of gunpowder as an equalizer among men reflects his tone, and the playful way in which he describes its role suggests he is gently goading Adams. The distinction he makes

---

[5]Thomas Jefferson to John Adams, 28 October 1813, *The Thomas Jefferson Papers, Series 1, General Correspondence, 1651–1827.* http://memory.loc.gov/ammem/collections/jefferson_papers/.

between natural and artificial aristocracies reinforces this point. Reading a letter aloud sometimes is helpful in evaluating tone or language.

To assess a letter's significance, the beginning historian should use other letters of the time as well as other contemporary sources to corroborate the interpretation found in the letter. In this example, was their discussion of aristocracy central to political discourse in the decade? When using correspondence as a source, the researcher should avoid whenever possible employing only a single letter. Ideas often evolve over time, and one letter, deprived of its context as part of a larger whole, may lead to erroneous assumptions. It is always important to try to read all the correspondence on a particular topic, especially if the letters extend over a long period of time. Correspondence is a vital resource for historical research and can offer many insights; however, like any other primary source, letters must be read critically and carefully.

Diaries, Memoirs, and Autobiographies

Diaries are among the most useful primary sources for examining the inner thoughts of past individuals. Although some may be subsequently published, all diaries offer the historian the advantage of an internal view into the mind of the author. Diaries are especially useful since they are rarely intended for the public, and as a result, are more likely to contain the private thoughts and views of an individual. Diarists often recount the day's events and their activities with candid thoughts. Clearly, a historian must analyze a diary in much the same way as any other primary source, but since the audience for any diary is the individual who wrote it, the author is much less likely to guard his or her comments. Although some diaries may be published, it is useful to locate and use the original diary since published diaries often are edited and sanitized for public consumption. For example, an unexpurgated version of *The Diary of Anne Frank* offers graphic insight into the life of a young Jewish girl hiding from Nazi occupiers in the Netherlands during World War II.

The private nature of a diary offers clear advantages over memoirs and autobiographies as a primary source. Although all such sources are useful, the memoir or autobiography is generally written for a public audience; as a result, it is more likely to cast the author in a favorable light. For example, Richard M. Nixon's memoirs say little about his involvement in Watergate. They are also reflective pieces produced after the events they describe.

Government Documents

Government documents offer perhaps the widest array of source types. The records kept by international, national, state, and local authorities over the centuries are voluminous and varied. These materials include, but are not limited to, legislation, resolutions, debates and speeches by government officials, records of government agencies, meeting minutes, cables, intelligence, court records, and census and statistical materials—which will be discussed later in this chapter. Increasingly, government documents are being made available digitally. For example, records of the United States Congress from 1774 to 1875 can be found in the American Memory website: http://memory.loc.gov/ammem/ amlaw/lawhome.html. The United Nations' website provides excellent documentation of its activities: http://www.un.org/documents/. Laws and resolutions help show an official position on a particular issue that often reflects underlying tensions within a society. An examination of laws may indicate emerging issues in a society, or may help to reveal power relationships during a time or place. For example, Dutch law requires the maintenance of their extensive system of dikes, largely as a result of the massive floods that inundated the Netherlands in 1953.

Speeches by government officials not only reveal how one individual viewed an important issue of the day, but they may also say much about the audience he or she is addressing. When used in conjunction with other documents, a speech may offer insights into the strength or weakness of a particular government or political figure. The partially opened Soviet archives offer a very different perspective of government operations from those released at the time events were taking place. Because of their very nature however, all government records must be used with great care.

Court records are especially useful for providing a window into the lives of people who may not have left written records. Some court records detail the activities of individuals who have run afoul of the law. They tend therefore to be hostile accounts or to present their subjects in a less than favorable light. Despite their potential difficulties, the types of cases prosecuted offer a useful window into the issues of concern in a particular age. The court proceedings of the Old Bailey in London offer an example of trial records available digitally. The cases in the collection, numbering more than 100,000, embrace the period from 1674 to 1834 (http://www.oldbaileyonline.org/). When used in conjunction with other sources, court proceedings add an important dimension to understanding the lives of everyday people.

Wills and Inventories

Wills and inventories provide a unique glimpse into the world of those who did not usually write. Since wills were often written shortly before death, they offer insights into what occupied a person's mind at that moment. Wills can provide information about family, religious attitudes, and what an individual valued and, if accompanied by an inventory, reveal useful information about possessions and debts. Inventories were official lists of possessions on hand at the time of death with an estimate of their value. Some inventories are particularly helpful because they provide a room-by-room listing of possessions. Such evidence is extremely useful for determining an individual's wealth, social status, and lifestyle. Comparing a number of inventories in the same place over time can reveal rising or declining standards of living in a certain community. Like so many other primary sources, wills and inventories only give a snapshot into an individual's life. They are imperfect; however, they are a vital primary source.

The typescript will of Margaret Brownson, dated 1 March 1665, found in the Church Documents section of the *Earls Colne, Essex: Records of an English Village,*

1375–1854 (http://linux02.lib.cam.ac.uk/earlscolne/) illuminates the value and limits of such evidence. Because the Earls Colne online data archive cross-references all digitized records, Margaret Brownson's marriage record survives, as do tax records and other documents that assist in reconstructing portions of her life and her place in the village. Shortly before her death, she dictated her last will:

> I Martha Brownson of Earls Colne do on the 1.3.1665 make and ordain this my last will and testament imprimis I give to Wm Harlakenden of the same parish esq the bed in the parlour and all things belonging thereto with the great chest also in the parlour and whatsoever he pleaseth of any small things I leave to his dispose item I give to mrs Owens one pair of sheets a wicker chair a wainscot glass case a brazen pestle and mortar my best stuff coat a box smoothing iron a say apron item to her maid all her small wearing linen great cupboard in the hall one little table all her earthenware an old skillet a brass kettle and all appurtenances to the dairy viz bellows firepan tongs etc one pewter dish over above and a bed with all belonging to it two feather pillows chair reel and wheel one long chest and with other things mr Harlakenden thinks fit item I give to mrs Josceling the screen as it stands by the chimney item I give to my cousin Jn Gulston 40s and to my cousin his brother 40s to my cousin Chrismas my best cloth waistcoat and 20s to her two daughters 10s each of them to my cousin Gulston her sister 20s and to her maid Ann Hutton 40s to my sister Everitt 20s to her two daughters 10s either of them to goodman Peak 5s all my debts I will to be truly paid and I appoint my loving friend Wm Harlakenden executor of this my will and if there remain any overplus of goods or money I give it to my cousin Jn Gulston to whom I give my long table in the hall and forms declared to be her last will and testament in presence of us Ralph Josselin ✗ Ann Hutton[6]

Her inventory, valued at £24 1s, was not broken down by items.

An analysis of Martha Brownson's will reveals its usefulness as a primary source. In the first part of her will Brownson allows Harlakenden to select or dispose of any small, unnamed items in the parlor and asks that he see that any surplus wealth and possessions are given to her cousin. The terminology employed to describe certain items—for example, her reference to "best stuff coat"—may suggest how she valued certain things. Specifying some individuals by name and omitting the names of others may reveal much about family structure. Many of the specific items noted in the will may be unfamiliar to modern readers and require the use of an etymological dictionary. Taken collectively, wills from a given area or time offer insight into the material world of a community and its social stratification. They tell about families, feuds, and friendships, and about what was valued in communities. Furthermore, wills sometimes speak to debts

---

[6]Martha Brownson of Earls Colne, widow, Wills (ERO D/ACW17/80 Martha Brownson 1664/5), http://linux02.lib.cam.ac.uk/earlscolne/.

owed and forgiven, and indicate significant relationships. They are but one type of social history document and historians would use them in conjunction with those exploring marriage negotiations and other varieties of evidence.

Statistical Records

Another important, and underutilized, primary source is statistical data, such as census and tax records. Such sources offer a measure of precision unavailable in other forms of written evidence. Knowing how many people were infected by a disease or migrated to a region, or how much they owned, is far more valuable than falling back on looser terms such as "some" or "many." Examining changing literacy levels or levels of employment in the same region over an extended period of time adds a dimension to understanding the past that is difficult to discern from other primary sources. Moreover, comparing statistical evidence of factors, such as demography, gender balance, ethnic makeup, and per capita income, can reveal trends over time not readily observable in other forms of evidence. Like other primary sources, statistical information must be carefully scrutinized. Researchers must know who generated the data and for what purpose. Who is the intended audience? Is there a point of view? What other evidence permits full conclusions from statistical data? How complete is the evidence? That is, were specific groups ignored? Underrepresented? What does the data reveal about the officials who gathered it or the society that generated it?

Some of the most readily accessible statistical evidence for any nation is census information. In the United States, census data has been compiled since 1790 and much of it is now available in online formats. The Geostat Center (http://fisher.lib.virginia.edu/collections/stats/histcensus/) provides easy access to this rich collection of data. Individual censuses may be examined and national or regional data isolated. The collection also permits sorting of variables and the creation of individual tables.

An examination of census materials for Suffolk County, Massachusetts, in the time period 1890–1920 can be helpful in explaining the strong nativist response to the Sacco and Vanzetti trial in 1921. The murder that took place just outside of Boston in 1920 reflected growing fears about immigrants in American cities. The accusation, trial, conviction, and execution of these two Italian immigrants was part of the "Red Scare" in the United States and had significant anticommunist and antisocialist overtones. There was a significant demographic shift in Suffolk County from 1890 to 1920. The number of native white males age 21 and over declined from 78,444 in 1890 to 59,998 in 1920, while the number of foreign born white males of the same age increased from 66,728 in 1890 to 122,176 in 1920. One of the fastest growing groups were those born in Italy, whose number increased from 4,799 in 1890 to 42,052 in 1920. The statistics alone do not indicate why suburban white Bostonians reacted so strongly, but they provide clear evidence of a seismic shift in population in the generation preceding the trial. When combined with other primary evidence surrounding the case, statistical evidence provides a clearer understanding of the social tensions behind nativism.

Newspapers and Periodicals

Newspapers are among the most commonly used primary sources. Part of their appeal is their availability in print, microform, and online formats. Most local libraries have actual copies or microfilm copies of area newspapers; major research libraries have substantial collections of historical newspapers. Many historical newspapers are online with the capability of searching for a specific article, or showing an entire newspaper page. One example of these online historical newspapers is *Harper's Weekly,* a mid-nineteenth-century serial: http://app.harpweek.com/. Despite their usefulness and widespread availability, newspapers should be used by beginning historians with caution. Although these sources provide a popular view into a time period, the fact that newspapers often report on events based on the evidence a reporter has collected gives newspapers and magazines some of the characteristics of a secondary source.

Many newspapers also have a point of view, which in some cases may be muted, but in other times and places this point of view is quite pronounced. Nineteenth-century United States newspapers were often mouthpieces for political parties, religious organizations, or social movements. The historian must rigorously apply the same critical evaluation about the author, the audience, and the historical context employed for other sources. When using newspapers to understand an event, it is best to corroborate with other primary sources on the same event. Newspapers are especially useful in examining a particular point of view. For example, any examination of the politics surrounding Jacksonian fiscal policy should include a review of leading Democratic newspapers from the period. Newspapers can also be of great use to historians interested in examining language as a means to recover meaning. A historian might carefully scrutinize an editorial from a particular time period, and, armed with a thorough knowledge of historical context, recover important and otherwise difficult-to-discern aspects of an event or time.

Oral Interviews

Oral interviews open another avenue to help historians understand and explain the past. They represent an exciting addition to existing primary source collections. Oral testimony, created with the assistance of a trained scholar, preserves individual recollections of past events. Because this source falls into the category of a created source—one intentionally generated through a planned and orchestrated oral interview—knowledge of the interviewer, intended audience, purpose, and point of view are critically important in weighing the value of the testimony. These oral sources must withstand the rigor of a critical evaluation like any other primary source.

One of the richest oral history collections began in the 1930s and sought to gather the accounts of former slaves, whose stories had largely been ignored as a source for the history of slavery in the United States. Housed in American Memory, *Voices from the Days of Slavery: Former Slaves Tell Their Stories* (http://memory.loc.gov/ammem/collections/voices/) gives a unique glimpse into the world of the former slaves. The interviewers are identified in the collection and there is information about each of them, as well as about each interview subject. Studied individually, the slave narratives offer significant insights into life experiences. One example is the testimony of Alice Gaston of Gee's Bend, Alabama, recorded in 1941 by Robert Sonkin. Her interview opens:

> Alice Gaston:?. We was talking about in the old war time, the old slavery time. I can remember when, uh, I can remember when the Yankees come through and, uh, they carried my father away and carried away, my si, two sisters and one brother. And, uh, they left me. And I can remember when my missus used to run in the garden, from the Yankees and tell us if they come, don't tell them where they at. Told, don't tell nobody where they at when they come and they all come and they told me, don't get scared now and tell them, where they is, where they is. I told them no, we told them no. And uh, when they come and ask for them I told them I didn't know there they was, and they was in the woods. And this was at the house. And my father, when my father left, he carried with the, he went away with the Yankees, and carried two, carried two, two girls and one son, the oldest one. Carried them with him. And he with the Yankees. And I can remember that. And uh, my old missus was named Mrs. M., and the master was name Mr. F. I.[*pause*]? Mr. F. I.[7]

Alice Gaston was a young child when the event she described took place, more than three-quarters of a century earlier. Despite her inability to recall her owner's names and the general nature of her account, it does depict the presence of Union forces and the separation of families, both of which deeply affected the lives of slaves. By studying this account and those of other African Americans from this region of Alabama and the South, greater knowledge and understanding of the world known only to slaves can be reconstructed. These narratives also illustrate the importance of studying many documents to gain an understanding of the larger group rather than focusing only on an individual interview. There may well be factual errors that trace to the memory loss between the event and the interview; however, the source remains critical because it is one of the few extant collections of African Americans describing their experiences in their own words.

Photographs and Maps

Visual evidence, like oral testimony, is an intentionally created primary source that requires careful scrutiny. When working with this form of evidence, researchers ask similar questions about **authorship, intended audience, purpose, perspective,** and **point of view** that they would of any other primary source. Paintings and photographs are the creations of the artist; yet, the pictures

---

[7]Interview with Alice Gaston, Gee's Bend, Alabama, 1941, *Voices from the Days of Slavery,* http://memory.loc.gov/ammem/collections/voices/. Another excellent oral history collection is *Born in Slavery: Slave Narratives from the Federal Writer's Project, 1936–1938,* http://memory.loc.gov/ammem/snhtml/snhome.html.

they produce offer another type of evidence of great use to researchers. These sources not only reveal important images; they also provide insights into the mind and world of the artist and the times. The composition of crowds at events may offer unique glimpses of different cultures and present information not intended by the artist or photographer.

A useful example of photographic evidence is found in a digital archive in American Memory. Ansel Adams, the preeminent American photographer, photographed the Japanese-American Manzanar Relocation Center in California and his works have been gathered and preserved digitally. They record aspects of daily life and experiences of the families interned during World War II. The following photograph captures Japanese Americans in line for lunch in 1943.[8]

Library of Congress, LC-DIG-ppprs-00173; Photograph by Ansel Adams

The black-and-white photograph illustrates the starkness of the camp and the regimented lives of its residents. It suggests the camp's isolation and documents a daily occurrence. The people seem comfortable in their surroundings and do not appear to be closely guarded. The visual evidence corroborates written accounts from those who lived in the camps, government accounts, contemporary newspapers, and other forms of evidence. The photographs also reveal what appealed to Adams. Photographs, moving pictures, and paintings provide researchers with an additional perspective on a topic under analysis.

Similar observations may be made about maps. All maps describing the world in 1600 are not necessarily the same. If the mapmaker was European, his

---

[8]"Mess line, noon, Manzanar Relocation Center, California," photograph by Ansel Adams, "Suffering under a Great Injustice": Ansel Adams Photographs of Japanese Americans at Manzanar," Library of Congress, American Memory, http://memory.loc.gov/pnp/ppprs/ 00100/00173v.jpg.

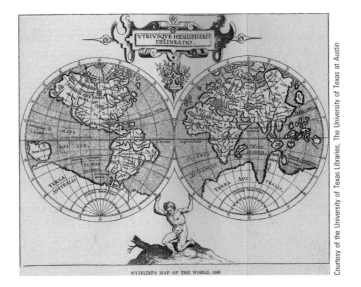

WYTFLIET'S MAP OF THE WORLD, 1598

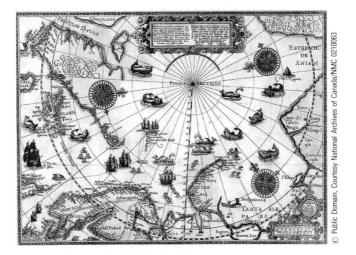

perspective and focal points may have differed profoundly from a Chinese or Arab cartographer. The axis of the world differs from place to place and the knowledge of places may not be identical. Maps, like other forms of visual evidence, are sources that must be scrutinized according to the same standards of evaluation.

The two global maps published by Cornelius Wytfliet[9] and Edward Wright[10] in the late sixteenth century show the status of cartography at the time.

---

[9]Wytfliet's Map of the World 1598, Perry-Castañeda Library Map Collection, The University of Texas at Austin, http://www.lib.utexas.edu/maps/historical/.

[10]Wright's World Map of 1598, reproduced from an 1880 facsimile, National Archives of Canada/NMC 0210063, http://www.collectionscanada.ca/explorers/.

Wytfliet's map is more detailed and speculates on the sizes and locations of land masses, while Wright's tends to focus more clearly on what has been explored and previously mapped. A comparison of these maps offers insight into the map-maker's knowledge of the world. When evaluating these maps, the historian should consider **audience** and **perspective.** Furthermore, the historian should try to discern similarities between the maps as well as the differences to better understand the mapmaker's world. How do these maps compare with maps of today; what did the late sixteenth-century cartographers know and not know about the world? A close study of maps can enhance any research project.

Artifacts

Physical evidence, in the form of the built landscape or objects remaining from a given society, constitutes another seldom studied resource. This kind of evidence survives in many forms and can enrich the historian's understanding of individuals and societies. In a sense, all other forms of historical evidence are artifacts from the past; however, buildings, furnishings, clothing, tools, coins, and the like are normally classified as artifacts. Physical remains help historians understand texture, weight, size, scale, and a host of other elements that may not be knowable from written or other types of sources. They help historians understand popular conceptions of themselves, their society, and their beliefs. For societies who left no written records (and for many who did), their artifacts can help historians understand their place in the human past.

At Sutton Hoo in Suffolk, England, archaeologists uncovered a ship burial laden with Anglo-Saxon artifacts from the seventh century. One of them was

an iron helmet, covered with tinned copper alloy panels[11] that serves as a good example of the kinds of information that may be learned from an analysis of artifacts. The helmet and the other relics from the buried vessel are now housed in the British Museum in London.

Made of iron, decorated in bronze, the helmet is one of four known to have survived from Anglo-Saxon times. It protected the ears, eyes, and neck from attack and was reinforced to protect the skull and nose. The mask illustrates the level of military technology at the time. It is a valuable complement to extant codes of Anglo-Saxon law that imposed stiff fines on those who damaged the critical faculties of warriors. The mask also reveals the level and quality of artisanship available in seventh-century Anglo-Saxon society.[12]

PRIMARY SOURCES IN A STUDENT PAPER

In his essay on rebuilding the city of London following the Great Fire, Jack Sheehan used a variety of primary source materials from his university library, interlibrary loan, and the Internet. Some of the sources helped him establish context while others formed the backbone of his argument. He found sources that explained the responses of those who observed the fire, as well as the ways in which the state and city responded to it. His interests were less in explaining the fire itself than in the problems involved in reconstructing the city. Jack's basic primary sources fall into three categories: contemporary newspapers, personal diaries, and government records. For the general narrative of the fire, he relied extensively on the *London Gazette*, a weekly newspaper. The editor observes that this was a special edition of the paper to give readers a brief account of the fire:

> On the second instant, at one of the clock in the Morning, there hapned to break out, a sad in deplorable Fire in *Pudding-lane,* neer *New Fish-street,* which falling out at that hour of the night, and in a quarter of the Town so close built with wooden and pitched houses spread itself so far before day, and with such distraction to the inhabitants and Neighbours, that care was not taken for the timely preventing the further diffusion of it, by pulling down houses, as ought to have been; so that this lamentable Fire in a short time became too big to be mastred by any Engines or working *neer* it. It fell out most unhappily too, That a violent Easterly wind fomented it, and kept it burning all that day, and the night following spreading itself up to *Grace-church-street* and downwards from *Cannon-street* to the Water-side, as far as the *Three Cranes in the Vintrey.*[13]

---

[11]Helmet from the ship burial at Sutton Hoo, Anglo-Saxon, early seventh century AD, from Mound 1, Sutton Hoo, Suffolk, England.

[12]The helmet may have been Scandinavian or produced by a Scandinavian craftsman. We are grateful to Dr. Sonja Marzinzik, Curator of Insular Early Medieval Collections, The British Museum, London, for her helpful commentary about the Sutton Hoo helmet.

[13]The *London Gazette,* 8 September 1666, http://www.exmsft.com/~davidco/History/fire1.htm.

The framework for analysis introduced earlier in this chapter—**author, audience, purpose, point of view, language,** and **significance**—helped focus Jack's questions about this passage and those that follow. The source is a newspaper issued under the authority of the English government. Though it has no author, whereas it is an official publication sanctioned by the state and is intended for widespread distribution, certain inferences may be made.

First, according to the source, the account is intended to provide English readers with a summary of how the fire began, its physical boundaries, and what it destroyed. Thus, its purpose is to inform. The passage concludes with a summary of the number of buildings and other structures. The story accomplishes these ends in clear, coherent fashion and the audience has a good sense of what transpired.

Second, the paragraph cited gives the reader significant specific information regarding why the fire spread so quickly. Even the winds worked against the firefighters and helped spread the destruction. The point of view is authoritative since the paper presents the position of the government and the author is privileged to precise information about the extent of the damage. Its tone is matter of fact. While the author quite naturally is shocked, he reports the events without editorializing or sensationalizing them. This conclusion is reflected in the balanced language of the passage as well. The account appeared right after the fire and its thoroughness enhances its significance as a resource for modern researchers. This account from an official London observer provides a balanced view. It is corroborated by other firsthand observers and reinforced by later scholars, therefore, lending credence to Jack Sheehan's conclusions.

The most detailed primary account of the London Fire is found in the diary of Samuel Pepys, another source used extensively in Sheehan's paper. A Londoner, Pepys kept the most extensive extant personal diary of the 1660s. His account is richly detailed, gossipy, and filled with unique insights about the times and its people that reinforce and expand upon other contemporary sources, including the *London Gazette*. He walked the streets during the fire and provided extensive commentary about the human suffering and property damage. The following extract from 2 September 1666 is typical of Pepys's coverage:

> Having stayed, and in an hour's time seen the fire rage every way, and nobody to my sight endeavouring to quench it, but to remove their goods and leave all to the fire; and having seen it get as far as the Steelyard, and the wind mighty high and driving it into the city, and everything, after so long a drought, proving combustible, even the very stones of churches, and among other things, the poor steeple by which pretty Mrs. (Horsely) lives, and whereof my old school-fellow Elborough is parson, taken fire in the very top and there burned till it fall down—I to Whitehall with a gentleman with me who desired to go off from the Tower to see the fire in my boat—to Whitehall, and there up to the King's closet in the chapel, where people came about me and I did give them an account dismayed them all; and word was carried in to

the King, so I was called for and did tell the King and Duke of York what I saw, and that unless his Majesty did command houses to be pulled down, nothing could stop the fire.[14]

In the case of this diary, there is an identified author and he is well known. Therefore, finding information about Samuel Pepys and establishing his credibility as an authority is far simpler than for anonymous sources. The diary was written in code and was thus not intended to be read by others. This fact enhances its likely accuracy as he had no cause to exaggerate to himself or about his contributions. Since Pepys's purpose in keeping the diary was for his personal edification, he did not have to concern himself with word count. Overall, his tone is even-tempered and conversational and what he includes—though richer in detail than most other contemporary accounts of the fire—agrees with their conclusions. Later historians have relied upon his observations; he appears again and again as a major source in their monographs about the 1660s.

Jack Sheehan also relies more fully on Pepys's account than any other diary of the times, though he is careful to corroborate the diarist's observations with those of other sources. The passage cited above offers clear evidence of what Pepys saw. It also points to Pepys's ability to contextualize what he observed and heard by making reference to people he knew and commenting on how the fire impinged on their lives. Sheehan's own paragraphs demonstrate an understanding of what he has read in the source and an ability to use his information to construct a sound narrative. Rather than quoting extensively, he employs the diary and other primary sources to illuminate the points he is making instead of simply quoting the source and leaving the reader to make the connection. Too often beginning researchers cherry-pick from primary sources, embedding direct quotations periodically throughout their paper. This practice should be avoided.

As he transitions from coverage of the Great Fire itself to an analysis of the process of recovery and rebuilding, Sheehan turns to a review of government orders, the political question of responsibility, and the plans proposed to restore the city. These sources are a blend of official and personal, those intended for the widest possible audience and those, like John Evelyn's diary, intended for his own edification. Some of the documents have a pragmatic and a political purpose. They inform the public of the government's plans for reconstruction, while at the same time they calm popular fears by showing the King has matters under control. These varied interpretations form the basic structure of Sheehan's argument and blend well with his secondary sources to build a solid case. It might have been improved had he examined more government papers and considered the political and legal issues surrounding rebuilding in more depth. Yet, the varieties of primary evidence and the efforts to corroborate their testimony with reference to other primary sources add to the authority of Sheehan's argument. Effective research must be rooted in as wide an array of primary sources as

---

[14]Samuel Pepys, *The Diary of Samuel Pepys, Volume VII, 1666,* edited by Robert Latham and William Matthews (Berkeley and Los Angeles: University of California Press, 1972), 269.

possible. Jack's research was conducted as part of a class assignment and was governed by time constraints. While he considered a number of primary sources, his work was by no means exhaustive.

CONCLUSION

This chapter defines primary sources and explains ways to analyze the diverse forms of evidence contained within them. The primary sources available to historians are virtually without limit and the opportunity to examine firsthand evidence is unparalleled. Beginning historians can access a veritable treasure chest of evidence types and use them to construct their arguments. With the finding aids and support documentation available online and in print, researchers can more readily use their critical faculties and imagination to study aspects of the past impossible for most a short generation ago. The volume is daunting and scholars must be conscious of what may reasonably be examined and studied closely to strengthen a particular project. They must weigh the number of examples required to make a compelling case without tipping the scale to make an argument that overwhelms a reader. The process of assembling and blending information to support a well-reasoned and well-written historical argument is found in the next chapter.

5

Writing

Writing is an ongoing process that starts when research begins. Although it seems that research and writing are independent tasks, they are not. Writing is to historical inquiry what oxygen is to life; it surrounds all that the historian does and one cannot practice history without writing. The writing process begins when a researcher enters an archive or library; it continues as he or she critically analyzes what has been gleaned from research; it informs further research on a topic; it enables students of history to develop a clear and organized understanding of the subject; and it provides a medium by which these students may clearly present their interpretation of the process or event they have examined. Writing history is a constant conversation: with the sources, with ideas, with other historians, and with one's self. No clear understanding of the past is possible without following a painstaking yet rewarding process of writing. Writing is the best way to learn about history.

BEGINNING THE WRITING PROCESS

Inexperienced historians still believe that writing is a process that begins after the research has been completed. For the uninitiated, this means after spending hours and hours reviewing the pertinent primary and secondary sources, the beginning researcher sits in front of a computer, notes in hand, and bangs out an essay that is "complete" with few revisions. Such an approach might be common, but it is seldom good writing. Nor is it good history. As the central component to the critical thinking process, writing should consume considerably more time than the hours spent researching. The final product is, after all, what is read and judged by others.

All historians must ask themselves several questions as they begin to write.

What is the Purpose of the Writing Assignment?   Writing a book review is different from writing a research paper or analyzing a document or preparing an
annotated bibliography. Some writing assignments have limitations. Book
reviews, for example, tend to be about 400–1,000 words in length and offer
critical evaluation of a single book. For larger writing assignments, some
instructors impose page limits or restrict the assignment to specific books or
sources. Formal research papers usually take the form of a scholarly journal
article, about 20–25 pages in length, with appropriate footnoting and bibliography. Beginning scholars should be aware of the writing assignment's purpose
as they begin their work.

- Who is the audience? Those individuals who read book reviews have different expectations than those who read a journal article, historiographic
  essay, or research paper. But in any case, historical writing is intended for
  peers—other historians.

- What voice should the paper take? Historical writing should always
  assume a scholarly tone or voice that presents a thoughtful interpretation
  of the past.

- What interpretation does the paper take? Many forms of historical writing
  offer interpretations. Historians read the sources (both secondary and
  primary), construct an argument supported by this evidence, acknowledge
  alternative interpretations, and demonstrate why their perspective is
  most suitable through a preponderance of evidence.

Early Writing

Historical writing is initiated in the "early writing" stage. This occurs when a
historian first begins to think about a topic. Initially, this might involve little
more than jotting down ideas on a subject. But such free-form thinking is irrel-
evant if uninformed. This preliminary investigation may begin with reading a
general source such as an encyclopedia or book chapter, but will quickly lead
to the important secondary sources described in Chapter 3. As the beginning
researcher reads these general and secondary sources on a subject, the ideas
about a topic begin to take shape and should begin to evolve into a group of
written questions. For many historians, this is a useful time to formulate a
prospectus.

Prospectus

The prospectus illustrates the conversation between research and writing. The
drafting of a prospectus is outlined in Chapter 2 as one of the first steps of the
research process, but it also is an early step in writing a research paper. Without fully reiterating what was written earlier, the prospectus is an informal
writing assignment in which the beginning researcher jots down initial ideas

and begins to formulate a series of questions about a topic based upon preliminary research. Ideally, such informal thinking committed to paper will allow the researcher to begin to develop a central question or hypothesis about the topic.

THE JURY OF OUR PEERS

Nearly all historians recognize that their work is eventually going to be submitted to their peers for scrutiny. It is essential, especially for beginning researchers, to make use of a peer reviewer while writing. Ideally, a peer reviewer is someone who either knows something about the subject, or someone who can discern a well-constructed, thoughtful essay supported by evidence. An effective peer is not one who reads the early drafts of a paper, stating, "That's great." Rather, it is someone who critically evaluates numerous aspects of the essay, offering constructive criticism on how it might be improved. It is often helpful to seek constructive criticism from the peer reviewer at all stages of the written work.

In evaluating another's writing, a peer reviewer should consider some of the following questions:

- How well organized is the essay? How might it be improved?
- How well written is the essay? Are the main points clearly presented? How might the draft be improved?
- What is the thesis of this paper? Is it clearly presented? How might it be improved?
- Does the author provide adequate background information and historical context for the topic? What suggestions would improve this section?
- What are the strengths and weaknesses of the essay?
- How might the topic be better developed?
- How well are primary sources and secondary works used? Are they adequate?
- How analytical is the paper? How interpretative?

Few activities are more valuable to any writer than a good peer review. Effective peer reviewing is, however, a two-way street. Constructive criticism from a peer, if heeded, can greatly improve a paper. Conversely, careful analysis of a peer's paper can help improve one's own analytical and writing skills.

THE SHORT INFORMAL ESSAY

One of the best ways to improve both critical thinking and writing skills is through writing short essays. Such essays force the writer to commit ideas to paper, but also to grapple with essential points. As a follow-up to a prospectus or as a reflection upon reading material, the short essay offers the author an opportunity to sharpen thoughts on a particular subject.

The simplest short essay assignment is the **summary.** Although even the most inexperienced historians believe that they can easily summarize a reading, many discover that when put to the task, they struggle. This is because an effective summary is succinct, and being succinct requires the writer to make difficult decisions about the material. Virtually anyone can offer a lengthy summary of a monograph they have read, a lecture they have heard, or a movie they have seen, but how many can do it in 300 words or fewer? Writing a summary requires the ability to express points clearly and concisely, as well as requiring the author to understand the material well enough to make choices about what is most important. Therefore, a quality summary describes the thesis and main points as well as includes important conclusions. Some short essays might also be useful for clarifying points concerning historical context, historiographical issues, or in considering the relationship between author and audience. These skills are essential for reading material, but they can improve the ability to take notes in class and can even lead to more effective note taking for a paper. Beginning researchers can quickly hone both their writing and critical thinking skills by performing such exercises. For example, writing short 100–150 word summaries of reading assignments forces the writer to grasp the most essential details. Among the most common forms of the short essay is the book review described in Chapter 3.

The short essay is essential to writing. As the beginning researcher works through secondary sources, he or she must be an active reader who thinks constantly about the material before committing preliminary ideas to paper. (The passive reader, by contrast, does little more than thoughtlessly transcribe material from one medium to another.) A short essay is most effective if it is an elaboration on the prospectus or on some aspect of the prospectus. Ultimately, such writing should yield a central question or hypothesis that will evolve into a clearly articulated thesis after further research and reflection.

THE FIRST PARAGRAPH

In many ways drafting the first paragraph of the paper is the culmination of the short writing assignment. Although not especially informal in its grammar or organization, the first paragraph is a rough draft that sets a paper's direction. The first paragraph serves as a rudimentary roadmap, but it also requires initial thoughts about the organization of the project.

Several elements are essential to a quality first paragraph. Like a good first impression, the opening paragraph must interest readers and draw them into reading further. Failure to do so may mean that the rest of the paper is ignored. Developing an interesting opening to an essay is a difficult task even for the most experienced writers. Many historians attract readers' interest by beginning with dramatic tension. For example, an essay explaining who fired the first shot at Lexington in 1775 might not begin with background causes, but might start with a brief description of the exchange of fire or the immediate aftermath of the event. In presenting this tension, the writer should offer a cursory sketch (no more than a few sentences) of historical context. Having briefly established a central tension that draws readers' interest and offers some background, it is important to next develop a central question that the paper will answer. Only after considerably more research, analysis, and writing of subsequent drafts will the beginning researcher be able to develop a thesis from this preliminary hypothesis. This statement of hypothesis (and eventually thesis) should appear by the end of the first paragraph. A thesis statement that appears early in the paper is an effective cue to the argument; it also serves as the central spine around which an essay is organized. The thesis must be stated clearly and it must be developed and supported with evidence throughout the paper. The paper, then, should be organized, and flow from one point to another, while periodically returning to the thesis as a touchstone.

At the end of the first paragraph, historians often include a **historiographic footnote.** This footnote offers a brief commentary on the most important secondary sources on the topic. The historiographic footnote tends to be organized with the most important general scholarly works on the time period or subject listed first, then it narrows to more specific secondary sources on the topic. After listing the scholarly works, most historians include a brief list of the most important primary sources on the topic. This feature offers readers a shorthand guide to the sources that shaped the approach to the topic.

Student Jack Sheehan follows these conventions in his first paragraph. He creates a tension, a curiosity about the subject by suggesting that plans to make London an ideal city could not be achieved. His thesis comes at the end of the first paragraph and is clear. The thesis elicits skepticism in the reader, while also allowing Sheehan to present several main points to be explored in his paper. Sheehan's first paragraph and historiographic footnote are below:

> In the year 1666, the city of London had already undergone a great amount of turmoil from an outbreak of the plague in the previous year. Adding to this disaster, the city caught fire in September, and the blaze grew to engulf a great number of buildings. These buildings included homes, churches, and public buildings. By the time the fire was extinguished more than half of the city lay in ruin. Life in London came to almost a complete standstill, as the city was prepared to be rebuilt from the ground up. Many architects and city planners worked on the rebuilding of the city over the years that followed. However, a plan to build a unified city of grandeur fell greatly short. Due to the elaborate plans, property laws, general disagreement, and the inability to coalesce

the plans into reality, London soon became the ideal city that was never realized.[1]

A first paragraph is an ideal short essay to submit to a peer for constructive criticism. Since the first paragraph sets the direction for the future development of the paper, a critical eye is essential to ensure that the paper is not on the wrong track. A good peer will review the first paragraph with some of the following points in mind:

- Did the opening sentences of the paragraph attract the reader's attention?
- Did the paragraph set the historical context?
- Can you identify the central question or hypothesis or thesis?
- Was the paragraph well written and well organized?
- Does the historiographic footnote present the major scholarly works on this topic?
- Was the correct footnote style used?

---

[1] The secondary books dealing with the rebuilding of the city are Elizabeth McKellar, *The Birth of Modern London: The Development and Design of the City, 1660–1720* (New York: St. Martin's Press, 1999); Neil Hanson, *The Great Fire of London in that Apocalyptic Year, 1666* (New York: John Wiley and Sons, 2002); Timothy Baker, *London: Rebuilding the City After the Great Fire* (London: Phillimore, 2000); Walter George Bell, *The Great Fire of London*, 2nd ed. (London: The Bodley Head, 1951); Jonathan Barry, *The Tudor and Stuart Town: A Reader in English Urban History 1530–1688* (London: Longman Publishing, 1990). The last source deals with the town structure and physical building. There also are a relevant number of articles on the topic as well, including M. A. R. Cooper, "Robert Hooke's Work as Surveyor for the City of London in the Aftermath of the Great Fire," *Notes and Records of the Royal Society of London* 51, no. 2 (1997): 161–174. See also 52, no. 1 (1998): 25–38 and 52, no. 2 (1998): 205–220; Charles Elliot, "Samuel Pepys' London Chronicles," *Smithsonian* 32, no. 4 (2001): 102–109; Phillippa Glanville, "The Topography of Seventeenth Century London; A Review of Maps," *Urban History Yearbook* (1980): 79–83; Frank T. Melton, "Sir Robert Clayton's Building Projects in London, 1666–1672," *Guildhall Studies in London History* 3, no. 1 (1977): 37–41; Alan Wykes, "The Great Fire of London," *British History Illustrated* 1, no. 1 (1974): 18–27. Other sources include A. L. Beier and Roger Finlay, eds., *London 1500–1700: The Making of the Metropolis* (New York: Longman Group Ltd., 1986); Frank E. Brown, "Continuity and Change in the Urban House: Developments in Domestic Space Organisation in Seventeenth Century London," *Comparative Studies in Society and History* 28 (1986): 558–590; Gregg Carr, *Residence and Social Status: The Development of Seventeenth Century London* (London: Garland Publishing, 1990); Robert Fishman, "The Origins of the Suburban Idea in England," *Chicago History* 13, no. 2 (1984): 26–36; Jack Lindsay, *The Monster City: Defoe's London, 1688–1730* (New York: St Martin's Press, 1978); Valerie Pearl, "Change and Stability in 17th Century London," *London Journal* 5, no. 1 (1979): 3–34; Keith Wrightson, *English Society 1580–1680* (New Brunswick, NJ: Rutgers University Press, 1982). Another facet that is examined in many sources is the growing population and expansion of London. See Jeremy Boulton, *Neighbourhood and Society: A London Suburb in the Seventeenth Century* (Cambridge and New York: Cambridge University Press, 1987); Michael Power, "Shadwell; the Development of a London Suburban Community in the Seventeenth Century," *The London Journal* 4, no. 1 (1978): 29–46. Primary sources come from Roland Bartel, ed., *London in Plague and Fire, 1665–1666: Selected Source Materials for College Research Papers* (Boston: D.C. Heath and Company, 1957); selected acts from the *Early English Books 1641–1671* Collection; Samuel Pepys, *Diary of Samuel Pepys*, eds. Robert Latham and William Matthews (Berkeley: University of California Press, 1970); John Evelyn, *The Diary of John Evelyn*, ed. W. Bray (London: M. W. Dunne, 1901) and the *London Gazette* (London), 2 September 1666–10 September 1666.

- What are your suggestions to improve the first paragraph and historiographic footnote?

ELEMENTS OF EFFECTIVE WRITING

Writing well is not a trait one is born with, although some individuals may have more innate ability in this area than others. Effective writing is the result of drafting, editing, rewriting, and polishing. While effective writing is difficult to describe, most readers know it when they see it. Most good writers developed an eye for good writing through a love of reading. The more that an individual reads the more attuned they become to clear writing. A beginning researcher might improve his or her writing skills by emulating the writing style and tone of a favorite historian.

TIPS FOR EFFECTIVE WRITING

Effective Writing Requires Hard Work   While there is no simple set of suggestions that can easily turn a weak writer into a good one (except practice through repetition), all types of effective writing share certain elements in common.

Know the Audience   It is essential for a writer to have a clear sense of the audience. Writing that might be appropriate in some venues might not be acceptable in others. Most historians assume that their audience consists of academic peers with an interest in scholarly deliberation. This requires writing in a serious tone and in a style that conforms to accepted scholarly practice. Scholarly journals or monographs provide clues to this standard.

Be Clear and Concise   Although many inexperienced writers attempt to impress their readers with flowery or obscure language, such writing belabors and clouds the point being made. Successful writers use clear, simple language, making even difficult concepts easy to understand. The active voice is the best means for making writing clear and more concise. Sentences that begin with a subject followed by a verb that acts upon an object are examples of the active voice; conversely, the passive voice places the object first in the sentence, followed by the verb, with the subject coming toward the sentence's end. While many novice writers may believe that the active sentence "He loved her" is too simple and brief, the passive version of this sentence "She was loved by him" indicates how wordy and occasionally confusing the passive voice becomes. The increase in the number of words adds nothing to the concept expressed and, indeed, in more complicated sentences can be confusing. One of the easiest ways to identify passive voice is to look for tenses of "to be" or "to have" as modifiers for other verbs. While these verb tenses are perfectly fine alone and are among the most used in the English language, when they stand in front of or near another verb, trouble lurks. For example, the above passive sentence includes the phrase "was loved." All writers should use sentences that clearly indicate the subject.

Be Organized   One of the most difficult tasks for any historian is to write in an organized, logical manner. It is important that an essay proceeds logically from sentence to sentence, from paragraph to paragraph, and from section to section. Whether a sentence, a paragraph, or a section of the paper, each is simultaneously discreet and connected with what came previously and what follows. One of the important aspects of creating a well-organized paper is to offer transitions from one point to another. This may require a clause at the end of one sentence or the beginning of the next to ease the transition, or sentences at the beginning and end of paragraphs that make the transition to the next paragraph.

Write in Sentences and Paragraphs   This point may seem almost too obvious to state, but many writers fail to follow this essential adage. All sentences should contain a subject and verb. Many sentences also include an object. Sentences which lack these essentials are known as **sentence fragments.** Perhaps more problematic are those sentences that have too many subjects, verbs, and objects. The **run–on sentence** is one which does not know when it is time to stop. A good rule of thumb to avoid run-on sentences is to place a period after a sentence that contains two clauses connected by the words "and," "but," or "however." The additional points may be closely connected, but they deserve a sentence of their own. Indeed, two sentences may reinforce an important point. It is also essential to have proper transitions between sentences. In some cases this can be accomplished by including a clause at the end of one sentence or the beginning of the next that makes for easier reading. Sometimes an entire sentence may be necessary to achieve this end.

   Paragraphs are somewhat more problematic. Paragraphs are like sentences in that they have a central point to make, but beginning researchers often do not know when to stop. Each major point deserves its own paragraph. One of the best means for making a paragraph a self-contained entity is through the use of topic and concluding sentences. A **topic sentence** in a paragraph serves as an introduction to the topic of the paragraph and is followed by sentences that illustrate this point. A **concluding sentence** briefly summarizes the paragraph. Not only are these useful for setting limits for a paragraph, but topic and concluding sentences are helpful to make the transition from one point to another.

Vary Words, Sentences, and Paragraphs   Even technically correct prose may not be especially good writing if it lacks variety. Most historians recognize when writing their first essay that some words are essential, but writing can become repetitious and boring if the same words are used over, and over, and over again. A **thesaurus** is a valuable tool that enables a writer to find words with the same meaning, thus adding variation to one's language. Similarly, the length of sentences should vary. A string of grammatically correct, short, declarative sentences is exhausting to read. Good writing varies between short sentences, long sentences, and compound sentences to maintain a reader's interest. Paragraphs should also vary in length for similar reasons. When writing, think of the reader; it should not be a chore or difficult to read history.

Words Matter   Effective writers take great care to select the right word for the occasion. Writers who try to impress by using longer, flowery, or obscure language often confuse their readers. They use inappropriate words, or, even words which if used correctly, may offend their readers with an approach that seems patronizing. Even the most experienced historians must regularly consult a dictionary or thesaurus to find just the right word that conveys precisely the point being made. Be sure to avoid words that suggest uncertainty or doubt. Historians often are tentative in what they can assert, but they should never write, "It appears that maybe it is time to possibly change strategies." Effective use of the language also means that even the most inexperienced scholars must avoid clichés (such as "a stitch in time saves nine"), colloquial, conversational language, or slang. One would never write, "When James Madison first met his future wife Dolley, he thought she was a hottie."

Word choice should also be precise. One of the most misused words in the English language is "feel" or "felt"; for example, "The beginning scholar felt she had written an excellent paper." But to feel is a sensory perception, such as a bee sting or a cold breeze; it is not thought. A more appropriate sentence might read, "The beginning scholar believed she had written an excellent paper" or perhaps, "The beginning scholar knew she had written an excellent paper." Effective writers are also economical in the use of language; never use ten words if fewer convey the point clearly. Finally, avoid contractions and abbreviations in all formal writing.

Avoid First and Second Person in Academic Writing   Writing in the third person provides two important benefits to an essay:

- It provides a sense of scholarly detachment from the subject that sets a tone of academic seriousness and evenhandedness.

- It avoids the first person. Authors, especially inexperienced authors who use the first person, often slip from clear prose to conversational language that is inappropriate for the task at hand.

Check for Agreement   Effective writing exhibits agreement and parallel construction. A singular noun must be accompanied by a singular verb, and a plural noun must be accompanied by a plural verb. For example, "The beginning historian was busy with her research" is grammatically correct, but "The beginning historian were busy with her research" is not. Authors should also attempt to be as consistent with tenses as possible. Most historians write about the past, so they make almost exclusive use of some form of the past tense in their writing. For example, "Mr. Lincoln determined to supply Fort Sumter after assuming the presidency. South Carolina officials responded by firing upon the fort" is grammatically correct, but "Mr. Lincoln determined to supply Fort Sumter after assuming the presidency. South Carolina officials respond by firing upon the fort" is not.

Quote Appropriately   Experienced historians use quotations to provide their readers with a sense of how a historical figure thought about or reacted to a specific situation. Many beginning researchers are much less effective in the way they use quotations. Quotations should be used to illustrate or provide specific evidence, not to make a point. The following hypothetical example highlights this issue. In discussing Robert E. Lee's reaction to the death of Stonewall Jackson, it would be better to write "Jackson's death stunned the general. Lee remarked, 'I have lost my right arm,'" instead of "Jackson's death led Lee to remark, 'I have lost my right arm.'"

Direct quotations should come from primary sources, and the writing should clearly identify the author or speaker of these words. Extensive, excessive, and awkward quotations should be avoided. Remember, quotations exist to enhance the narrative, not to take up space or make it more cumbersome.

Use Proper Punctuation   Poor punctuation can mar otherwise fine writing. Over-use of commas or semicolons often indicates poor punctuation, generally the result of an inexperienced writer. All writers regularly consult a grammar manual for appropriate use. Over-punctuation can often contribute to choppy writing that is painful to read.

Proofread and Edit   The most important piece of advice for beginning researchers is to proofread and edit. And proofread and edit. And proofread and edit. Proof-reading and editing requires looking at different aspects of the paper. A beginning researcher might initially proofread for organization, then proofread for content, then proofread for writing and grammar. The final proofread should be done aloud as the ear picks up errors often missed by the eye. A more detailed examination of proofreading and editing can be found in Chapter 6.

TYPES OF WRITING

All historians make use of four basic approaches to writing. While they go by a variety of names, for our purposes, they are **narration, description, interpretation,** and **persuasion.** The first two, narration and description, are often closely related and provide a visceral sense of an event or period. The second two, interpretation and persuasion, are similarly interdependent, but function on a more intellectual level. Historical writing requires all four methods to be effective. Although each method is different, they often overlap and intertwine. For that reason, a brief explanation of the four methods and their usefulness is necessary.

Narration

Narration is a critical element of history that tells what happened in the past—the series of events that when combined narrates the story. Thus, the historian must resurrect past events and organize these events in a manner that the reader can follow. The key to narration is to tell a good story about what happened.

The beginning researcher should consider several ideas when narrating events.

- Narration has a purpose beyond simply telling what happened. Like the thesis statement, narration must create curiosity in the reader to want to continue reading. It introduces information that will be explained later.

- The beginning researcher should tell the story in a manner that enables the reader to understand what happened. Be efficient in this presentation: what to include or not include are critical decisions. Too much detail will burden the reader with unnecessary information, while too little will leave the reader wondering what actually transpired. Provide sufficient information so that the reader can make connections later in the paper, or so they can understand the analysis of events.

- Tell the story from multiple perspectives, if possible. This is particularly important if various viewpoints are to be addressed, or if historians provide differing interpretations of the events. Where possible, the beginning researcher should reveal the contradictions and tensions in the sources, while trying to remain faithful to retelling what happened.

In the following selection, Jack Sheehan weaves a lively narrative of the London Fire with a vivid description of its impact.

> During the fire, there was a great deal of chaos. People were running from their homes leaving all of their valuables behind. Many of the lower class stayed until the last seconds before they ran to the river and caught boats to get across to the opposite bank. The confusion was heightened with the darkness on the first night, when the fire broke out. The *London Gazette* describes a great amount of yelling and confusion, and nobody knowing quite what to do. People were trying to move their valuables from their homes in the city to areas that were untouched by the fire, such as churches. The mass confusion was present throughout the entire time the fire raged, and then continued for some time afterwards. Soon after the fire, before the embers had cooled, the people suspected plots of various kinds, and looked to convict someone for what had occurred. The chance appeared in a French Huguenot, who claimed to have started the fire all by himself. He was later convicted and sentenced to death. Even though spots were still burning, the inhabitants now faced a daunting task of rebuilding the entire city from the ground up. Very quickly it was apparent that some had plans to build the city in a new and elaborate style, much different from that of the city in ruins.[2]

Description

Description is a vivid presentation that appeals to the senses. It describes the way things smell, look, feel, taste, and sound. Description provides a sensory perception of the situation in the past so that readers can relate to these past events through their own experiences. For example, those who have spent time outside on a cold winter day might better understand the situation facing the Continental Army encamped at Valley Forge in the winter of 1777–78. Or, those who have canoed on a river or hiked in the wilderness, might have a better appreciation of the Lewis and Clark expedition. Description can also help the reader visualize different circumstances.

---

[2]Pepys, v. 7, 268, 270, 277; The *London Gazette;* Bell, 23; Wykes, 25; Hanson 59, 170.

Words can describe the confusion, the jumble of a battlefield, the acrid smell of gunpowder. They can also present the loneliness of life on the frontier, or the mixed emotions of European immigrants as they were processed though Ellis Island.

Description can also be used to explain geography. Any discussion of European colonialism in East Asia must address the geographical importance of cities such as Shanghai and Hong Kong. Similarly, it would be hard for any reader to understand the Battle of Gallipoli in 1915 without a description of the surrounding terrain.

It is important that beginning researchers use narration and description carefully.

- Narration and description should not dominate a paper. They are devices, methods to draw the reader into the topic and to provide the reader with enough information to understand the situation.

- The beginning researcher should provide sufficient information, but not overwhelm the reader with a blizzard of excessive detail. The basic question at this juncture is, "What does the reader need to know at this point in the paper in order to understand later sections?"

- Description should be based directly on the sources or what can be inferred from them. **Never** make up information. Be as historically accurate as possible.

Interpretation

This method of writing, which is intertwined with persuasion, explains or analyzes the meaning of events or ideas. **Interpretation** most often involves a close analysis of primary sources to determine, as best as possible, **why** something happened. The beginning researcher defines terms or ideas in a historical context and seeks to explain past writings and actions for the present-day reader to understand. Such analysis often produces different interpretations of past events, based on the weight of the primary source evidence. The goal is to advance a convincing interpretation supported by such evidence.

The beginning researcher should consider the following elements in interpretative writing.

- **Interpretation is central to historical writing.** The analysis of human actions is often complex and must be fully explained. There are often contradictions or exceptions that must be considered and evaluated. Such critical thinking requires marshalling evidence to support an interpretation, while also acknowledging—and sometimes refuting—other existing viewpoints.

- Historians are critical readers of the scholarship on their topic. They must be alert to the interpretations that are presented. Sometimes it is best to write down a brief description of the scholar's interpretation, as it will be helpful in developing a historiographic footnote or an annotated bibliography. Remember, be skeptical of the sources. Understanding the various scholarly interpretations will enable the beginning researcher to confidently develop an interpretation based on the weight of the primary source evidence.

■ Beginning researchers should present their interpretations carefully and in an organized and logical manner. Make sure that the interpretation is consistent throughout the paper. Make use of evidence to support the interpretation, while also acknowledging that other interpretations and contradictions in the primary sources exist.

Persuasion

Modern academic writing must contain a thesis. While persuasion may actually form a small part of the paper, it is likely to be the most important part. **Persuasion** is the argument and the evidence which supports it. Persuasive writing is easiest to locate in the introduction, where the thesis is first stated, and in the conclusion, where the thesis is restated and subsidiary conclusions are presented. But persuasion will also appear throughout the paper. Historians interpret evidence throughout the course of their written arguments to clarify how they use evidence. The thesis functions as the framework of a historical essay; the reader must be frequently reminded about the thesis and be shown how the evidence supports such an assertion.

Student Jack Sheehan effectively uses all four forms of historical writing in his conclusion: narration, description, interpretation, and persuasion.

> Even though none of the plans were undertaken, London was still rebuilt to a better standard than it had held previously. The roads were now wider, the houses safer, and the streets cleaner. The social impacts of the fire and fear of what was to happen to the city had driven the people to their breaking points. The people did not seek a magnificent work for themselves; instead they sought a functioning economic area that was safe from any more tragedy. It is this mindset that forced Parliament, the King, and city officials to rebuild the area in a manner that incorporated safety precautions and also speediness. Although fires still struck the city on a regular basis, no significant damage was done to London until the mid-twentieth century. More important than the actual design of London as it stands today are the thoughts and ideas that the committee of men in the latter half of the seventeenth century dreamed of how the city would look. So, whether the city was built according to the ideal plans or not, the seeds of the progressive city planning had been planted, and it would not be long before others noticed, but the dream of an ideal city of London died within a year of the fire.

ORGANIZATION

The first paragraph discussed earlier in this chapter implies a form of organization by providing a central core for a paper. Historians generally follow the writing of their first paragraph by creating a roadmap of what should follow. All essays, whether a scholarly journal article, a critical biography, or a scholarly monograph, contain the same basic elements as the classic five-paragraph essay: an introduction, the body of the paper, and the conclusion. This might be presented as the argument (introduction), support for the argument with evidence (body), and restating the argument and summarizing subsidiary arguments (conclusion). Often, a historian begins with a brief outline that can be gradually fleshed out as he or she conducts more research. But most essays eventually contain the following sections.

Introduction   Although the first paragraph attempts to elicit the reader's attention while also introducing the thesis and the main focus of the essay, a good introduction should seamlessly continue by offering the reader historical background and context. Some scholars devote a paragraph or more to what select previous historians have written on the topic by briefly acknowledging the schools of thought or interpretations. This section often explains how their particular argument complements or challenges the earlier interpretations. One of the great difficulties for many beginning researchers is knowing how much material to include. Since the historical past is a foreign country, it is important to help the reader make sense of that different place. The best place to begin is to provide historical background. The development of this historical background may be organized in a variety of ways, but often it begins with more general comments about the historical time and place, which are followed by information that is more focused on the event or process described. In a monograph, establishing context may take a chapter or more; in a 20-page essay it usually consumes several pages. The best rule of thumb is to provide enough historical background so that the reader can make sense of the event. Jack Sheehan's 18-page narrative on the rebuilding of London after the Great Fire provides an excellent example of how to provide historical background. He begins by telling the reader something about London prior to the fire, and then transitions to the prevalence of fire in the city. He proceeds to focus on the event that is the catalyst for the process described in his paper, the fire itself and its immediate impact. By devoting several pages to the subject, Sheehan gives the reader a sense of seventeenth-century London, the prevalence of fires during the time, and the causes and immediate impact of this particularly destructive fire. The stage has been appropriately set for Sheehan to delve into the body of his paper. One of the hallmarks of an effective introduction is that it is difficult to tell when the introduction ends and where the body of the paper begins.

Body   The most important part of any historical essay is the body. Here, the historian narrates the story of what happened, describes the sights and sounds that can make the past come to life, elaborates on points that would otherwise remain obscure, explains and interprets the significance of various points, and presents the core of evidence that supports the argument or rebuts evidence that might point to other possible conclusions.

The organization of this part of the paper is critical to presenting a clear and coherent argument. Historians generally have two choices for organizing a paper—**chronological** or **thematic.** If the beginning researcher organizes his or her paper chronologically, events taking place contemporary to one another might need to be presented thematically. Conversely, if the thematic approach is chosen, material under each theme will likely be organized chronologically. Effective organization makes for a more coherent essay; it helps to show cause and effect more clearly.

Conclusion   The conclusion is the researcher's last opportunity to make his or her point. It is the lasting impression of the research paper. Most conclusions offer a summary of the major points made in the paper. They often contain a restatement of the thesis. Some historians like to include this restatement in either the first or last paragraph of their conclusion. A conclusion should also tie up any loose ends, elaborate on the points that support the thesis, and may offer suggestions for further research on the topic.

THE FIRST DRAFT

Because writing is a way to analyze critically, historians—novice and experienced—should begin to write a first draft long before they complete their research. A beginning researcher said it best:

> "Write! Get something down. It forces you to grapple with the sources and scholarship. Besides, a working draft, no matter how poor, is better than nothing. It is easier to edit and rewrite than to stare at a blank piece of paper or computer screen and hope something happens."

Since historians write from primary sources, a good rule of thumb is to write after completing most of the secondary source reading and at least some of the primary source research. The first draft is precisely that—a draft. As such, it need not be particularly formal, nor does it need to cover all aspects of a topic, nor does it need to be especially well organized. The draft is simply an effort to get ideas down on paper. For most historians, producing a draft essay is a messy affair. It is full of gaps in logic and information. The important point is to get ideas down on paper. A historian should attempt to follow many of the conventions discussed earlier in this chapter, but an effective draft attempts to present ideas as clearly as possible, although it may not be perfectly written and organized. The first draft is a conversation between the beginning researcher, his or her sources, and the draft itself. Thus, the draft may also include questions, comments about points that need additional evidence, or more thorough analysis. These might be stated parenthetically, in boldface or italics in the text, or placed in a footnote. A draft should be clear enough that a fellow historian can read it and provide commentary on strengths and weaknesses. It should also include footnotes to indicate where information, ideas, and direct quotes have been obtained. No draft is perfect; hence its name.

It is absolutely essential to review one's own first draft and have a peer read it as well. A review of a draft essay is often something of a draft itself. It may offer less commentary on writing for the simple fact that the essay is a draft. But a good peer will offer considerable constructive criticism about the essay's strengths and how the essay might be improved. Authors should review their own work with the same critical eye. Some of the questions to keep in mind in reviewing a draft include the following:

- Is the historical background or context sufficient?
- What are the strengths of the essay?
- What points would you like more information about?
- Is the thesis clearly presented? Does the subsequent evidence support the thesis?
- How might the paper be better organized? How might it be better developed? Were there any sections that were not clear? What were they?
- What suggestions would improve the writing and organization?
- How well are primary sources and secondary sources used?
- How analytical is the paper?
- What are the initial conclusions? Does the evidence support them?

REVISING AND EDITING

The first draft should **never** be a final draft. Following the author's own review of the essay coupled with peer comments, a beginning historian will discover that the first draft needs considerable work before it can be submitted as a final paper. Early reviews of one's work often reveal that important pieces of essential evidence are missing, that the thesis might need modification because of some initially fuzzy thinking, that the research has excluded some types of potentially useful sources, or that the organization and writing need improvement. Because historical writing is a conversation between the author and the sources, most beginning researchers' first step after receiving peer comments is to conduct further research.

The additional research must be integrated into the paper, but editing and rewriting involves more than simply plugging more information into the same narrative. As the beginning researcher finds more evidence, it is essential to consider the extent to which the new material supports the thesis. Often, a draft or the research conducted subsequent to the draft review will turn up information that refutes or at least casts doubt on some initial assertions.

Revising and editing also requires attention to writing and organization. Historians revise for content, then consider their analysis, argument and conclusions, and then review their essay for clarity of expression, effective organization, appropriate grammar, and proper word choice. Since it is virtually impossible for anyone to catch every problem in just one reading, good historians continually revise and edit, based on their own reviews and those of their peers. Many historians find it useful to have a peer consider specific requests for constructive criticism. Such a request might ask about the quality of the argument, or the essay's organization or use of sources. The important point is that beginning researchers should seek additional constructive criticism of their work and should continue to revise and edit until the essay reaches a final stage.

THE ORAL PRESENTATION

After several rounds of drafting, editing, and revising, historians generally present a polished, but not yet final version of their research to an audience of their peers. The oral presentation is among the most daunting parts of the drafting and editing process, but it is essential to receive constructive criticism to improve an essay. It can be one of the most rewarding aspects of the entire writing process.

Oral presentations vary little from those delivered in a small, friendly seminar to sessions at a large professional conference. There are several ideas to keep in mind in preparing the oral presentation.

- Understand the kind of presentation to be made. Prepare accordingly. Is the purpose simply to offer information about the topic? Is the presentation a persuasive argument that presents only one side of an issue? Is it designed to solicit questions or open a dialogue on the topic?

- Know the audience. How much knowledge and understanding do they have of the topic? This will dictate how much, or how little, historical background to provide. It will also determine how much explanation is needed.

- Know the time limitation for the presentation. Is the presentation to be 10 minutes, 15 minutes, 20 minutes? It takes about 2½ minutes to read one typed, double-spaced page of text. Will the text be read or presented from an outline? Will the presentation make use of visuals or maps? Will presentation software be used? If so, is there a reason for using it? When using such software, make certain to test it before the actual presentation.

- As the topic is introduced, be certain to open with something that makes the audience want to listen. A brief description of a specific event that captures the central tension of the essay is very effective. Can the audience easily discern the thesis or major thrust of the presentation? In the introduction, do voice and demeanor convey confidence and credibility? Will the presentation convey knowledge of the topic?

- How will the presentation be organized? Can the audience follow the argument easily? Is there a clear separation between points? Does the presentation flow naturally from one idea to the next? Are the meaning and purpose of the presentation clear?

- Is there sufficient evidence to support the thesis? Were direct quotations identified and clearly presented? Statistics? Was evidence displayed or circulated in handouts? Were sources referenced, especially the primary evidence?

- Was the topic presented enthusiastically? Could the audience hear clearly? Were varieties of pitch, intonation, and pace of delivery employed to avoid a monotone?

- Were the pronunciation and articulation clear? Avoid vocal distractions such as repetitive use of "you know" or "like." Avoid visual distractions like running hands through your hair or flipping hair. Use good posture before the audience. Do not slouch or lean upon the podium.

- Was good visual contact maintained with the audience?

- Reach conclusions. Make certain to return to the main points of the argument. Did the presentation come to closure?

- Presentations should allow time for questions from the audience. What did the audience have to say during the questions and comments? All constructive criticism should be taken seriously. Such comments can be used to improve subsequent drafts of the paper.

Preparation for an oral presentation is obviously central to its success. Careful attention to each element offers an opportunity to showcase what has been learned and to share enthusiasm for the topic with the audience. The same level of preparation and attention to detail will also produce a written paper that reflects the same high standard.

The paper has now evolved from a vague idea scribbled on paper, to a first draft, to a nearly final paper—at all stages aided by the constructive criticism of peers as well as one's own proofreading and editing. The final paper is the next and concluding step in the process. The following chapter discusses many of the last points to consider as the beginning historian completes the essay.

SUGGESTED READINGS

Bailyn, Bernard. *On the Teaching and Writing of History: Responses to a Series of Questions.* ed. Edward C. Lathem. Hanover, NH: University Press of New England, 1994.

Hacker, Diane. *A Writer's Reference.* Boston: Bedford/St. Martin's, 2003.

McArthur, Tom, and Roshan McArthur. *Concise Oxford Companion to the English Language.* Oxford and New York: Oxford University Press, 2005.

Rampolla, Mary Lynn. *A Pocket Guide to Writing in History,* 5th ed. Boston: Bedford/St. Martin's, 2007.

Safire, William. *Fumblerules: A Lighthearted Guide to Grammar and Good Usage.* New York: Doubleday, 1990.

Strunk, William, and E. B. White, *The Elements of Style,* 4th ed. Boston: Pearson Education, 2005.

Zinsser, William K. *On Writing Well: An Informal Guide to Writing Nonfiction,* 7th ed. New York: HarperCollins, 2006.

6

Finishing the Paper

Polishing a successful research project into finished form demands a different set of skills than those involved in research and writing; yet, they are every bit as critical to the work's ultimate success. It is, after all, the final version of a research paper that will be read and subsequently evaluated. The last review of a paper is a tedious and time-consuming process that requires careful attention to detail. It also requires an understanding of—and precise adherence to—the discipline's conventions. Beginning researchers must follow this fundamental aspect of research and writing, especially in the rush to meet deadlines.

This chapter will emphasize the principal aspects of finishing a project successfully: accurately completing the necessary scholarly apparatus (footnotes and bibliography according to *The Chicago Manual of Style* or its abbreviated form, *A Manual for Writers of Term Papers, Theses, and Dissertations* by Kate L. Turabian); reviewing a suggested checklist of the paper's mechanical and stylistic elements necessary for the final written presentation. Beginning researchers should be thinking of these matters throughout the research and writing process; however, they assume a more central place as the project nears completion.

FOOTNOTES

When historians read scholarly monographs and journal articles, they quickly understand that footnotes are an essential part of the work. Footnotes assist the audience in following the thought processes and questions posed by fellow scholars to shape their arguments. The reader also learns how other historians use information. Reading footnotes carefully and thinking about the ways historians use evidence transfers readily when beginning researchers frame their own studies and give form to their own arguments. Footnotes, then, are fundamental to historical analysis. Whenever writing takes place, footnoting should be done simultaneously to document the sources used. Three basic questions are central to footnoting: Why do researchers footnote? What do they footnote? How do they footnote?

Why Do Researchers Footnote?

Footnotes serve several purposes in the research paper and appear in several varieties.

- The most common type of footnote may be called a **citation footnote.** These footnotes inform the audience where the author found the evidence that supports a particular argument or case. Since historical scholarship is a collaborative effort, identifying the sources and crediting the works of others is a fundamental responsibility for all students of history. In footnoting, historians acknowledge publicly how previous scholarship has strengthened and influenced their interpretation.

- Footnoting primary sources indicates that the researcher has examined the original materials and used them fully to substantiate an argument.

- Footnotes provide audiences with the ability to locate, analyze, and corroborate the evidence used in the paper, and enable them to determine the validity of the conclusions reached. Footnotes, therefore, credit primary and secondary sources to establish reliability for the historian's argument.

In sum, the historian uses footnotes to credit his or her sources. Footnotes are part of an ongoing series of conversations the researcher has undertaken with the sources and the readers. They help the historian better understand the quality of an argument and inform readers about the level of care that has gone into the selection of evidence to support conclusions.

Another type of footnote is the **explanatory footnote.** Historians use explanatory footnotes in several ways. As the name suggests, this footnote form helps to further explain material, terms, individuals, places, or ideas that are mentioned in the paper. The explanatory footnote usually contains a few simple sentences that enhance or clarify a point presented in the text. A general rule for using an explanatory footnote is as follows: in the author's judgment, this information would disrupt the narrative flow of the paper, or is an interesting aside that may not be appropriate for presentation within the body of the paper. For example, if someone is named in the paper and that individual is not well known, the historian may want to provide some brief, biographical information about this person. Less familiar places may also be identified, or terms may be defined. The explanatory footnote can also be used to clarify sources, to comment on historical and historiographical discrepancies, or to explain foreign language material. In all instances, the explanatory note is included to enhance understanding. Explanatory footnotes are another illustration of active conversations between the historian and the evidence. If the conversations are sustained, it is more likely that the researcher will identify elements of the argument that would be improved with the introduction of an explanatory note.

The **historiographic footnote** is the third footnote form. It is usually one of the first footnotes in a research paper or scholarly article, often appearing at the conclusion of the first paragraph. There is a detailed explanation of the purpose and composition of the historiographical footnote in Chapter 5; an example appears early in Jack Sheehan's paper in Appendix B. The historiographic footnote illustrates the historian's familiarity with the extant secondary literature.

What Do Researchers Footnote?

One of the most difficult concepts for less experienced historians to grasp is when to footnote. There are two possible approaches to footnoting. The first is to foot-note each sentence or sentences containing information taken from a specific sec-ondary or primary source. Whenever a direct quotation is used, it must be footnoted. This approach works best during the draft writing stage of the paper. It allows the author to see the sources and it facilitates editing since the footnote is clearly linked to sentences that may be edited or perhaps moved to another part of the paper. It also gives beginning researchers confidence that any ideas or words not their own have been attributed to the appropriate source. Because historians use many sources in crafting a paper, this approach also means that many paragraphs will contain a number of footnotes.

A second approach, and one increasingly used by scholars, is the multiple-citation footnote. This footnote appears at the end of each paragraph. It lists the various sources employed to write the paragraph, with the sources generally arranged in the order of their appearance in the paragraph. This ordering allows the reader to determine with some degree of certainty the source used to write a particular part of the paragraph. Even if the historian employs a direct quotation from a primary source, it too should be included in a multiple-citation footnote. The multiple-citation footnote is preferable to having a discrete footnote for each sentence or groups of sentences within a paragraph. Although it reduces the number of footnotes in the paper, it still provides the necessary documentation. A semicolon (;) is used to separate one citation from another in the multiple-citation footnote.

The following are examples of the two approaches to footnoting as demon-strated with a paragraph from Jack Sheehan's paper. The first paragraph shows the approach of footnoting each sentence or sentences:

> In the aftermath of the fire many different plans were proposed right away.[1] Plans such as Christopher Wren's, Robert Hooke's, and John Evelyn's were submitted within days of the fire. These men who submitted the plans were to become very influential in the rebuilding of the city.[2] In this overall scheme of rebuilding there are multiple steps, and the first step is to survey the city. So, the plans to rebuild were put on

---

[1] M. A. R. Cooper, "Robert Hooke's Work as Surveyor for the City of London in the Aftermath of the Great Fire," *Notes and Records of the Royal Society of London* 51, no. 2 (1997): 162–164.

[2] Timothy Baker, *London: Rebuilding the City After the Great Fire* (London: Phillimore, 2000), 14.

hold until a committee was appointed and a survey of the entire area was accomplished. Appointed to the committee were Christopher Wren, who was the head architect; Robert Hooke; and Edward Woodroffe, who died and was replaced by John Oliver—all were appointed as surveyors. The survey was taken very seriously by those involved. Proclamations were issued stating that all areas needed to be surveyed, that the rubble should be piled up and area cleared within 15 days, the persons did not need to pay a fee, and the residents could present evidence in their favor. The committee saw the need for stricter regulations in the building codes, wider streets, and a uniform city. These elements, if implemented correctly, would improve the quality of life for all.[3] However, before these elements could be realized, a number of problems would occur.[4]

The following shows the same paragraph using the multiple-citation footnote:

In the aftermath of the fire many different plans were proposed right away. Plans such as Christopher Wren's, Robert Hooke's, and John Evelyn's were submitted within days of the fire. These men who submitted the plans were to become very influential in the rebuilding of the city. In this overall scheme of rebuilding there are multiple steps, and the first step is to survey the city. So, the plans to rebuild were put on hold until a committee was appointed and a survey of the entire area was accomplished. Appointed to the committee were Christopher Wren, who was the head architect; Robert Hooke; and Edward Woodroffe, who died and was replaced by John Oliver—all were appointed as surveyors. The survey was taken very seriously by those involved. Proclamations were issued stating that all areas needed to be surveyed, that the rubble should be piled up and area cleared within 15 days, the persons did not need to pay a fee, and the residents could present evidence in their favor. The committee saw the need for stricter regulations in the building codes, wider streets, and a uniform city. These elements, if implemented correctly, would improve the quality of life for all. However, before these elements could be realized, a number of problems would occur.[5]

---

[3]Corporation of London, "By the Order to the Rebuilding of the city . . .," *Early English Books 1641–1700* (London: Printed by James Fletcher).

[4]Alan Wykes, "The Great Fire of London," *British History Illustrated* 1, no. 1 (1974): 25–26.

[5]M. A. R. Cooper, "Robert Hooke's Work as Surveyor for the City of London in the Aftermath of the Great Fire," *Notes and Records of the Royal Society of London* 51, no. 2 (1997): 162–164; Timothy Baker, *London: Rebuilding the City After the Great Fire* (London: Phillimore, 2000), 14; Corporation of London, "By the Order to the Rebuilding of the city . . .," *Early English Books 1641–1700* (London: Printed by James Fletcher); Alan Wykes, "The Great Fire of London," *British History Illustrated* 1, no. 1 (1974): 25–26.

The only exception that some historians make to using the multiple-citation footnote is the block-indented quotation. It is often footnoted immediately after the quoted material with the citation referring to the single, specific source. Scholarly writing convention suggests that when a direct quotation exceeds four typed lines, it should be indented from the left-hand margin, and the quotation marks removed. A good rule to follow is to introduce the block-indented quotation and reference the author. Block-indented quotations may be single-spaced or double-spaced; however, the same format must be used consistently. The footnote number should appear outside the punctuation following the block quotation. Block-indented and other quotations should be used judiciously to illustrate arguments made by the researcher; they do not replace the arguments themselves. When using any direct quotation, be extremely careful to check each word to make certain it appears in the text exactly, including punctuation and spelling,[6] as found in the source.

Plagiarism Failure to footnote appropriately may result in charges of **plagiarism,** which is academic dishonesty of the highest order. Plagiarism is when an author claims words, thoughts, ideas, or interpretations that are not his or her own. This act may be committed consciously or inadvertently; either way, it is plagiarism. In most instances, plagiarism involves carelessness in paraphrasing, quoting, or citing evidence.

The American Historical Association website includes a full, clear explanation of the issues involved in plagiarism and how to avoid them. It also includes a fine article intended for beginning researchers.[7] Both should be studied carefully as a reminder to document all the works used in writing any portion of the paper. It is not only a good habit; it is also ethical, professional behavior.

How Do Researchers Footnote?

Many different style manuals specify footnote form, and, it seems, nearly every scholarly discipline observes its own style format.[8] Historians prefer *The Chicago Manual of Style*, 15th ed. (Chicago: University of Chicago Press, 2003). A copy of this style manual can be found in most college libraries and many also have abridged versions with samples available linked to the library's homepage. It is also available through subscription at: http://www.chicagomanualofstyle.org/home.html. *The Chicago Manual of Style* has been condensed into a more manageable form by Kate L. Turabian in *A Manual for Writers of Term Papers,*

---

[6]Any error, such as misspelled words, factual mistakes, etc., in direct quotations should be followed by [*sic*]. The Turabian manual indicates that [*sic*] is either italicized or underlined.

[7]The American Historical Association, "Statement on Professional Standards," Chapter IV, Plagiarism, http://www.historians.org/pubs/Free/ProfessionalStandards.cfm; Michael Rawson, "Plagiarism: Curricular Materials for History Instructors," http://www.historians.org/governance/pd/Curriculum/plagiarism_defining.htm.

[8]For example, most English Literature scholars follow the Modern Language Association (MLA) style, while most psychologists observe the American Psychological Association (APA) style.

Theses, and Dissertations, 6th ed. (Chicago: University of Chicago Press, 1996). Both manuals include clear explanations of types of footnotes as well as examples. Beginning researchers should be consistent in following *Chicago Manual*/Turabian style throughout the research paper, including the bibliography.

One of the strengths of *Chicago Manual*/Turabian style is its unobtrusiveness. Within the narrative of the paper, a footnote is simply indicated by a super-scripted (raised one-half letter) number that appears after the punctuation mark. Most software programs perform this task automatically when the footnote function is enabled. The actual text of the footnote can appear at the bottom of the page, or as an endnote at the end of the paper. The advantage of footnotes is the ease of having them at the bottom of each page while reading through the text, instead of flipping back and forth from the text to the endnotes. Historians prefer *Chicago Manual*/Turabian style because it allows for long citations of sources, or explanation, or commentary on sources at the bottom of the page or the end of a paper without disrupting the narrative flow of the paper.

The first time a source is cited, a complete footnote citation is required. A typical footnote for a book should contain the following information:

- Author's name, generally first name, middle initial, last name, followed by a comma.

- Full title of the book in italics. No punctuation follows the title.

- Publication information is enclosed within parentheses: city of publication, followed by state abbreviation unless it is a well-known city like Boston, followed by a colon (:); name of the publisher, followed by a comma; and year of publication. After the last parenthesis, place a comma.

- The page or pages cited, followed by a period. Often no p. or pp. is required.

Each footnote should be single-spaced, with a double-space between foot-notes. Typically the first line of a footnote is indented one tab stop (like the beginning of a paragraph). The footnote number is superscripted in both the text and the actual footnote. Most word processing programs automatically handle these tasks. The author's name should be flush with the footnote number (there should be no space between the number and the author's name).

The following examples cover the major types of footnotes that appear in *Chicago Manual*/Turabian style. For a complete listing, beginning researchers should consult these references directly. When working to complete footnotes for any research project, a copy of either *The Chicago Manual of Style* or Turabian should be close at hand and regularly consulted to make certain that the form used is consistent with the standard.

Books

1. Single author book

[1]Elizabeth McKellar, *The Birth of Modern London: The Development and Design of the City, 1660–1720* (New York: St. Martin's Press, 1999), 221.

[2]David M. Kennedy, *Freedom from Fear: The American People in Depression and War, 1929–1945* (New York: Oxford University Press, 1999), 363.

Both examples include the full title of each book as it appeared on the title page. Beginning researchers who sometimes cite directly from sources like WorldCat or online library catalogs, often overlook this point. The form used on these online reference works may differ dramatically in style from what appears on the title page. This difference is most common in matters of capitalization and punctuation.

2. Subsequent (short-title) footnote reference for second or later references

In subsequent footnotes that refer to an earlier cited work, list only the author's last name and page number.

[3]McKellar, 219.
[4]Kennedy, 232.

However, in instances where an author has published more than one work on a subject, or where a different author with the same last name has published a source **used in the paper,** the short title should include key words from the title of the book or article as well as the author's last name.

[5]Kennedy, *Freedom from Fear*, 323.

The same short title must be used consistently throughout the paper.

3. Two or more authors

If a book has two or three authors, list the full names of these individuals in the order they appear on the title page of the book.

[6]J. L. Hammond and Barbara Hammond, *The Village Labourer, 1760–1832: A Study in the Government of England Before the Reform Bill* (London: Longman, Green and Company, Ltd., 1911), 26–29.

If a book has more than three authors, use the term "and others" after the first author's name instead of listing each author separately.

[7]James West Davidson and others, *Nation of Nations: A Concise Narrative of the American Republic*, 4th ed. (Boston: McGraw-Hill, 2006), 471.

4. Editor(s) as author(s)

When citing an editor as an author, the format is similar to that used for author(s), except the abbreviation "ed." or "eds." is added to indicate that the work has been edited.

[8]Lloyd deMause, ed., *The History of Childhood* (New York: The Psychohistory Press, 1974), 41–57.
[9]A. L. Beier and Roger Finlay, eds., *London 1500–1700: The Making of the Metropolis* (London and New York: Longman Group Ltd., 1986), 28.

5. Author's work edited or translated

Scholars often edit writings such as diaries and memoirs for publication. In this case, the editor is selecting and editing the work of another author.

[10]*The Diary of John Quincy Adams, 1794–1845: American Political, Social, and Intellectual Life from Washington to Polk,* ed. Allan Nevins (New York: Longman, Green and Company, 1928), 244.

Works originally published in another language are often translated to facilitate wider scholarly use. When such works are cited in footnotes, it is important to credit the author, but also to acknowledge the translator. In some cases, there may be more than one translator and all should be referenced by name. Such citations inform the audience that the book was originally published in another language.

[11]Philippe Ariès, *The Hour of Our Death,* trans. Helen Weaver (New York: Alfred A. Knopf, 1981), 222.

6. Edition other than first

Second and subsequent editions of a book may include significant revisions and modifications; thus, it is important to specify the edition actually used.

[12]Walter George Bell, *The Great Fire of London,* 2nd ed. (London: The Bodley Head, 1951), 17.

7. Multivolume work

[13]Robert Hamlett Bremner, ed., *Children and Youth in America: A Documentary History,* vol. 2, *1866–1932* (Cambridge, MA.: Harvard University Press, 1971), 61–74.

8. Published correspondence

Many historians make use of published correspondence that has been collected and edited by scholars. A letter from one correspondent to another appears as follows:

[14]Oliver Cromwell to Sir William Spring and Mr. Barrow, 28 September 1643, *Oliver Cromwell's Letters and Speeches with Elucidations,* ed. Thomas Carlyle, vol. 3 (New York: Peter Fenelon Collier, Publisher, 1897), 166–169.

Articles

1. Scholarly journal article

Scholarly journal articles are one of the most important secondary sources. They should be cited as follows:

[15]Gregory D. Massey, "The Limits of Antislavery Thought in the Revolutionary Lower South: John Laurens and Henry Laurens," *Journal of Southern History* 63, no. 3 (August 1997): 522–523.

Increasing numbers of scholarly journals appear in online format such as JSTOR. Some scholars opt to indicate this format in their footnote.

[16]Gregory D. Massey, "The Limits of Antislavery Thought in the Revolutionary Lower South: John Laurens and Henry Laurens," *Journal of Southern History* 63, no. 3 (August 1997): 522–523. http://www.jstor.org/.

2. Article in published collections

[17]Christopher Clark, "The Consequences of the Market Revolution in the American North," in *The Market Revolution in America: Social, Political and Religious Expressions, 1800–1880*, ed. Melvyn Stokes and Stephen Conway (Charlottesville, VA: University Press of Virginia, 1996), 24.

3. Article in popular magazine (author named)

Popular magazines are often useful primary sources for historians.

[18]William Bradford Huie, "The Shocking Story of Approved Killing in Mississippi," *Look*, 24 January 1956, 46–50.

4. Article in popular magazine (author unnamed)

[19]"Making the Black Sox White Again," *Literary Digest*, 20 August 1921, 13–14.

5. Article in newspaper (author named)

[20]Bob Woodward and B. C. Colen, "Bugging Case Suspect Is Free on Bail," *Washington Post*, 24 June 1972, p. C1.

In footnoting material taken from newspapers, the use of p. or pp. is acceptable. This is one of the few instances in Turabian where p. or pp. is used.

6. Article in newspaper (author unnamed)

[21]"Pacifists Condemn and Praise Wilson," *New York Times,* 11 February 1917, p. 6.

7. Article in newspaper, place of publication not included in title

If the newspaper title does not indicate place of publication, or if the location of the city is not readily apparent from the newspaper name, the city name and state should be included within parentheses following the newspaper title.

[22]"State of Maine!," *Eastern Argus* (Portland, ME), 14 March 1820, p. 3.

Government Publications

1. Presidential papers

[23]"Farewell Radio and Television Address to the American People," *Public Papers of the Presidents of the United States: Dwight D. Eisenhower, 1960–61* (Washington, DC: Government Printing Office, 1961), 1035–1040.

2. Testimony before a congressional committee

[24]Congress, Senate, Subcommittee on Unemployment Relief, "Statement of Miss Dorothy Kahn," *Hearings before the Senate Subcommittee on Unemployment Relief, Senate Committee on Manufacturers*, 72nd Cong., 1st sess. (28 December 1931), 73–77.

3. Congressional committee report

[25]Congress, *Report of the Joint Committee on Reconstruction*, 39th Cong., 1st sess. (Washington, DC: Government Printing Office, 1866), 435.

4. Congressional debates

[26]Congress, Senate, Albert J. Beveridge, "Policy Regarding the Philippines," 56th Cong., 1st sess., *Congressional Record* (9 January 1900), 704–712.

5. Supreme Court

[27]*Brown v. Board of Education of Topeka, Kansas*, 347 U.S. 483 (1954).

6. Other

[28]Public Record Office, "Marc Antonio Giustinian, Venetian Ambassador in France, to Doge and Senate," 12 October 1666, *Calendar of State Papers and Manuscript, Relating to English Affairs, Existing in the Archives and Collections in Venice, and in Other Libraries of Northern Italy 1202–[1675]* (London: Longman, Green, Longman, Roberts, and Green, 1864), no. 87, 86.

Electronic Sources   The proliferation of web-based sources has been a boon to historical research. Students of history should understand that the historical profession has yet to settle on an accepted standard for documenting information taken from websites. Like traditional footnotes, the reference to an electronic source should contain the following information:

- Author's name
- Title of document in quotation marks
- Title of complete work in italics (if relevant)
- Date of publication
- URL of the website

1. Website

[29]Hannah Spires, "Killing: Infanticide, 16 January 1751," *The Proceedings of the Old Bailey* Ref.: t17510116-52. http://www.oldbaileyonline.org/.

[30]Thomas Jefferson to James Madison, 28 August 1789, *The Thomas Jefferson Papers, Series 1, General Correspondence, 1651–1827.* http://memory.loc.gov/ammem/collections/jefferson_papers/.

2. E-mail message

Personal e-mail messages are treated as written correspondence and are cited similarly.

[31]Michael Roth to John Smith, 22 February 2003, "Re: A Note on Polish Immigrant Sources," personal e-mail.

3. Listserv or newsgroup message

Many Listservs and newsgroups archive messages that can be readily accessed. These archives contain valuable insights and information on various topics. These messages should be cited in a manner similar to unpublished papers.

[32]Phil VanderMeer, "Re: WWI Era Harassment of Germans," 12 February 2003, http://www2.h-net.msu.edu/~shgape/.

In the cases of online newspapers, online journals, and online book reviews, some scholars find it acceptable to cite these materials without reference to the specific website. Check with your instructor or editor to determine their preference.

Other Sources

1. Unpublished dissertation or thesis

[33]James Munro McPherson, "The Abolitionists and the Negro During the Civil War and Reconstruction" (PhD diss., Johns Hopkins University, 1963), 28.

[34]David G. Bloom, "Divergent Paths: John L. Lewis, Walter Reuther and World War II" (MA thesis, James Madison University, 1996), 45.

2. Manuscript collections

[35]Samuel E. Dutton to Reuel Williams, 14 July 1807, Folder 11, Box 2, Reuel Williams Papers, Maine Historical Society, Portland, ME.

[36]Diary of Henry L. Stimson, 9 December 1941, Henry L. Stimson Diaries, George C. Marshall Library, Lexington, VA.

3. Video

[37]*Cold War, 23: The Wall Comes Down, 1989*, prod. Sir Jeremy Isaacs and Pat Mitchell, 47 min., Turner Original Productions, 1998, videocassette.

4. Interview

[38]James McPherson, "Fresh Air from WHYY," interview by Terry Gross (National Public Radio 22 June 2004) http://www.npr.org/.

5. Interview by author of paper

[39]John Baugh, president of SYSCO Foodservices, interview by author, 15 October 2004, Houston, TX, tape recording in author's possession.

6. Indirect source (quoted in)

In some instances a primary source is located in a scholarly work. While it is always preferable to read the original source, sometimes this is not possible. When citing such a source it is important to attribute the secondary work that contains the primary source material.

[40]J. C. Peoples to A. W. Buchanan, December 12, 1890, J. A. Rose Papers, The University of Texas Library, Texas Archives Division, Austin, TX, quoted in Norman Pollack, ed., *The Populist Mind* (Indianapolis: Bobbs-Merrill Company, 1967), 22–23.

Historiographic Footnote

Here is another example of a historiographic footnote. It comes from student Darci Mitchell's paper on women in Oneida, a Utopian community in upstate New York. She addresses the larger issue of religion in upstate New York, shows works on Utopian communities of the time period, focuses specifically on the Oneida community, then provides an introduction to some primary sources.[9]

---

[9]For a good overview of the Burned-Over District of New York, see Michael Barkun, *Crucible of the Millennium: The Burned-Over District of New York in the 1840s* (Syracuse, N.Y.: Syracuse University Press, 1986), and Whitney Cross, *The Burned-Over District: The Social and Intellectual History of Enthusiastic Religion in Western New York, 1800–1850* (New York: Harper Torchbooks, 1950). To read more on Utopian communities consult Arthur Eugene Bestor, Jr., *Backwoods Utopias: The Sectarian and Owenite Phases of Communitarian Socialism in America: 1663–1829* (Philadelphia: University of Pennsylvania Press, 1950); Robert S. Fogarty, *American Utopianism* (Itasca, I.L.: F. E. Peacock Publishers, 1972); Ira L. Mandelker, *Religion, Society, and Utopia in Nineteenth-Century America* (Amherst, M.A.: University of Massachusetts Press, 1984); John McKelvie Whitworth, *God's Blueprints: A Sociological Study of Three Utopian Sects* (London: Routledge & Kegan Paul, 1975); Robert S. Fogarty, *All Things New: American Communes and Utopian Movements, 1860–1914* (Chicago: University of Chicago Press, 1990); and Robert S. Fogarty, *Dictionary of American Communal and Utopian History* (Westport, C.T.: Greenwood Press, 1980). For information on the history of the Oneida Community, refer to Maren Lockwood Carden, *Oneida: Utopian Community to Modern Corporation* (Baltimore: The Johns Hopkins Press, 1969); Constance Noyes Robertson, *Oneida Community: An Autobiography, 1851–1876* (Syracuse, N.Y.: Syracuse University Press, 1970); Robert S. Fogarty, *Daily Journal of Oneida Community*, volumes 1–3: *The O.C. Daily*, volumes 4–5 (Philadelphia: Porcupine Press, 1975); Louis J. Kern, *An Ordered Love: Sex Roles and Sexuality in Victorian Utopias: The Shakers, the Mormons, and the Oneida Community* (Chapel Hill, N.C.: University of North Carolina Press, 1981); Spencer Klaw, *Without Sin: The Life and Death of the Oneida Community* (New York: Allen Lane, 1993); and Oneida Community, *Handbook of the Oneida Community, 1867 & 1871, Bound w/Mutual Criticism* (New York: AMS Press, 1976). Finally, for information on the women's role at Oneida, see Lawrence Foster, *Women, Family, and Utopia: Communal Experiments of the Shakers, the Oneida Community, and the Mormons* (Syracuse, N.Y.: Syracuse University Press, 1991); Robert S. Fogarty, *Desire and Duty at Oneida: Tirzah Miller's Intimate Memoir* (Bloomington, I.N.: Indiana University Press, 2000); Victor Hawley, "Special Love/Special Sex: An Oneida Community Diary," *New York History* 76, no. 1 (1995): 108–110; Stewart Hall Holbrook, "When Sex Flourished in Oneida," *American Mercury* 40 (February 1961): 202–208; Jessie Catherine Kinsley, *A Lasting Spring: Jessie Catherine Kinsley, Daughter of the Oneida Community* (Syracuse, N.Y.: Syracuse University Press, 1983); Mary P. Ryan, *Cradle of the Middle Class: The Family in Oneida County, New York, 1790–1865* (New York: Cambridge University Press, 1981); and Harriet M. Worden, *Old Mansion House Memories, by One Brought Up In It* (Oneida, N.Y.: np, 1950).

Explanatory Footnote

In the sample student paper, Jack Sheehan describes one of the proposed plans for reconstructing the city and mentions large, "merchant mansion houses." If he stopped in the text to explain why they were to be constructed farther from the street, he would clutter the narrative. Instead, he provides a brief, explanatory note to inform the reader.

[1]The mansion houses had to be pushed back from the street in order to have room for a courtyard leading up to the house.

Sometimes explanatory footnotes are used to provide additional information about the topic, or to act as an aside to the reader. They can also be used to describe discrepancies in the sources as well as comment on scholarly interpretations.

BIBLIOGRAPHY

A bibliography is the last part of a paper, and it reveals much about the research process. It indicates the extent of the research, the kinds and types of sources that were used, and the different disciplines that helped inform the study. The proper bibliographic citation is necessary so that interested readers might find and read the sources for themselves. As emphasized earlier, bibliographies are valuable for finding sources on particular topics. Finally, the bibliography provides a window to the research for the paper, while also allowing the reader to make a discerning judgment about that research. Having a complete bibliography is therefore essential to a finished piece of research.

Beginning researchers should create a **selected bibliography.** A selected bibliography only includes those sources—both primary and secondary—that were cited (footnoted) in the paper. Historians do not pad or inflate the bibliography with sources that were consulted but not actually footnoted.

There are three basic types of bibliographies.

Standard Bibliography   The simplest is the standard bibliography, which is a listing of works used in the paper. It is arranged into subcategories beginning with a listing of primary sources, followed by secondary works. The primary sources category may be further subdivided into the following order: unpublished materials, published materials, and newspapers. Secondary sources are often subdivided into the categories of books, journal articles, and unpublished works. In each category and subcategory, sources are arranged alphabetically.

Annotated Bibliography   The annotated bibliography is more useful to students of history. Its arrangement is the same as a standard bibliography, but each entry has an annotation or critical commentary. The annotation should be brief, usually not more than three lines of text. It indicates the author's coverage of the subject, the historical interpretation, and the overall value of the work.

Bibliographic Essay   The bibliographic essay provides commentary about sources in a narrative format. Rather than arranging sources in alphabetical order, the bibliographic essay is arranged by topic or subject in paragraph form. The beginning researcher determines how the sources are organized in this essay. The bibliographic essay must be readable, informative and, like the annotated bibliography, provide critical analysis of the sources. It is helpful to the author of the paper because he or she must have a good sense of the works in order to write about them in a clear narrative style. Constructing a bibliographic essay is a good exercise in learning history by writing. But the essay is also useful to the historian's audience because of its topical or thematic organization.

Since students of history know they must prepare a bibliography, it is important that they arrange the required information as they conduct their reading and research. Maintaining a computer file of works consulted is a good starting point, as is preparing bibliographic note cards. It is useful to indicate the call number of a book in this file, as the work may need to be located again after it has been returned to the library. A typical bibliographic entry contains the following information:

- Author's last name, followed by a comma, generally first name, middle initial, then a period.
- Full title of the book in italics. Place a period after the title.
- Publication information: city of publication, followed by a colon (:); name of the publisher, followed by a comma; and year of publication. Place a period after the publication date.

Guiding Points

What follows is a basic guide for considering annotations, comments in the bibliographic essay, or remarks in the historiographic footnote, especially for secondary or interpretive works. Keep the answers to these questions on the bibliographic note card or the computer file for later use.

1. What is the author's point of view? Examine the book's preface or introduction for clues or information.
2. What is the author's thesis? Authors of books often indicate the thesis of the study in the preface, while authors of articles usually do so in the first paragraph.
3. What evidence supports the thesis? Examine the bibliography to determine the variety and kinds of sources that were used.
4. What is the value of this study? This is the judgment of the scholarly work.

Examples of Bibliographical Citations

Books

1. Single author book

Note that all lines after the first one are indented one tab stop.

Kennedy, David M. *Freedom from Fear: The American People in Depression and War, 1929–1945*. New York: Oxford University Press, 1999.

McKellar, Elizabeth. *The Birth of Modern London: The Development and Design of the City, 1660–1720*. New York: St. Martin's Press, 1999.

2. Two or more authors

Davidson, James West, William E. Gienapp, Christine Leigh Heyrman, Mark H. Lytle and Michael B. Stoff. *Nation of Nations: A Concise Narrative of the American Republic*, 4th ed. Boston: McGraw-Hill, 2006.

Hammond, J. L., and Barbara Hammond. *The Village Labourer, 1760–1832: A Study in the Government of England Before the Reform Bill*. London: Longman Green and Company, Ltd., 1911.

3. Editor(s) as author(s)

Beier, A. L. and Roger Finlay, eds. *London 1500–1700: The Making of the Metropolis*. London and New York: Longman Group Ltd., 1986.

deMause, Lloyd, ed. *The History of Childhood*. New York: The Psychohistory Press, 1974.

4. Author's work edited or translated

Ariès, Philippe. *The Hour of Our Death*. Translated by Helen Weaver. New York: Alfred A. Knopf, 1981.

The Diary of John Quincy Adams, 1794–1845: American Political, Social, and Intellectual Life from Washington to Polk. Edited by Allan Nevins. New York: Longman, Green and Company, 1928.

5. Edition other than first

Bell, Walter George. *The Great Fire of London*, 2nd ed. London: The Bodley Head, 1951.

6. Multivolume work

Bremner, Robert Hamlett, ed. *Children and Youth in America: A Documentary History*. 3 vols. Cambridge, M.A.: Harvard University Press, 1970–1974.

7. Published correspondence

Cromwell, Oliver. *Oliver Cromwell's Letters and Speeches with Elucidations,* ed. Thomas Carlyle. 3 vols. New York: Peter Fenelon Collier, Publisher, 1897.

Articles

1. Scholarly journal article

Massey, Gregory D. "The Limits of Antislavery Thought in the Revolutionary Lower
   South: John Laurens and Henry Laurens." *Journal of Southern History* 63, no. 3
   (August 1997): 495–530.

Increasing numbers of scholarly journals appear in online format such as
JSTOR. Some scholars opt to indicate this format in their footnote.

Massey, Gregory D. "The Limits of Antislavery Thought in the Revolutionary Lower
   South: John Laurens and Henry Laurens." *Journal of Southern History* 63, no. 3
   (August 1997): 495–530. http://www.jstor.org/.

2. Article in published collections

Clark, Christopher. "The Consequences of the Market Revolution in the American
   North." In *The Market Revolution in America: Social, Political and Religious Expressions,
   1800–1880*, ed. Melvyn Stokes and Stephen Conway, 23–42. Charlottesville, V.A.:
   University Press of Virginia, 1996.

3. Article in popular magazine (author named)

Huie, William Bradford. "The Shocking Story of Approved Killing in Mississippi." *Look*,
   24 January 1956, 46–50.

4. Article in popular magazine (author unnamed)

"Making the Black Sox White Again." *Literary Digest*, 20 August 1921, 13–14.

5. Article in newspaper

When more than one article is used from a newspaper, indicate the name of
the newspaper and the range of dates of the articles used in the paper.

> *Eastern Argus* (Portland, M.A.). 14 March 1820–28 March 1820.
>
> *New York Times.* February 1917–April 1918.
>
> *Washington Post.* June 1972.

Government Publications

1. Presidential papers

Public Papers of the Presidents of the United States: Dwight D. Eisenhower, 1960–61.
   Washington, DC: Government Printing Office, 1961.

2. Testimony before a congressional committee

U.S. Congress. Senate. Subcommittee on Unemployment Relief. "Statement of Miss
   Dorothy Kahn." *Hearings before the Senate Subcommittee on Unemployment Relief, Senate
   Committee on Manufacturers.* 72nd Cong., 1st sess., 28 December 1931.

3. Congressional committee report

U.S. Congress. *Report of the Joint Committee on Reconstruction.* 39th Cong., 1st sess. Washington, DC: Government Printing Office, 1866.

4. Congressional debates

U.S. Congress. Senate. Albert J. Beveridge, "Policy Regarding the Philippines." 56th Cong., 1st sess. *Congressional Record* (9 January 1900).

5. Supreme Court

Brown v. Board of Education of Topeka, Kansas. 347 U.S. 483 (1954).

6. Other

United Kingdom. Public Record Office. "Marc Antonio Giustinian, Venetian Ambassador in France, to Doge and Senate," 12 October 1666. *Calendar of State Papers and Manuscript, Relating to English Affairs, Existing in the Archives and Collections in Venice, and in Other Libraries of Northern Italy 1202–[1675].* London: Longman Green, Longman, Roberts, and Green, 1864.

Electronic Sources

1. Website

If only one citation from a website is used, cite as follows:

Spires, Hannah. "Killing: Infanticide, 16 January 1751." *The Proceedings of the Old Bailey* Ref.: t17510116-52. http://www.oldbaileyonline.org/.

If more than one document is used from a website, then indicate the collection as follows:

The Thomas Jefferson Papers, Series 1, General Correspondence, 1651–1827. http://memory.loc.gov/ammem/collections/jefferson_papers/.

2. E-mail message

Roth, Michael to John Smith. "Re: A Note on Polish Immigrant Sources," 22 February 2003, personal e-mail.

3. Listserv or newsgroup message

VanderMeer, Phil. "Re: WWI Era Harassment of Germans," 12 February 2003, http://www2.h-net.msu.edu/~shgape/.

Other Sources

1. Unpublished dissertation or thesis

Bloom, David G. "Divergent Paths: John L. Lewis, Walter Reuther and World War II." MA thesis, James Madison University, 1996.

McPherson, James Munro. "The Abolitionists and the Negro During the Civil War and Reconstruction." PhD diss., Johns Hopkins University, 1963.

2. Manuscript collections

Lexington, Virginia. George C. Marshall Library. Henry L. Stimson Diaries.

Portland, ME. Maine Historical Society. Reuel Williams Papers.

3. Video

Cold War, 23: The Wall Comes Down, 1989. Produced by Sir Jeremy Isaacs and Pat Mitchell. 47 min. Turner Original Productions, 1998. Videocassette.

4. Interview

McPherson, James. "Fresh Air from WHYY." Interview by Terry Gross (National Public Radio, 22 June 2004). http://www.npr.org/.

5. Interview by author of paper

Baugh, John. Interview by author, 15 October 2004. Tape recording. In author's possession.

Annotated Bibliography

The annotated bibliography is far more valuable to the audience than a simple list of sources consulted because it includes a brief commentary about each source. The typical annotation is no more than three lines of text, though some variations in length are acceptable. Drawing upon the notes and answers to the "guiding points" questions that were written on bibliographic note cards or the computer file, annotations to the sources can be developed readily. The organization of an annotated bibliography is the same as the standard bibliography, with primary sources listed in alphabetical order first, then secondary sources listed in alphabetical order.

Student Jack Sheehan's annotated bibliography illustrates the usefulness of this bibliographic form. His annotations are brief but descriptive. The audience gains a sense of the varieties of historical interpretations and the nature of the primary evidence used. Jack Sheehan's annotated bibliography appears at the end of his paper located in Appendix B.

Bibliographical Essay

The bibliographical essay is presented in essay format with a narrative flow. It contains a brief review of the primary and secondary sources used to write the paper. The organization and style for entries is different from the standard and annotated bibliographies. While primary sources are still addressed first in the bibliographic essay, the traditional alphabetical organization is dropped. The author of the bibliographic essay decides how to organize the material. Some approaches include grouping sources around particular topics, themes, issues, personalities, or interpretations. A brief commentary about the sources is an essential component of the essay. Like the annotated bibliography, it is useful to draw upon the notes and answers to the "guiding point" questions that were placed on the note cards or in the bibliographic file. Because of the essay format, the bibliographic entry takes a form similar to a footnote. A typical bibliographic essay entry uses a different format from other bibliographic forms. It should contain the following information:

- Author's name, generally first name, middle initial, last name, followed by a comma.

- Full title of the book in italics. No punctuation after the title.

- Publication information enclosed within parentheses: city of publication, followed by a colon (:); name of the publisher, followed by a comma; and year of publication

Below is student Jack Sheehan's bibliographic essay, which conforms to the appropriate style of such an exercise.

Bibliographic Essay

The Great Fire of London was one of the significant events of the Restoration and it has attracted broad scholarly attention. There is a rich variety of evidence available to historians, especially relating to the themes of the fire and plans for reconstruction of London, urban growth in the city, and social forces operating during the period. Obviously, such a dramatic event drew considerable comment from contemporaries and attracted widespread attention. The best primary work from the time is Samuel Pepys's diary: Samuel Pepys, *The Diary of Samuel Pepys*, eds. Robert Latham and William Matthews (Berkeley: University of California Press, 1970). This standard edition is in 10 volumes and encompasses the entire diary of Pepys. A second work on Pepys's diary is Robert Latham, ed., *The Illustrated Pepys: Extracts From the Diary* (Berkeley: University of California Press, 1978). It is a great companion to the full diary, citing specific important entries, and also adding illustrations to provide a greater understanding of place. There are numerous other diaries from this time period including John Evelyn's *The Diary of John Evelyn*, ed. William Bray (London: M. Walter Dunn, 1901), which covers from 1620 to 1706, and gives insight into a great amount of detail on the major events in Restoration London. Another diary is John Milward's *The Diary of John Milward*, ed. Caroline Robbins (Cambridge: Cambridge University Press, 1938). He was a Member of Parliament in 1666, and wrote about its proceedings until 1668. This diary has little to do with the social aspects of London and focuses on the political proceedings in stark difference from Pepys's diary. In addition to the accounts present in the diaries, there is also a great account from the

London Gazette: *The London Gazette* (London: Printed by Tho. Newcomb, 2 September–10 September 1666). This paper, although slanted in its view, gives a description of the area burnt, the extent of the damage, and how the fire spread. Other accounts of the fire and rebuilding are contained in the State Papers Venetian: Public Record Office, *The Calendar of State Papers and Manuscripts, Relating to English Affairs, Existing in the Archives and Collections in Venice, and in Other Libraries of Northern Italy 1202–[1675]* (London: Longman, Green, Longman, Roberts, and Green, 1864), which shows a foreign view of what was happening to London, and describes the social and political problems of the time.

After the fire, many acts were passed. These included Corporation of London, *By the Order of Rebuilding the City* . . . (London: James Fletcher, Guildhall Library Collection: *Early English Books, 1641–1700*); Robert Hanson, *Where as in and by the additional act of Parliament for rebuilding the city of London, it is enacted that the Lord Maior and Court of Alderman shall be thereby empowered and required to cause all and every shed, shops, and other buildings . . . to be taken down and removed . . .* (London: Printed by Andrew Clark, Guildhall Library Collection: *Early English Books, 1641–1700*); and William Hooker, *This court taking into their consideration that the utmost time appointed for the taking down and removing all such sheds, shops, and other like buildings, which have been erected since the late dismal fire . . .* (London: printed by Andrew Clark, Guildhall Library Collection: *Early English Books, 1641–1700*). These acts were enacted to promote the building of the city in a timely fashion while producing a desirable result.

A number of collections house primary material. Roland Bartel, ed., *London in Plague and Fire 1665–1666: Selected Source Materials for College Research Papers* (Boston: D.C. Heath and Company, 1957), contains useful information including letters as well as proclamations by Charles II. A similar work is Andrew Browning, ed., *English Historical Documents 1660–1714* (New York: Oxford University Press, 1953), which contains a large amount of personal accounts regarding the major events in that time period.

Among the secondary resources are numerous books on the fire and the rebuilding of London. One of the best is Timothy Baker, *London: Rebuilding the City After the Great Fire* (London: Phillimore, 2000). It goes into great detail on the design of the buildings. Another excellent work on the fire is Walter George Bell, *The Great Fire of London*, 2nd ed. (London: The Bodley Head, 1951). This volume deals with the effects of the fire and the problems that resulted during the rebuilding. T. F. Reddaway, *The Rebuilding of London After the Great Fire* (London: Edward Arnold and Co., 1951), reveals the influence of Bell. He wrote about the reconstruction and the problems encountered. The last book that deals with the rebuilding and city planning is Elizabeth McKellar, *The Birth of Modern London: The Development and Design of the City, 1660–1720* (New York: St. Martin's Press, 1999). McKellar deals with urban space development as London returned to its former glory. Another book that deals with the social aspects of the fire and rebuilding is Neil Hanson, *The Great Fire of London in that Apocalyptic Year, 1666* (New York: John Wiley and Sons, 2002). Hanson goes to great depths to show the hardships that people faced following the fire.

Some scholarly articles are worthy of mention. The first and most useful is M. A. R. Cooper, "Robert Hooke's Work as Surveyor for the City of London in the Aftermath of the Great Fire," *Notes and Records of the Royal Society of London* 51, no. 2 (1997): 161–174; continued in 52, no. 1 (1998): 25–38; and 52, no. 2 (1998): 205–220. The series highlights Hooke's work in rebuilding the city, and emphasizes the disputes that occurred as well as aspects of the daily life of Hooke. Another extremely useful article was Alan Wykes, "The Great Fire of London," *British History Illustrated* 1, no. 1 (1974): 18–27. He examined the fire itself closely, and added a great part to the discussion of the plans that were presented afterwards. His focus is on the plan put forward by Sir Christopher Wren. Frank T. Melton, "Sir Robert Clayton's Building Projects in London, 1666–1672," *Guildhall Studies in London History* 3, no. 1 (1977): 37–41, examines the fact that capitalists did not play a major role in the rebuilding of London; rather reconstruction depended more on the resources provided by private artisans. A final article by Nicholas Hudson, "Samuel Johnson, Urban Culture and the Geography of Postfire London," *SEL Studies in English Literature 1500–1900* 42, no. 3 (2002): 577–600, gives a retrospective view of London that focuses on the missed opportunities during rebuilding.

Several works deal with the growth around London as the city steadily expanded. A great introductory study is Jonathan Barry, ed., *The Tudor and Stuart Town: A Reader in English Urban History 1530–1688* (London: Longman Publishing, 1990). This collection of articles gives the reader a strong background in the period and in urban history. A second important book in this field is Jeremy Boulton's *Neighbourhood and Society: A London Suburb in the Seventeenth Century* (London: Cambridge University Press, 1987). This is a micro-history that describes the effects of growth on a London suburb. Numerous articles in this field have been published since 1978. The first is Michael Power, "Shadwell: The Development of a London Suburban Community in the Seventeenth Century," *The London Journal* 4, no. 1 (1978): 29–46. His article is also a micro-history that shows the growth through the period of the fire. Robert Fishman, "The Origins of the Suburban Idea in England," *Chicago History* 13, no. 2 (1984): 26–36, examines the overall growth of the suburbs, and the architectural styles used. Frank E. Brown, "Continuity and Change in the Urban House: Developments in Domestic Space Organisation in Seventeenth Century London," *Comparative Studies in Society and History* 28 (1986): 558–590, studies how the houses were laid out, including the floor plans. This work probably never would have been written unless the article Phillippa

Glanville, "The Topography of Seventeenth Century London; A Review of Maps," *Urban History Yearbook* (1980): 79–83, had been published. Glanville examines the change in London by comparing different maps.

Other works attempt to examine the sociological factors operating in the city during the period. John Richardson, *The Annals of London: A Year-by-Year Record of a Thousand Years of History* (Berkeley: University of California Press, 2000), is an account of the people and the politics in London since 1065. One of the major works on the seventeenth century that provides great perspective on the social order is Keith Wrightson, *English Society 1580–1680* (New Brunswick: Rutgers University Press, 1982). Wrightson studies the family structure, social relations, and population of England in the period before and after the fire. A. L. Beier and Roger Finlay, eds., *London 1500–1700: The Making of the Metropolis* (New York: Longman Group Ltd., 1986), surveys the growth, economy, and social ideas of the age. Gregg Carr, *Residence and Social Status: The Development of Seventeenth Century London* (London: Garland Publishing, 1990) deals with the population of London. Finally, Jack Lindsay, *The Monster City: Defoe's London, 1688–1730* (New York: St. Martin's Press, 1978) details the fashions of the day and gives insight into the way people lived in the late seventeenth century. Two articles provide glimpses into the daily life of the times. Charles Elliot, "Samuel Pepys' London Chronicles," *Smithsonian* 32, no. 4 (2001): 102–109, is a popular account of the life and times of the great diarist while Valerie Pearl, "Change and Stability in 17th Century London," *London Journal* 5, no. 1 (1979): 3–34, shows how society changed over the entire seventeenth century, and how urban realities overcame traditions.

HISTORIOGRAPHIC ESSAY

By definition, **historiography** is the study of how historians interpreted a particular topic and the ways in which their work may be characterized. It is not the study of the actual events or personalities; rather, it examines the secondary studies of various scholars. The historiographic essay differs from the bibliographical essay in one essential way: it reviews only secondary sources.

The essay begins with an introduction that sets the context and outlines the major issues, interpretations, or other patterns that will be used to explain the works of those scholars whose works will be discussed. One method is to approach the topic chronologically, beginning with those scholars who first addressed the topic, then considering in a systematic way how and why interpretations changed over time. In some cases, new information came to light causing a reinterpretation of an area. In others, historians began asking different questions of the same or similar evidence.

The historiographic essay groups major and lesser historians according to their approaches, methods, or types of conclusions. It seeks to explain how historians once viewed a topic and why interpretations have changed. Thus, it must describe each work and analyze its place along a continuum. What does each work contribute to the subject? What new interpretations or fresh examination of evidence is offered? How does each use evidence? What kinds of evidence does each rely upon? It may also seek to place the works of particular historians in specific categories or schools: Marxist, Annales, postmodern.

To modify Jack Sheehan's essay into an historiographic one, it would be necessary to revise the introduction, eliminate the primary source references in the first paragraph, and regroup the discussion of secondary sources either chronologically or topically. Greater emphasis would be placed upon a critical analysis of each book and article with the author explaining the various interpretations and schools, as well as the uses of evidence.

FINAL CHECKLIST

Once the scholarly apparatus is complete and proofread for accuracy, beginning researchers examine the entire paper one final time to make absolutely certain they have satisfied all the criteria necessary to produce the desired best effort. A comprehensive checklist recording each component helps beginning researchers make certain they have completed each part. It is also helpful to have a peer read the final paper critically. The checklist may seem pedestrian, but it is a significant step in the successful paper writing process. It may be adapted to suit individual needs; however, it does illustrate important aspects that are often ignored.

Proofread!   While it is enticing to rely on the automatic spelling and grammar functions of most word processing programs, it is far better to reread the finished paper aloud and slowly to yourself. The ear will often pick up awkward constructions the eye may miss. It is also a good idea to have a peer read the paper. If a peer does not understand a point or a paragraph, the point or paragraph should be made clearer.

Be sure to proofread more than once. Does the introductory paragraph provide some historical context? Is there a clear thesis statement? Is the thesis evident throughout the paper? Does the evidence support the argument? Does the paper have a conclusion? How well organized is the paper? How well does the paper make transitions between points?

Is the Paper Grammatically Correct?   Many software programs contain both spelling and grammar functions that can assist the beginning researcher in the proofreading process. It is also prudent to consult a grammar guide. Historians should consult these throughout the writing and proofreading process. British English spellings in sources (labour, for instance) will be changed in most spell check programs. In quoted material, if an electronic program modifies the spelling or grammar, the result will be an error.

Are the Arguments Clear and Supported by Solid Evidence?   By this point in the process, the beginning researcher has read and reviewed the arguments several times; there may be a temptation to read through the points in haste. It is important to read closely and check each argument against the specific evidence used to support it. Has anything that would strengthen the case been left out? Is there other evidence that might help clarify the case?

Are the Correct Elements on the Title Page?   A title page should be the first page of the paper. A page number should not appear on this page. The title page should include your name, title of the paper, and date. If the research is being prepared as part of a course assignment, include the semester of the course, course name and number, and instructor's name. See Appendix B for an example.

Number the Pages   Number the pages of your paper. Software programs can place page numbers easily in a variety of locations; just be consistent in the location.

Is an Appendix Needed?   Does the paper need an appendix for materials that add to the paper but cannot be included, such as images, maps, or lengthy documents?

Check the Footnotes/Endnotes   Footnotes should appear at the bottom of each page; endnotes should appear after the text of the paper. They should be numbered consecutively. Historians follow *Chicago Manual*/Turabian format when documenting materials in a footnote/endnote. Use a short-title footnote/endnote after a full citation.

Check the Bibliography   The bibliography should be divided into two sections—primary sources and secondary sources. If annotated or an essay, the bibliography should include the author's interpretation as well as the usefulness of the work. The bibliography should conform to *Chicago Manual*/Turabian format.

Once the historian has completed the steps outlined in the previous chapters, and has reviewed his or her work numerous times, the paper can be submitted to the jury of peers for their consideration and it will add to the continuing conversation about the historical past.

Conclusion: The Continuing Conversation

When a piece of original research is systematically completed, as described in Chapters 1 through 6, there is a sense of genuine satisfaction and accomplishment. The research, interpretation, and writing processes have combined imagination and creativity with rigorous discipline. All of the relevant primary and secondary sources have been located and analyzed. The evidence has been used to develop a series of explanations and arguments that have added to the knowledge and appreciation of an aspect of the past. Those who read or hear the study and examine the sources critically can readily trace the structure and outline of the research, verifying the reliability of the findings.

Chapter 1 introduced the question "What is history?" and provided the tools necessary to practice it. It presented an overview of historical interpretations and approaches used by historians to study the past. By understanding these various approaches, historians better appreciate their own perspectives and theoretical foundations. In the process of studying the past, researchers add their own scholarship to the totality of historical knowledge. They have become part of an ongoing conversation about the discipline.

The second chapter presented a systematic framework to conduct historical research. The "research trail" offered an exhaustive approach to collecting all relevant, potential sources found in standard reference works and online databases. The trail also identified specific reference works that are essential to researching any topic successfully. Following this process fully, researchers can be confident that they have found all pertinent primary and secondary evidence and are prepared to begin a thorough analysis of that evidence.

Chapters 3 and 4 discussed the interpretation and analysis of secondary and primary sources. Chapter 3 explored the steps involved in understanding historical context, historiographical interpretations, and methodological approaches. By critically reading these works, researchers learn the importance of context, that historical interpretations may change over time, and that there are various ways to interpret similar evidence. Knowledge of secondary sources enable the researcher to better engage the essence of history—primary sources. Chapter 4 examined primary sources and illustrated the ways historians evaluate them. The interpretation of secondary and—especially primary—evidence provides the flesh and bones of historical analysis.

The fifth and sixth chapters explored the writing processes, finishing the paper, and appropriate attribution of evidence. The writing chapter discussed shorter writing assignments and placed particular emphasis on the importance of drafting, proofreading, peer reviewing, editing/revising, presenting orally, and ultimately producing a written essay. The final chapter described how and why historians cite evidence and offered numerous examples of how to acknowledge sources for notes and bibliographic purposes.

Observing the suggestions made in the preceding chapters can transform beginning researchers into apprentice historians. The completion of the paper does not end the process; rather, it begins the next stage in an ongoing conversation about the past. It may lead to additional questions or approaches to the topic. If others choose to do so, they can be guided by the work to build on or modify its conclusions. The research is a part of a continuing dialogue with other historians about the past; at this point the beginning researcher has now crossed a threshold to become an apprentice historian. Not all will continue along this path; however, learning to research, analyze, read critically, organize thoughtfully, and write effectively has benefits for citizens as well as scholars.

Appendix A

A Reference Librarian's Guide to Historical Reference Works

CREATED AND MAINTAINED BY PATRICIA HARDESTY, JAMES MADISON UNIVERSITY

TABLE OF CONTENTS

A. Guides to Historical Literature

B. Bibliographies of Bibliographies

C. Bibliographies/Indexing and Abstracting Services

D. National Bibliographies and Verification Sources

E. Newspaper/Periodical Sources

F. Dictionaries/Encyclopedias/Handbooks

G. Historiography

H. Statistical Sources and Tables

I. Historical Atlases

J. Biography

K. Annuals/Yearbooks

L. Primary Sources

M. Guides to Manuscripts

N. Treaties

O. Law

P. Directories

Q. Book Reviews

R. Public Opinion Sources

S. Speeches

T. Oral History

U. Style Manuals

V. Government Document Indexes

W. Additional History Handouts

A. GUIDES TO HISTORICAL LITERATURE

Balay, Robert, ed. *Guide to Reference Books*. 11th ed. Chicago: American Library Association, 1996.
(Ref Z 1035.1 G89 1996)
The standard source for reference books published in the United States. Subject coverage is universal with the accent on scholarly reference tools. Arranged by broad subjects with many subcategories. Annotated.

Beisner, Robert L. ed. *American Foreign Relations Since 1600*. Santa Barbara, CA: ABC Clio, 2003. 2 vol.
(Ref E 183.7 .G84 2003).
A masterful annotated bibliographic guide to the historiography of U.S. foreign relations. Each chapter has a detailed table of contents outlining the categories of bibliographic sources included; e.g., primary material, bibliographies, biography, and subtopics. Excellent indexes.

Bengtson, Hermann. *Introduction to Ancient History*. Berkeley: University of California Press, 1970.
(Ref D 59 B413 1970).
Still a standard guide to ancient history. A translation from the German original, German-language works dominate the bibliographies.

Blazek, Ron. *United States History: A Selective Guide to Information Sources*. Englewood, CO: Libraries Unlimited, 1994.
(Ref E 178 B58 1994).
Along with the Prucha title (see below) this guide is the current standard for American history. Seven chapters are sources of general importance, U.S. history—topics and issues, diplomatic history, military history, social and cultural history, regional history, and economic history. This is an excellent guide highlighted by outstanding annotations.

Butler, L. J., ed. *Modern British History: A Guide to Study and Research*. London and New York: I. B. Tauris, 1997.
(D16.4 G7 M63 1997).
Crosby, Everett U. *Medieval Studies: A Bibliographical Guide*. New York: Garland Publisher, 1983.
(Ref CE 351 C76 1983).
Crosby is the most current scholarly guide to medieval studie. This work contains some 9,000 entries on monographs in European languages. Entries include brief descriptive and evaluative annotations. The guide is divided into 138 geographical and topical chapters.

de Graaf, Lawrence B. "Clio's Neglected Tools: A Taxonomy of Reference Works for American History." *The History Teacher*. 25, no. 2 (February 1992): 191–231.
(Periodical).
A historian's approach to listing the major reference sources in American history. Commentary with each section.

DeWitt, Donald L., comp. *Guides to Archives and Manuscript Collections in the United States: An Annotated Bibliography.* Westport, CT: Greenwood Press, 1994.
(Ref CD 3022 A2 D48 1994).
Covers over 2,050 published guides to archives mainly in the United States, with one chapter noting guides to foreign repositories with U.S.-related holdings. Most sections are topical; e.g., ethnic minorities and women, fine arts collections, political collections, etc. Annotated entries.

Ford, P. *A Guide to Parliamentary Papers: What They Are, How to Find Them, How to Use Them.* 3rd ed. Totowa, NJ: Rowman and Littlefield, 1972.
(Ref CD 1063 F6 1972).

Fritze, Ronald H. *Reference Sources in History: An Introductory Guide.* 2nd ed. Santa Barbara, CA: ABC-CLIO, 2004.
(Ref D 20 F75 2004).
Fritze is the standard guide to history research, with comprehensive coverage of geographic areas and time periods. International in scope. Excellent annotations supplement the 930 entries, which are arranged by type of resource.

Hanke, Lewis, ed. *Guide to the Study of United States History Outside the U.S., 1945–1980,* 5 vol. White Plains, NY: Kraus International Publications, 1985.
(Ref E 175.8 G85 1985).
Published under the auspices of the American Historical Association, this work uses essays and bibliographies to describe materials and sources on American history in other countries. Archival materials are noted. Foreign languages are included. Useful because much of the material is not covered in bibliographies and indexes in the United States.

Hardy, Lyda M. *Women in U.S. History: A Resource Guide.* Englewood, CO: Libraries Unlimited, 2000.
(Ref HQ 1410 H364 2000).
One section lists sources by chronological period and by category; e.g., women's movement. Second section includes categories such as sports, work, historiography.

Hefner, Loretta, comp. *The WPA Historical Records Survey: A Guide to the Unpublished Inventories, Indexes, and Transcripts.* Chicago: Society of American Archivists, 1980.
(Ref E 173 H43 1980).
Arranged by state and repository, a listing of the holdings of each repository.

Hessenbruch, Arne, ed. *Reader's Guide to the History of Science.* London: Fitzroy Dearborn, 2000.
(Ref Q 125 R335 2000).
Alphabetical arrangement of topics such as genetics, big bang theory, medical ethics, as well as entries on countries and individuals. A guide to the best secondary literature, with a good index and cross-references.

Higham, Robin D., ed. *A Guide to the Sources of British Military History.* Berkeley: University of California Press, 1971.
(Ref DA 50 G85).

Supplemented in 1988 with a work edited by Gerald Jordan
(Ref DA 50 G85 supp 1988).

Higham, Robin, ed. *Researching World War I: A Handbook.* Westport, CT: Greenwood
Press, 2003.
(Ref D 522.4 R47 2003).
Up-to-date handbook with long bibliographic essays, each by a different
scholar, followed by extensive bibliographies.

Hill, Edward E., comp. *Guide to Records in the National Archives of the United States Relating
to American Indians.* Washington, DC: National Archives and Record Services,
General Services Administration, 1982.
(Ref E 93 H642 1981).
Arranged by National Archives record group, this guide lists and describes
collections available at the Archives. Comprehensive coverage.

Larsen, John C., ed. *Researcher's Guide to Archives and Regional Sources.* Hamden, CT:
Library Professional Publications, 1988.
(Ref CD 3021 R47 1988).
In 14 topical chapters, Larsen presents issues important to regional research;
contains some bibliographic sources. Chapter titles include oral history, car-
tographic sources, business records, etc.

Leab, Daniel J., ed. *Labor History Archives in the United States: A Guide for Researching and
Teaching.* Detroit, MI: Wayne State University Press, 1992.
(Ref HD 8066 L22 1992).
Description of the labor holdings of 40 libraries, archives, and historical soci-
eties. Published sources and manuscript holdings are noted.

Loades, David, ed. *Reader's Guide to British History,* 2 vol. New York: Fitzroy Dearborn,
2003.
(Ref DA 34 .R43 2003).
Arranged alphabetically by topic, a guide to the best secondary literature on
British history, broadly defined. Covers prehistory to the time of publication,
and all constituent parts of the British Isles. At the front of vol. 1, alphabetical
and thematic lists of entries; at the back of vol. 2, a list by author of all books
referred to in the entries, a general index, and cross-references. This is one in
a series of excellent guides to secondary historical literature published by
Fitzroy Dearborn. Others in the series include *Reader's Guide to American History* and *Reader's Guide to the History of Science.*

Martin, Fenton S. *How to Research Elections.* Washington, DC: CQ Press, 2000.
(Ref JK 1976 M373 2000).
This annotated guide and bibliography offers comprehensive coverage of
American elections. An introductory part lists primary sources, secondary
sources, and finding tools, including Internet sources. A second part is a bib-
liography by topic; e.g., campaign finance, voting participation, etc.

Martin, Fenton S. *How to Research the Supreme Court.* Washington, DC: Congressional
Quarterly, 1992.
(Ref KF 8741 A1 M36 1992).

This guide has major sections on primary and secondary sources, including web sources. The guide concludes with a "selected bibliography" on all members of the Supreme Court. Martin has a companion work entitled *The U.S. Supreme Court: A Bibliography* (1990) at Ref KF 8741 A1 M37 1990. This comprehensive, although unannotated, bibliography of over 9,400 entries (monographs, journal articles, and dissertations) looks at all areas of Supreme Court endeavor.

Moody, Suzanna, ed. *The Immigration History Research Center: A Guide to Collections.*
New York: Greenwood Press, 1991.
(Ref E 184 A1 U58 1991).
A guide to the immigration collection at the University of Minnesota. The emphasis is on Central and East European immigration during the late nineteenth and early twentieth centuries. Twenty-four different national groups are included. Within each national group there are sections describing individual manuscript collections, a bibliography of monographic holdings, and a list of newspapers.

Morehead, Joe. *Introduction to United States Government Information Sources.* Englewood, CO: Libraries Unlimited, 1999.
(Ref Z 1223 Z7 M67 1999).
The best, current introduction to using government documents. Arranged generally by agency, Morehead includes sections on the Government Printing Office, statistical sources, historical background, etc. For advanced information on government documents see also Schmeckebier (see below).

Muccigrosso, Robert. *Term Paper Resource Guide to Twentieth-Century United States History.* Westport, CT: Greenwood Press, 1999.
(Ref E 741 M83 1999).
For 100 events, the compilers give background, suggestions for a term paper, reference sources, general sources, specialized sources, audiovisual sources, Internet sources, etc. Useful.

Neagles, James C. *Confederate Research Sources: A Guide to Archives Collections.* Salt Lake City, UT: Ancestry Pub., 1986.
(Ref E 487 N3 1986).
A scholarly presentation of the Confederacy and the records it produced.

Neagles, James C. *The Library of Congress: A Guide to Genealogical and Historical Research.* Salt Lake City, UT: Ancestry Pub., 1990.
(Ref E 180 N4 1990).
A comprehensive guide, with annotated bibliography, to the historical collections at the Library of Congress (LC), although many sources listed are also available outside of the LC. Arranged by topic and geographical area.

Newman, Debra L. *Black History: A Guide to Civilian Records in the National Archives.* Washington, DC: National Archives Trust Board, General Services Administration, 1984.
(Ref E 185 N576 1984).

This guide details the available collections on Black Americans at the National Archives.

Plischke, Elmer. *U.S. Foreign Relations: A Guide to Information Sources*. Detroit, MI: Gale Research Co., 1980.
(Ref JX 1407 P52 1980).
A major guide and bibliography for foreign relations. This annotated guide has sections on diplomacy and diplomats, conduct of U.S. foreign relations, official sources and resources, and memoirs and biographical material. Scholarly. See also the Beisner entry (see above).

Prucha, Francis P. *Handbook for Research in American History: A Guide to Bibliographies and Other Reference Works*. 2nd ed., rev. Lincoln: University of Nebraska Press, 1994.
(Ref E 178 P782 1994).
A major guide to American history research. Twenty topical chapters with short introductions on such topics as general guides, guides to newspapers, oral history materials, followed by titles of interest. Some annotations.

Quatannens, Jo Anne. *Senators of the United States, A Historical Bibliography: A Compilation of Works by and about Members of the United States Senate, 1789–1995*. Washington, DC: Government Printing Office, 1995. (Gov Doc Microfiche. Y 1.1/3:103–34).
A comprehensive bibliography to sources on U.S. Senators. A companion volume entitled *Guide to Research Collections of Former United States Senators, 1789–1995: A Listing of Archival Repositories Housing the Papers of Former Senators, Related Collections, and Oral History Interviews* is at Gov Doc Microfiche Y 1.1/3:103–35.

Richards, Michael D., ed. *Term Paper Resource Guide to Twentieth-Century World History*. Westport, CT: Greenwood Press, 2000.
(Ref D 421 R47 2000).
For 100 key world history events of the twentieth century, the author provides an overview along with key primary and secondary sources.

Schick, Frank L. ed. *Records of the Presidency: Presidential Papers and Libraries from Washington to Reagan*. Phoenix, AZ: Onyx Press, 1989.
(Ref CD 3029.82 S35 1989).
An excellent guide to researching the presidency and individual presidents. The first section details agencies that work with presidential records, guides to their records, etc. Additional sections look at presidential papers at the Library of Congress, papers in historical societies and special libraries, and the presidential libraries administered by the National Archives. Scholarly. Additional guides to aspects of the presidency and presidents include *Presidential Libraries and Collections* by Fritz Veit (1987) at Ref CD 3029.82 V45 1987 and *A Guide to Manuscripts in the Presidential Libraries* compiled by Dennis A. Burton (1985) at Ref CD 3029.82 B87 1985.

Schmeckebier, Laurence F. *Government Publications and Their Use*. 2nd rev. ed. Washington, DC: Brookings Institution, 1969.
(Ref Z 1223 A7 S3 1969).

Although published over 30 years ago, this guide remains the standard for a detailed understanding of how to use government documents from a historical perspective. See the entries under Morehead and Sears for current guides to government documents.

Sears, Jean L. and Marilyn K. Moody. *Using Government Information Sources: Electronic and Print.* 3rd ed. Phoenix, AZ: Onyx Press, 2001.
(Ref Z 1223 .Z7 S4 2001).
A practical guide that deals with specific types of government research searches; e.g., subject, agency, statistical. Includes special techniques section, which includes legislative history and treaties.

Slavens, Thomas P. *Sources of Information for Historical Research.* New York: Neal Schuman, 1994.
(Ref D 20 S42 1994).
Over 1,100 detailed annotated entries are contained in this bibliography. Arrangement is by Library of Congress call number. The scope of this work is international. An excellent source for key books used in historical research.

United States. Congress. House of Representatives. *A Guide to Research Collections of Former Members of the United States House of Representatives, 1789–1987,* ed. Cynthia Pease Miller. Washington, DC: Office of the Bicentennial of the United States, House of Representatives, 1988. (Gov Doc Y 1.1/7:100–171).
Information on collections related to ca. 3,300 former House members, whose papers are scattered widely. Also located in the Serial Set #13874.

United States. Congress. Senate. *Guide to Research Collections of Former United States Senators, 1789–1995.* ed. Karen Dawley Paul. Washington, DC: Superintendent of Documents, GPO, 1995. (Gov Doc Sen. Doc. 103rd, 35th).
A guide to repositories holding senatorial papers. For each repository it notes dates of coverage and collection size. An appendix lists repositories by state and the names of senators they hold. This is Serial Set #14218.

United States. Library of Congress. *Special Collections in the Library of Congress: a Selective Guide.* ed. Annette Melville. Washington, DC: Superintendent of Public Documents, GPO, 1980.
(Ref Z 733 U58 U54 1980).
A guide to ca. 270 major collections at the Library of Congress. Each collection is described with its scope and contents featured. Scholarly.

United States. National Archives and Records Administration. *Guide to the Records of the United States House of Representatives at the National Archives, 1789–1989.* ed. Charles E. Schamel. Washington, DC: U.S. House of Representatives, 1989.
(Gov Doc Y 1.1/3:100–42).
This guide is to the several committees that have served in the House. Appendices include such areas as a bibliography, glossary, microform publications of House records, etc.

United States. National Archives and Records Service. *A Guide to Pre-Federal Records in the National Archives.* comp. Howard H. Wehmann. Washington, DC: National

Archives and Records Administration, 1989.
(Ref CD 3045 W44 1989).
Most National Archives records relate to the period after the Constitution went into effect, 4 March 1789. This lists earlier records; e.g., Continental and Confederation Congresses, Constitutional Convention, Continental Army and Navy records, etc.

Vandercook, Sharon. *A Guide to British Documents and Records in the University of Virginia Library*. Charlottesville, VA, Reference Department, University of Virginia Library, 1972.
(Ref CD 1042 V363 1972).

Webb, William H. *Sources of Information in the Social Sciences: A Guide to the Literature*. 3rd ed. Chicago: American Library Association, 1986.
(Ref H 61 W433 S64 1986).
Webb is an excellent source for an overview of history. The chapter on history is introduced by subject specialists discussing the core sources of monographic literature for major episodes in history; e.g., American Civil War. This is followed by sections on topics such as key reference books, bibliographies, organizations, journals, etc.

Wigdor, Alexandra K. *The Personal Papers of Supreme Court Justices: Descriptive Guide*. New York: Garland Pub., 1986.
(Ref KF 8744 W55 1986).
An example of a guide for researching Supreme Court justices. Alphabetical arrangement by justice. Information includes location, size, access restrictions, provenance, and description of the collection.

B. BIBLIOGRAPHIES OF BIBLIOGRAPHIES

Beers, Henry P. *Bibliographies in American History, 1942–1978: Guide to Materials for Research*. Woodbridge, CT: Research Pubs., 1982. 2 vol.
(Ref E 178 B39 1982).
The standard source for a bibliography of bibliographies in American history. Ca. 12,000 entries are for monographs, parts of books, journal articles, and government documents. The 1942 edition, at the same call number, should be used for comprehensive coverage. It lists an additional ca. 7,500 entries.

Besterman, Theodore. *A World Bibliography of Bibliographies . . .* Totowa, NJ: Rowman and Littlefield, 1965–1966. 5 vol.
(Ref Z 1002 B5684).
A masterful and comprehensive bibliography of bibliographies containing some 117,000 entries covering the full span of human endeavor. Arranged by subject with thousands of individuals included. The final volume is an index. All languages and from the advent of printing.

Bibliographic Index. New York: H. W. Wilson, Co., 1937–.
An excellent source for bibliographies, updated semi-annually with annual cumulations. Indexes substantial bibliographies published in monographs and journal articles, covering all subject areas and time periods.

Bibliographies in History: An Index to Bibliographies in History Journals and Dissertations... Santa Barbara, CA: ABC-CLIO, 1988. 2 vol.
(Ref E 178 B52 1988).
Volume 1 covers the United States and Canada while volume 2 covers the rest of the world. Coverage is from 1954 in journals and 1974 for dissertations. Ca. 5,000 entries are available. Annotated.

Coulter, Edith M. *Historical Bibliographies: A Systematic and Annotated Guide.* Berkeley: University of California Press, 1935.
(Z 6201 A1 C8 1935).
Although dated, Coulter's scholarly work has research value for early bibliographies. Ca. 800 entries.

Newman, Richard, comp. *Black Access: A Bibliography of Afro-American Bibliographies.* Westport, CT: Greenwood Press, 1984.
(Ref E 185 N578 1984).
This lists both books and journal articles. Alphabetical arrangement with subject index.

C. BIBLIOGRAPHIES/INDEXING AND ABSTRACTING SERVICES

America: History and Life. Santa Barbara, CA: ABC-CLIO, Inc., 1954–present. (Online Library Subscription Database).
Comprehensive indexing and selective abstracting of the international scholarly literature treating the history and culture of the United States and Canada in all historic periods. Covers journal articles (from over 2,400 journals), book reviews from a subset of those journals, film and video reviews, dissertation listings. Complemented by the *Historical Abstracts* (see below).

l'Année Philologique. Paris: Société Internationale de Bibliographie Classique, 1959–present. (Microfiche, 1924–1973; Bound, 1983–1998, Ref Index/Abstracts). (Online Library Subscription Database).
An index with abstracts to scholarly work (books and articles) covering all aspects of Greco-Roman antiquity from the 2nd millennium BCE through the early middle ages (ca. 500–800 CE). Covers Greek and Latin language and linguistics, Greek and Roman history, literature, philosophy, art, archaeology, religion, mythology, music, science, early Christian texts, numismatics, papyrology. Absolutely essential for ancient history. See http://www.library.arizona.edu/help/tutorials/lannee/ for help in using this rather strange search interface.

Arksey, Laura. *American Diaries: An Annotated Bibliography of Published American Diaries and Journals*. Detroit, MI: Gale Research, 1983. 2 vol.
(Ref CT 214 A73 1983).
The standard bibliography to American diaries. Ca. 6,000 published diaries are arranged chronologically from 1492–1980. The diaries are listed for the year in which the diary began. Extensive indexing.

Asamani, J. O. *Index Africanus*. Stanford, CA: Hoover Institution Press, 1975.
(Ref DT 3 A73 1975).
Lists ca. 25,000 journal articles in Western languages published between 1885 and 1965. Following a general section the bibliography is divided by country and then by topics.

Bibliographie Annuelle de l'Histoire de France du Cinquième Siècle à 1958. Paris: Éditions du Centre national de la recherche scientifique, 1975–present.
(Ref DC 38.B5).
Covers books and articles. Has indexes by time period, subject, and authors' names.

Bibliography of Asian Studies. Ann Arbor, MI: Association for Asian Studies, 1946–present. Annual.
(Ref DS 5 B49).
Also available online in the library subscription database, JSTOR, as part of two journals, *The Far Eastern Quarterly* and *The Journal of Asian Studies*.
This is the standard bibliography on Asian studies, covering scholarship in European languages. The bibliography appeared in *Far Eastern Quarterly* between 1941–1956, and in the *Journal of Asian Studies* for 1956–1966. Thereafter, and until 1991, it appeared as a separate printed bibliography. It is now only available online.

Bibliography of British History. Oxford: Clarendon Press,
(Various editors, dates of publications, locations in Reference).
This excellent, though dated series is produced under the direction of the American Historical Association and the Royal Historical Society of Great Britain. Among the volumes are the following:

- Tudor Period, 1485–1603 (Ref DA 315 .R28 1959)
- Stuart Period, 1603–1714 (Ref DA 375 .D25 1970)
- Eighteenth Century, 1714–1789 (Ref DA 498 .P37 1977)
- 1789–1851 (Ref DA 520 B75 1977)
- 1851–1914 (Ref DA 530 H46 1976)
- 1914–1989 (Ref DA DA 566 R62 1996)

Combined Retrospective Index to Journals in History. Washington, DC: Carrollton Press, 1977. 11 vol. (In print only, Ref Abstract/Index).
Dissertation Abstracts. Ann Arbor, MI: University Microfilms, 1952–present. (Online Library Subscription Database).

Dissertation Abstracts International lists and provides abstracts for most dissertations produced in the United States since 1861. The original research and extensive bibliographies make dissertations valuable to the student. Dissertations can often be borrowed on interlibrary loan.

Expanded Academic ASAP. Foster City, CA: Information Access Company, 1999–present (Online Library Subscription Database).
A multidisciplinary database containing indexing, selective abstracting, and full-text for many scholarly journals as well as popular magazines.

Filby, P. William. *A Bibliography of American County Histories*. Baltimore, MD: Genealogical Pub. Co., 1985.
(Ref E 180 F54 1985).
Arranged by state and county, Filby's work lists significant published county histories. It also includes some regional historical studies. This should be used with the comprehensive *United States Local Histories in the Library of Congress: A Bibliography* (see below).

Foreign Affairs Bibliography: A Selected and Annotated List of Books on International Relations. New York: Published for the Council on Foreign Relations by Harper, 1919/1932–present.
(Ref JX 1391 F73).
An excellent annotated bibliography of monographs on foreign affairs. Topical sections cover the full range of foreign affairs. Various European languages. This has been published ca. every 10 years. It is kept current by a bibliography in each issue of the journal, *Foreign Affairs*.

Friedel, Frank B. *Harvard Guide to American History*. Cambridge, MA: Belknap Press of Harvard University Press, 1974. 2 vol.
(Ref E 178 F77 1974).
Although dated, this title remains a standard bibliographic guide to American history. Topical sections cover the full range of American history. The "best" sources are listed. Well indexed.

Goehlert, Robert U. *Members of Congress: A Bibliography*. Washington, DC: Congressional Quarterly, 1996.
(Ref JK 1030 A2 G568 1996).
Books, articles, dissertations, and essays are listed in this alphabetically arranged bibliography.

Griffin, Appleton P. C. *Bibliography of American Historical Societies*. Washington, DC: American Historical Association, 1907.
(Ref E 172 A60 1905 v.2).
An important bibliography for pre-twentieth-century American history. Griffin indexed all major historical society periodicals up to 1905. Although the arrangement is awkward for a researcher today, the indexing and content make this a useful tool. *Writings on American History* (see below) partially continues Griffin.

Handbook of Latin American Studies. Gainesville: University of Florida Press, 1935–present.
(Online Public Access Database at http://lcweb2.loc.gov/hlas/. In print at Ref F
1408 H262;).
A comprehensive and essential scholarly bibliography to all areas of Latin
America. Beginning with 1964, the volumes on social sciences and human-
ities are published in alternate years. The online version is updated weekly.
What the printed version lacks in currency, however, it makes up for in
ease of use.

Historical Abstracts. Santa Barbara, CA:, ABC-CLIO, Inc. 1954–present. (In print form,
1955–1966, Ref Abstract/Index). (Online Library Subscription Database).
An index with abstracts to more than 2,000 periodicals on world history
from 1450 to the present, *excluding* the United States and Canada. This
source does not index book reviews, but does index review articles.

Index Islamicus. London: Mansell, 1983–present.
(Online Library Subscription Database). (Online, 1905–present; in print, 1976–, Ref
Abstract/Index).
Indexes books, journal articles, book chapters, reviews, some online sources.
Coverage is comprehensive and scholarly, covering all countries of the world
where Islam is the majority faith, as well as Muslim minorities living
elsewhere.

Journal of American History. Bloomington, IN: Organization of American Historians, 1964–
present. (See *Periodical Locator* for available formats). (Published 1914–1964
as *Mississippi Valley Historical Review*).
Each issue has a bibliography of current journal articles and dissertations
arranged by subject. See *Journal of Southern History* for an additional example
of a bibliography in a journal.

Larned, Josephus N. *The Literature of American History: A Bibliographical Guide.* New York:
F. Ungar Pub. Co., [1966] reprint of the 1902 edition.
(Ref E 178 L3 1966).
An important bibliography for pre-twentieth century American history.
Useful for its listing of source material and the critical annotations to the
citations.

Lee, Lloyd, ed. *World War II in Europe, Africa, and the Americas, with General Sources.*
Westport, CT: Greenwood Press, 1997.
(Ref D 743.42 .W67 1997).
Lincove, David A., comp. *Reconstruction in the United States: An Annotated Bibliography.*
Westport, CT: Greenwood Press, 2000.
(Ref E 668 L56 2000).
Comprehensive in its coverage, Lincove has ca. 3,000 entries of books,
essays, journal articles, doctoral dissertations, and masters theses.

Matthews, William. *British Diaries: An Annotated Bibliography of British Diaries Written
Between 1442 and 1942.* Gloucester, MA: P. Smith, 1967.
(PR 1330 .M38 1967).

Miller, Gordon W. *Rockingham: An Annotated Bibliography of a Virginia County*. Harrisonburg, VA: Harrisonburg-Rockingham Historical Society, 1989.
(Ref F 232 R7 M5486 1989).
An example of a historical bibliography at the county level. Comprehensive coverage of books, articles, maps, etc. Topical arrangement. For the online supplement, go to: http://www.lib.jmu.edu/rockbib/index.htm.

The Nazi Era, 1919–1945: A Select Bibliography of Published Works from the Early Roots to 1980. Helen Kehr comp. London: Mansell, 1982.
(DD 253.25 K4 1982)

Norton, Mary B., ed. *The American Historical Association's Guide to Historical Literature*. 3rd ed. New York: Oxford University Press, 1995. 2 vol.
(Ref D 20 A55 1995).
This two-volume guide is an excellent handbook for world history. Arranged in 48 topical sections, this work contains extensive bibliographies, mostly covering English-language publications published between 1961 and 1992. Each bibliographic section is preceded by a short essay that provides an overview of the development of the topic at hand. Earlier editions are at Ref D 20 .A55 (1961) and Ref D 20. A55 (1931).

Poole, William Frederick. *Poole's Index to Periodical Literature, 1802–1906*. New York: Peter Smith, 1938. (Online Library Subscription Database, *19th Century Masterfile*; also in print, Ref Abstract/Index).
Similar in scope to *The Readers' Guide to Periodical Literature* (see *Wilson OmniFile* below), this resource indexes popular magazines of the nineteenth century.

The Royal Historical Society Bibliography. 1900–. (Online Public Access Database at http://www.rhs.ac.uk/bibl/bibwel.asp).
A rich online source that indexes scholarship on the British Isles during all historical periods, including books, articles in journals, and articles in books. Incorporated into the database are pre-1900 entries from a number of print sources, notably several important bibliographies published by Oxford University Press.

Swem, Earl G., comp. *Virginia Historical Index*. Roanoke, VA: Stone Printing and Manufacturing Co., 1965 reprint of the 1934 ed. 4 vol.
(Ref F 221 S93 1965).
An outstanding bibliography for Virginia history, this source provides deep indexing of seven important journals and legal publications relating to Virginia. Mandatory for locating historical research on Virginia published prior to 1930.

Trask, David F. *A Bibliography of United States–Latin American Relations Since 1810*. Lincoln: University of Nebraska Press, 1968.
(Ref F 1418 T7 1968).
At the same call number is the 1979 supplement compiled by Michael Meyer. Together these bibliographies are the most comprehensive guide to this literature. Over 15,000 books, articles, and dissertations are listed. There are both chronological and country sections.

United States. Library of Congress. General Reference and Bibliography Division. *A Guide to the Study of the United States of America* . . . Washington, DC: Library of Congress, 1960. (Ref Z 1215 U53).
A selective bibliography listing major works on American history, broadly defined. About 6,500 annotated entries cover divisions such as diplomatic, education, science, etc.

United States. Library of Congress. *United States Local Histories in the Library of Congress: A Bibliography.* ed. Marion Kaminkow. Baltimore, MD: Magna Carta Book Co., 1975–1976. 5 vol.
(Ref E 180 U59 1975).
An exhaustive bibliography of local histories. Arranged by Library of Congress call number, which places all books within a geographical hierarchy. Useful in biographical and genealogical research.

Wieczynski, Joseph L., ed. *The Gorbachev Bibliography, 1985–1991: A Listing of Books and Articles in English on Perestroika in the USSR.* New York: Norman Ross Pub., 1996. (Ref DK 286 W54 1996).
This work covers English-language books and articles (primarily scholarly articles) on Gorbachev and perestroika.

Wilson OmniFile Full Text Mega. Bronx, NY: H. W. Wilson Co., 1982–present. (Online Library Subscription Database).
Among other indexes, this database combines Humanities Abstracts, Readers' Guide Abstracts, and Social Sciences Abstracts. In addition, it includes the full-text subset of Art Abstracts. Includes *Vital Speeches of the Day* (see below in *Speeches* section).

Work, Monroe N. *A Bibliography of the Negro in Africa and America.* New York: H. W. Wilson Co., 1928.
(Ref E 185 W67 1928).
This excellent bibliography, arranged topically, has ca. 17,000 entries, covering documents, books, articles, maps, pamphlets, etc.

Writings on American History. Washington, DC: American Historical Association, 1902–1961. Annual.
(Ref E 178 L331).
Until the publication of *America: History and Life,* this was the most exhaustive index to scholarly work on American history. Includes books, essays in books, dissertations, journal articles. Chronological and subject arrangement, with an author index. A cumulative index for 1902–1940 is available. Not published 1904, 1905, 1941–1947.

D. NATIONAL BIBLIOGRAPHIES
AND VERIFICATION SOURCES

National bibliographies are massive compilations of all items published in a given country. They are standard sources for verifying citations for interlibrary loan requests. More and more of the information contained in printed national bibliographies can be found in online library catalogs.

British Museum. Department of Printed Books. *General Catalogue of Printed Books to 1955.* compact ed. New York: Readexex Microprint Corporation, 1967.
(Biblio Z 921 B8753).
This is the British national bibliography, listing all titles held by the British Museum to 1955 and supplemented through 1970.

Global Books in Print. New Providence, NJ: R. R. Bowker, n.d.
(Online Library Subscription Database).
The standard source for determining books published in the United States that are currently in print. Includes selective reviews.

The National Union Catalog Pre-56 Imprints. Washington, DC: Library of Congress, 1968–1980. 754 vol.
(Biblio Z 881 A1 U372).
Published by the Library of Congress, this monumental publication (known as the *NUC*) aimed to list all printed materials published before 1956 and owned by any of 700 research libraries in the United States and Canada. It lists, in author order, over 13 million books, pamphlets, maps, atlases, and music held by the Library of Congress and other libraries. The entries include variant editions and usually note the U.S. libraries that own the source. This title is especially useful for historical and literary research to verify a book's existence and/or multiple editions. There is no subject access to the items listed. The *NUC* has been partially superseded by the next listing for *WorldCat.*

WorldCat. Dublin, OH: OCLC, 1997.
(Online Library Subscription Database).
This cooperative catalog maintained by thousands of libraries worldwide contains descriptions of over 46 million items.

E. NEWSPAPER/PERIODICAL SOURCES

Brigham, Clarence S. *History and Bibliography of American Newspapers 1690–1820.* Westport, CT: Greenwood Press, 1975. 2 vol.
(Ref PN 4861 B86 1976).
Brigham's work covers the early years and is used as a predecessor to Gregory (see below). Over 2,000 newspapers are identified. Brigham has lengthy descriptions of the newspapers, noting editors and publishers. Institutions with holdings are noted.

Cappon, Lester J. *Virginia Newspapers 1821–1935: A Bibliography with Historical Introduction and Notes.* Charlottesville, VA: The Institute for Research in the Social Sciences, 1930.
(Ref F 230 C28 1936).

Cappon's work was compiled prior to the introduction of microfilming in this country. This is an example of a guide to all newspapers published in a state. Cappon lists the dates of publication along with libraries holding individual issues. He notes the various publishers, by date, and even has bibliographical information noting his sources.

Gregory, Winifred, ed. *American Newspapers 1821–1936: A Union List of Files Available in the United States and Canada.* New York: Kraus Reprint Corp., 1967 reprint. (Ref PN 4855 A53 1967).
Originally published in 1937, this comprehensive directory predates microfilming of newspapers. Arranged by state and city, the available issues are keyed to holding libraries.

Milner, Anita C. *Newspaper Indexes: A Location and Subject Guide for Researchers.* Metuchen, NJ: Scarecrow Press, 1977–1982. 3 vol. (Ref AI 3 M5 1977).
Although quite dated, Milner's work remains the most comprehensive guide to indexed newspapers. Since only major newspapers are indexed commercially, this guide is valuable for noting small and regional papers that have some indexing. To determine if a given newspaper is indexed, you may need to check locally.

New Serials Titles: A Union List of Serials Commencing Publication After December 31, 1949. Washington, DC: Joint Committee on the Union List of Serials, Library of Congress, 1953–.
(Biblio Z 6945 U5 S42).
Periodicals beginning since 1950 are listed in this comprehensive source. International in coverage.

Ulrichsweb.com. Ulrich's International Periodicals Directory. New Providence, NJ: R. R. Bowker, nd.
(Online Library Subscription Database).
A major source for current periodicals published worldwide. Over 125,000 titles are listed. Includes contact information, lists sources where a periodical is indexed, and notes if a periodical is refereed (peer-reviewed). Available from 1942–1993, with some years lacking, as *Ulrich's International Periodicals Directory* and *Ulrich's Periodicals Directory* at Z 6941 U5. Other major sources for periodicals include *The Serials Directory* at Ref Z 6941 S464 and *The Standard Periodical Directory* at Ref Z 6951 S78.

Union List of Serials in Libraries of the United States and Canada. 3rd ed. Washington, DC: Joint Committee on the Union List of Serials, Library of Congress, 1965. 5 vol. (Biblio Z 6945 U45 1965). Complemented and updated online by *WorldCat* (Library Subscription Database).
The print source lists periodicals published prior to 1950, and held in 950 libraries. Coverage is international and comprehensive, with over 150,000 titles. A good choice to determine the existence of a periodical published prior to 1950. *WorldCat* contains records describing most serial publications, including those in the printed *Union List*. It also lists the precise holdings of

many libraries. To access this information in *WorldCat,* click on "Libraries worldwide that own item."

United States. Library of Congress. *Newspapers in Microform: Foreign Countries, 1948–1983.* Washington, DC: Library of Congress, 1984.
(Ref PN 4731 U515 1984).
Lists non-U.S. newspapers that are available on microforms. Arranged by country and city. This lists newspapers back into the eighteenth century.

United States Newspaper Program. Dublin, OH: OCLC, 1987.
(Website at http://www.neh.gov/projects/usnp.html).
This cooperative program aims to locate, catalog, and preserve on microfilm, all newspapers published in the United States. This website provides links to most state programs, providing the researcher with lists of available newspapers. Records for these newspapers are included in *WorldCat.*

F. DICTIONARIES/ENCYCLOPEDIAS/ HANDBOOKS

World History

Krech III, Shepard, ed. *Encyclopedia of World Environmental History.* New York: Routledge, 2004. 3 vol.
(Ref GF 10 E63 2004).
Entries on the expected and the unusual, from acid rain to Protestantism to zoos. Each entry has a bibliography.

Langer, William L. *Encyclopedia of World History*... 5th rev. ed. Boston: Houghton Mifflin, 1972.
(D21. E578 1972).
A classic source that has the reputation for being the best manual of history ever published. It covers all time periods and geographic areas with an emphasis on post-1500 Western civilization. Arranged chronologically, this manual includes maps, lists of kings and rulers, and some genealogical tables. This has been updated by Peter N. Stearns's *The Encyclopedia of World History: Ancient, Medieval, and Modern Chronologically Arranged.* A Completely Revised and Updated Edition of the Classic Reference Work Originally Compiled and Edited by William L. Langer. 2001 (Ref D 21 E578 2001).

McNeill, William H., ed. *Berkshire Encyclopedia of World History.* Great Barrington, MA: Berkshire Pub. Group, 2005. 5 vol.
(Ref D 23 B45 2005).
A scholarly work with the particular perspective of the interactions of people and events over time and place. Bibliographies end the entries.

Europe

Cook, Bernard, ed. *Europe Since 1945: An Encyclopedia.* 2 vol. New York: Garland Pub., 2001.
(Ref D 1051 E873 2001).

While arranged alphabetically, there is a subject guide at the front of vol. 1, as well as a chronology of political events. Scholarly, signed articles, but rather brief bibliographies.

Dewald, Jonathan, ed. *Europe 1450 to 1789: Encyclopedia of the Early Modern World*. New York: Scribner's, 2004. 6 vol.
(Ref D 209 .E97 2004).
Helpful chronology in vol. 1. Illustrated, with bibliographies, and extensive index in vol. 6.

Frucht, Richard, ed. *Encyclopedia of Eastern Europe from the Congress of Vienna to the Fall of Communism*. New York: Garland Pub., 2000.
(Ref DJK 6 E53 2000).
There are seven long articles on the primary countries: Poland, Hungary, Czechoslovakia, Albania, Bulgaria, Romania, and Yugoslavia. Shorter articles cover individuals, culture, geography, trends, etc. Bibliographies emphasize English works.

Gardiner, Juliet, ed. *The Columbia Companion to British History*. New York: Columbia University Press, 1997.
(Ref DA 34 H64 1997).

Gutman, Israel, ed. *Encyclopedia of the Holocaust*. 4 vol. New York: Macmillan, 1990.
(Ref D 804.3 .E53 1990).
Detailed treatment of the Holocaust, with excellent bibliographies that emphasize En-glish-language publications. At end of vol. 4, a glossary, chronology, tables, and index.

Historical Dictionaries of French History. Series published by Greenwood Press.
(Various call numbers).
The books in this series are similarly organized. Signed articles, in alphabetical order, contain brief bibliographies. A chronology and index are at the back. Here are a few representative volumes:

- Connelly, Owen, ed. *Historical Dictionary of Napoleonic France, 1799–1815*. Westport, CT: Greenwood Press, 1985.
  (Ref DC 201 .H673 1985).

- Newman, Edgar Leon, ed. *Historical Dictionary of France from the 1815 Restoration to the Second Empire*. New York: Greenwood Press, 1987. 2 vol. (Ref DC 256 .H57 1987).

- Echard, William E., ed. *Historical Dictionary of the French Second Empire, 1852–1870*. Westport, CT: Greenwood Press, 1985.
  (Ref DC 276 H57 1985).

Jackson, George, ed. *Dictionary of the Russian Revolution*. New York: Greenwood Press, 1989.
(Ref DK 265 D49 1989).
Scholarly signed articles with bibliographies. Maps and chronology at the back.

Cannistraro, Philip V., ed. *Historical Dictionary of Fascist Italy*. Westport, CT: Greenwood Press, 1982.
(Ref DG 571 A1 H57 1982).
Signed articles with short bibliographies. Useful appendices at the back.

Fritze, Ronald H., ed. *Historical Dictionary of Stuart England, 1603–1689.* Westport, CT: Greenwood Press, 1996.
(Ref DA 375 .H57 1996).

Kern, Robert W., ed. *Historical Dictionary of Modern Spain, 1700–1988.* New York: Greenwood Press, 1990.
(Ref DP 192 H57 1990).
Scholarly articles with bibliographies. At the end of the volume, a substantial chronology and bibliography.

Zabecki, David T., ed. *World War II in Europe.* New York: Garland Pub., 1999. 2 vol.
(Ref D 740 .W67 1999)
Somewhat confusing in its organization, this is an excellent encyclopedia with a good index. Illustrated, with good maps and tables. The articles have up-to-date bibliographies (English-language books only).

United States

Cayton, Mary Kupiec and Peter W. Williams, eds. *Encyclopedia of American Cultural & Intellectual History.* New York: Charles Scribner's Sons, 2001. 3 vol.
(Ref E 169.1 E624 2001).
A scholarly encyclopedia with signed articles and bibliographies. Arranged chronologically.

Cayton, Mary Kupiec, Elliott J. Gorn, and Peter W. Williams, eds. *Encyclopedia of American Social History.* New York: Scribner, 1993. 4 vol.
(Ref HN 57 E58 1993).
The major reference source on American social history, this encyclopedia has signed articles with bibliographies. About 180 lengthy essays discuss the topics. Comprehensive index.

Ciment, James, ed. *Encyclopedia of the Great Depression and the New Deal.* Armonk, NY: Sharpe Reference, 2001. 2 vol.
(Ref E 806 C543 2001).
Entries include thematic essays and entries on government topics, international affairs, biographies, and document texts. Bibliographies provided.

Cooke, Jacob Ernest, ed. *Encyclopedia of the North American Colonies.* New York: Charles Scribner's Sons, 1993. 3 vol.
(Ref E 45 E53 1993).
The standard, scholarly encyclopedia to North American colonization. Arranged by topic, the entries include bibliographies. Coverage is for all nations that had colonies. A chronology is printed in volume 1. Comprehensive index.

Current, Richard N., ed. *Encyclopedia of the Confederacy.* New York: Simon & Schuster, 1993. 4 vol.
(Ref E 487 E55 1993).
Comprehensive coverage of the Confederacy is provided in this encyclopedia. Individuals, battles, and topics are included. Signed articles by leading

scholars. Bibliographies accompany the articles. Appendices include the Confederate Constitution, etc. Illustrated.

DeConde, Alexander, Richard Dean Burns, and Fredrick Logevall, eds. *Encyclopedia of American Foreign Policy*. New York: Scribner, 2002. 3 vol.
(Ref E183.7 E52 2002).
The lengthy articles have bibliographical essays. Comprehensive index.

Finkelman, Paul, ed. *Encyclopedia of the United States in the Nineteenth Century*. New York: Charles Scribner's Sons, 2001. 3 vol.
(Ref E 169.1 E626 2001).
A scholarly encyclopedia with bibliographies for alphabetically arranged entries.

Greene, Jack, ed. *Encyclopedia of American Political History: Studies of the Principal Movements and Ideas*. New York: Scribner, 1984. 3 vol.
(Ref E 183 E5 1984).
About 90 topics are covered in this scholarly work. The lengthy, signed essays contain bibliographies. Useful for an understanding of basic themes and movements in American political history.

Heidler, David S. and Jeanne T. Heidler, eds. *Encyclopedia of the American Civil War: A Political, Social and Military History*. Santa Barbara, CA: ABC-CLIO, 2000. 5 vol.
(Ref E 468 H47 2000).
An outstanding, and current, encyclopedia of the Civil War. This complements *Encyclopedia of the Confederacy* (see above).

Jentleson, Bruce W. and Thomas G. Paterson, eds. *Encyclopedia of U.S. Foreign Relations*. New York: Oxford University, 1997. 4 vol.
(Ref E 183.7 E53 1997).
This scholarly encyclopedia has bibliographies with articles. Volume 4 has a chronology of foreign relations activity from 1754 to 1996, statistical tables, and a bibliography of reference works.

Kammen, Carol, and Norma Prendergast. *Encyclopedia of Local History*. Walnut Creek, CA: AltaMira Press, 2000.
(Ref E 180 K25 2000).
Some bibliographies, websites, and organization contact information are provided. Appendices have information on ethnic groups, religious groups, state historical organizations, and National Archives facilities.

Kane, Joseph Nathan, ed. *The American Counties: Origins of Names, Dates of Creation and Organization, Area, Population, Historical Data, and Published Sources*. 3rd ed. Metuchen, NJ: Scarecrow Press, 1972.
(Ref E 180 K3 1972).
The major section lists each county and notes information as when established, recent population, size, county seat, who the county was named for, and (when available) published major county histories.

Kutler, Stanley I. ed. *Dictionary of American History*. 3rd. ed. New York: Charles Scribner's Sons, 2003. 10 vol.
(Ref E 174 D52 2003).

The standard scholarly dictionary in American history. Encyclopedic in nature, with long articles and brief bibliographies. Comprehensive index. Volume 9 contains a series of historical maps with commentary, and a lengthy selection of primary source documents.

Levy, Leonard W. and Louis Fisher, eds. *Encyclopedia of the American Presidency*. New York: Simon & Schuster, 1994. 4 vol.
(Ref JK 511 E53 1994).
The standard, scholarly work on the presidency. The signed articles contain brief bibliographies. Individuals, themes and concepts, congressional topics, laws, etc. are included. Appendices include the Constitution, tables on the presidents with sections on personal information, their cabinets and other officials, and basic election statistics; and an index to legal cases.

Porter, Glenn, ed. *Encyclopedia of American Economic History: Studies of the Principal Movements and Ideas*. New York: Scribner, 1980. 3 vol.
(Ref HC 103 E52).
A scholarly work with long articles. Coverage is nineteenth century to date. Extensive bibliographies.

Roller, David C. and Robert W. Twyman, eds. *The Encyclopedia of Southern History*. Baton Rouge: Louisiana State University Press, 1979.
(Ref F 207.7 E52).
An outstanding collection of articles that includes biographical sketches, maps, statistical tables, etc. The entries contain brief bibliographies.

Other Regions

Embree, Ainslie T., ed. *Encyclopedia of Asian History*. New York: Scribner's, 1988. 4 vol.
(DS 31 E53 1988).
Entries covering Asia, broadly defined to include Central Asia, the Indian subcontinent, Indonesia, and the Philippines. Bibliographies targeted to educated nonspecialists.

Shillington, Kevin, ed. *Encyclopedia of African History*. New York: Fitzroy Dearborn, 2005. 3 vol.
(Ref DT 20 E53 2005).
Alphabetical arrangement, with index. Up-to-date bibliographies for each entry.

Tenenbaum, Barbara A., ed. *Encyclopedia of Latin American History and Culture*. New York: Scribner's, 1996. 5 vol.
(Ref F 1406 E53 1996).
Coverage of Latin America, including Brazil and all parts of the Western Hemisphere that had at one time formed part of the Spanish Empire. Bibliographies for each entry.

Other Criteria

Cancik, Hubert and Helmut Schneider, eds. *Brill's New Pauly: Encyclopaedia of the Ancient World: Antiquity*. Leiden, Germany and Boston: Brill, 2002–present.
(Ref DE5 .N4813 2002).
This English translation of the masterful German work, *Der Neue Pauly: Enzyklopädie der Antike*, is still in progress.

Encyclopedia Judaica. New York: Thomson/Gale, 2006.
(Ref DS 102.8 E496).
The standard English language encyclopedia on all aspects of Jewish studies. Ca. 25,000 signed articles are presented. Bibliographies are included. Updated with annual and decennial yearbooks. New edition expected in early 2007.

Grant, Michael and Rachel Kitzinger, eds. *Civilization of the Ancient Mediterranean: Greece and Rome*. New York: Scribner's, 1988. 3 vol.
(Ref DE 59 C55 1988).
Comprehensive coverage of the classical world. About 100 lengthy essays are featured. The index ties specific topics to the major essays.

Kohn, George Childs, ed. *Dictionary of Historic Documents*. New York: Facts on File, 2003.
(Ref D9 K63 1991).
An alphabetically arranged list of documents with brief definitions. International coverage from all time periods. Over 2,200 documents.

Martin, Richard C., ed. *Encyclopedia of Islam and the Muslim World*. New York: Thomson/Gale, 2004. 2 vols.
(Ref BP40 E525 2004).
The best scholarly work on Islam in the English language. Whereas most articles are in Arabic, transliterated according to an unusual system, use the separate indexes for easiest access to pertinent articles. Still in publication, this work contains signed articles with bibliographies.

Strayer, Joseph R., ed. *Dictionary of the Middle Ages*. New York: Scribner, 1982–1989. 13 vol.
(Ref D 114 D5 1982).
The standard encyclopedia on the Middle Ages. Alphabetical arrangement with ca. 5,000 entries. Signed articles with bibliographies.

G. HISTORIOGRAPHY

Bentley, Michael, ed. *Companion to Historiography*. London: Routledge, 1997.
(Ref D 13 .C626 1997).
Lengthy essays on the historiography of different periods and places, concentrating on trends in the recent past.

Bola, Lucian, ed. *Great Historians of the Modern Age: An International Dictionary*. New York: Greenwood Press, 1991.
(Ref D 14 G75 1991).
This source features ca. 700 deceased historians from the nineteenth and twentieth centuries. Arranged by 38 geographic or national areas. Has a European and male bias. Includes bibliographies.

Boyd, Kelly, ed. *Encyclopedia of Historians and Historical Writing*. Chicago: Fitzroy Dearborn Publishers, 1999. 2 vol.
(Ref D 14 E53 1999).
Entries on historians, study topics, and historical concepts. Each historian entry has a bibliography of principal writings; all entries include citations for further reading. An important historiographical source.

Kinnell, Susan K., ed. *Historiography: An Annotated Bibliography of Journal Articles, Books, and Dissertations*. Santa Barbara, CA: ABC-CLIO, 1987. 2 vol.
(Ref D 13 .H58 1987).
Richardson, R. C., comp. *The Study of History: A Bibliographical Guide*. 2nd ed. Manchester and New York: Manchester University Press, 2000.
(Ref D 13 R44 2000).
Richardson offers a bibliography of historiography. Following an overview of general works, the bibliography is arranged by time period.

Ritter, Harry. *Dictionary of Concepts in History*. Westport, CT: Greenwood Press, 1986.
(Ref D 13 R49 1986).
Brief definitions with essays are featured in this work. Bibliographies accompany the entries. Useful for a quick understanding of a term or concept.

Williams, Robert C. *The Historian's Toolbox: A Student's Guide to the Theory and Craft of History*. Armonk, NY: M. E. Sharpe, 2003.
(Ref D 16 W62 2003).
This reference work looks at history, how to research it, and how to write history. Examples are presented.

Woolf, D. R., ed. *A Global Encyclopedia of Historical Writing*. New York: Garland, 1998.
(Ref D 13 .G47 1998).
Entries include biographies of historians, surveys of national or regional historiographies, and articles on concepts.

H. STATISTICAL SOURCES AND TABLES

United States

America Votes. Washington, DC: Governmental Affairs Institute, Congressional Quarterly, 1956– . Biennial.
(Ref JK 1967 A8).

The standard source for detailed voting statistics since 1956. Contains presidential, gubernatorial, senatorial, and congressional statistics. Additional election statistical sources include:

- *Presidential Elections Since 1789.* 5th ed. Washington, DC: Congressional Quarterly, 1991. (JK 524 C65 1991).

- Burnham, W. Dean. *Presidential Ballots, 1836–1892.* Baltimore: Johns Hopkins University Press, 1955.
  (Ref JK 524 B8).

- Robinson, Edgar E. *The Presidential Vote, 1896–1932.* Stanford: Stanford University Press, 1934. (Ref JK 524 R6 1947).

- Robinson, Edgar E. *They Voted for Roosevelt: The Presidential Vote, 1932–1944.* Stanford: Stanford University Press; London: G. Cumberlege, Oxford University Press, 1947. (JK 1967 R6).

- Scammon, Richard M. *America at the Polls: A Handbook of American Presidential Election Statistics, 1920–1964.* Pittsburgh: University of Pittsburgh Press, 1965. (Ref JK 524 G6) Also an edition covering the years 1968–1984.

Carter, Susan and others, eds. *Historical Statistics of the United States: Earliest Times to the Present.* Cambridge and New York: Cambridge University Press, 2006. 5 vol. (Ref HA 202 H57 2006).
Used with the *Statistical Abstract of the United States* (see below), this covers the complete time period of American history. Over 12,500 time series are provided. Comprehensive coverage.

Historical Census Browser.
(Public Access Database at http://fisher.lib.virginia.edu/census/).
Detailed U.S. census information by state and county from 1790–1960. Permits selection of single or multiple variables to construct data lists.

ICPSR.
The Inter-university Consortium for Political and Social Research is an example of a numeric database. Although much of the data is based on recent sources, there are historical research possibilities. To view descriptions of the datasets, see http://www.icpsr.umich.edu/.

Kurian, George Thomas, ed. *Datapedia of the United States, 1790–2000: America Year by Year.* Lanham, MD: Bernan Press, 1994.
(Ref HA 202 K87 1994).
This book is based on the *Statistical Abstract of the United States* and the *Historical Statistics of the United States: Colonial Times to 1970.* Kurian has taken what he considers the most important series and repackaged them into 23 subject areas.

United States Bureau of the Census. *Statistical Abstract of the United States.* Washington, DC: U.S. Dept. of Commerce, Social and Economic Statistics. Administration, Bureau of the Census, 1878– . Annual.
(Ref HA 202 A35). Also in Microfiche and in Storage.

The standard, detailed source for statistics covering most areas of endeavor. In addition to the statistics, most tables note where the full statistical information is located.

Other Areas

Great Britain, Central Statistical Office, *Statistical Digest of the War*. London: HM Stationary Office, 1951.
(Ref HA 1125 .A53)
Statistics for Great Britain during World War II.

Mitchell, B. R. ed. *British Historical Statistics*. Cambridge and New York: Cambridge University Press, 1988.
(Ref HA 1134 M58 1988).

Mitchell, B. R. ed. *International Historical Statistics: Africa, Asia & Oceania, 1750–2000*. Houndmills, Basingstoke, Hampshire; New York: Palgrave Macmillan, 2003.
(Ref HA 4675 M552 2003).

Mitchell, B. R., ed. *International Historical Statistics: Europe, 1750–2000*. Houndmills, Basingstoke, Hampshire; New York: Palgrave Macmillan, 2003.
(Ref HA 1107 M5 2003).

Mitchell, B. R., ed. *International Historical Statistics: The Americas, 1750–2000*. Houndmills, Basingstoke, Hampshire; New York: Palgrave Macmillan, 2003.
(Ref HA 175 .M55 2003).

United Nations. *Statistical Yearbook*. Annual. 1948– .
(Ref HA 12.5 U63).
This is the standard source for international statistics since World War II. Coverage lacks comprehensiveness. Since 1971, this has been updated by *The Monthly Bulletin of Statistics*.

I. HISTORICAL ATLASES

Adams, James T., ed. *Atlas of American History*. New York: Scribner, 1943.
(Ref G 1201 S1 A2 1978).
An outstanding atlas of American history. Black-and-white maps are featured in this atlas covering diverse topics. No commentary.

Allen, James P., ed. *We the People: A Atlas of America's Ethnic Diversity*. New York: Macmillan, 1988.
(Ref G 1201 E1 A4 1988).
A scholarly work on immigration and ethnic studies. Over 100 maps accompany the commentary and analysis.

Barker, Felix. *The History of London in Maps*. New York: Cross River Press, 1992.
(Oversize G 1819 L751 B24 1992).

Barraclough, Geoffrey, ed. *The Times History of the World*. 5th ed. London: Times Books, 1999.
(Ref G 1030 T54 1999).

The standard atlas today covering the full sweep of world history. Arranged in chronological sections, this atlas takes a modern approach in treating history beyond the Western world.

Bayly, C. A., ed. *Atlas of the British Empire*. New York: Facts on File, 1989. (Ref DA 16 A8 1989).

The Harper Atlas of World History. New York: Harper and Row, 1987. (Ref G 1030 G68513 1987).
A good atlas with chronologies and narrative. Emphasis on Europe and the United States.

Lathrop, J. M. *An Atlas of Rockingham County, Virginia: From Actual Surveys*. Harrisonburg, VA: Harrisonburg-Rockingham Historical Society, 1992. (Ref G 1293 R7 L3 1982).
An example of county and state atlases that were produced after the Civil War for some of the states. Detailed information has value for many areas of historical research including genealogy.

Lobel, M. D., ed. *Historic Town: Maps and Plans of Towns and Cities in the British Isles, With Historic Commentaries From Earliest Times to 1800*. Vol. 1– . Baltimore: Johns Hopkins University Press, [1969–]. (Oversize G 1814 A1 H5).

Martis, Kenneth C. *The Historical Atlas of United States Congressional Districts, 1789–1983*. New York: Free Press; London: Collier Macmillan, 1982. (Ref G 1201 F9 M3 1982).
An atlas of outline maps showing congressional districts by Congress, 1789–1983. Commentary and analysis accompanies the maps. There are descriptions of each district's geographic composition.

Paullin, Charles O. *Atlas of the Historical Geography of the United States*. Washington, DC: Carnegie Institution of Washington and the American Geographical Society of New York, 1932. (Ref G 3701 S1 P3).
Although published in 1932, Paullin remains the most important and comprehensive American historical atlas. The wide range of topics covered include environment, boundaries, exploration, society, economy. The maps include commentary. Indexed.

Shepherd, William R. *Historical Atlas*. 4th ed. New York: Barnes and Noble, 1956. (Ref G 1030 S4 1956).
Strictly an atlas, with little or no commentary, Shepherd's has been a standard historical atlas for several generations. Shepherd's remains superior for Europe, but other atlases are better for the non-European world.

Talbert, Richard J. A., ed. *Barrington Atlas of the Greek and Roman World*. Princeton: Princeton University Press. (Ref G 1033 .B3 2000 with two supplements).
A scholarly and beautifully produced atlas. The supplements provide a map-by-map directory with an introduction to each map. For each place name,

there is information on the period(s) with which it is associated, its modern name, and a bibliography.

United States. Military Academy, West Point. Department of Military Art and Engineering. *The West Point Atlas of American Wars*. New York: Praeger, 1959. 2 vol. (Ref G 1201 S1 U5 1959).
Detailed maps, including commentary, of American wars through the Korean War.

J. BIOGRAPHY

American National Biography. New York: Oxford University Press, 1999. 24 vol. (Online Library Subscription Database at (http://www.anb.org/articles/home.html); also in print, Ref CT 213 .A68 1999).
This standard biographical dictionary covers deceased Americans. This updates the *Dictionary of American Biography* (see below) which had been the standard source (but did not include women or people of color). Bibliographies supplement the biographical sketches.

Biographical Dictionary of the United States Congress, 1774–present. (Online at http://bioguide.congress.gov/biosearch/biosearch.asp)
(Ref JK 1010 U5 1989)
A massive compilation of members of Congress with biographical sketches. Some contain bibliographies. Also useful for its listing of each Congress with the leaders and their positions. This is followed by a listing of members of Congress by state.

Biography and Genealogy Master Index. Detroit, MI: Gale Publishing.
(Online Library Subscription Database).
An index to ca. three million individuals. About 900 sources are indexed.

Biography Index. New York: H. W. Wilson Co., 1946– .
(Online Library Subscription Database).
An index to biographical information in journal articles and books.

Biography Resource Center. Farmington Hills, MI: Gale Group.
(Online Library Subscription Database).
A comprehensive database of biographical information on over 320,000 people from throughout history, around the world, and across all disciplines and subject areas. Contains the text of the *Dictionary of American Biography* (see below).

Burkett, Randall K. et al., eds. *Black Biography, 1790–1950: A Cumulative Index*. 3 vol. Alexandria, VA: Chadwyck-Healey, 1991.
(Ref E 185.96 B528 1991).
An outstanding collection of ca. 31,000 biographies from 297 source books. The index is necessary to locate the citation to the documentation on 1,068

microfiche. Volumes 1–2 of the index are arranged alphabetically and list place of birth and date, gender, occupation, religion, and location on the microfiche. Volume 3 is the index to the full set. It lists the 297 sources in addition to place of birth, occupation, religion.

Current Biography Yearbook. New York: H. W. Wilson Co., 1940– .
(Ref CT 100 C8).
Published monthly with annual cumulations. International coverage with the emphasis on the United States. All vocations. In addition to the sketch, a bibliography enhances its use.

Dictionary of American Biography. New York: Scribner, 1928– . 20 vol. plus supplements.
(Ref E 176 D56; also online in *Biography Resource Center*, an Online Library Subscription Database).
Until publication of the *American National Biography* (see above), this had been the standard source for deceased Americans, and remains a vital source. The supplements bring this up to 1980. In addition to the authoritative signed biographical sketches, there are excellent bibliographies.

Matthew, H. C. G. and Brian Harrison, eds. *Oxford Dictionary of National Biography*. New York: Oxford University Press, 2004. 60 vol.
(Ref DA 28 .O95 2004).
Completely new edition of the *Dictionary of National Biography (DNB)* (see above). Biographies of over 50,000 deceased persons whose lives were connected with the British Isles.

Muccigrosso, Robert, ed. *Research Guide to American Historical Biography*. Washington, DC: Beachem Publishing, 1988–1991. 5 vol.
(CT 214 R47 1988).
A major biographical source covering over 500 individuals. Volumes 1–3 are arranged alphabetically with prominent Americans in many areas of endeavor. Volume 4 has Native Americans and minorities and volume 5 has explorers, entertainers, Colonial and Civil War figures. Entries contain a chronology of the person's life, activities of historical significance, principal biographical sources, evaluation of primary sources, a list of museums and societies remembering the individual, and bibliography of sources.

The National Cyclopedia of American Biography . . . Clifton, NJ: J. T. White, 1893–1984. 63 vol.
(Ref E 176 N27).
An excellent historical biographical dictionary. Unsigned sketches and no bibliographies. Not arranged in alphabetical sequence. An index volume is available.

The New York Times Obituary Index. New York: New York Times, 1970–1980, 2 vols.
(Ref CT 213 N47 v.1).
The print resource indexes the *New York Times* obituaries for the years 1858–1968. The full-text *New York Times: Historical* is available online in *Research Databases*. It is possible to limit your search to obituaries.

Slocum, Robert B., ed. *Biographical Dictionaries and Related Works: An International Bibliography of More Than 16,000 Collective Biographies*... 2nd ed. Detroit, MI: Gale Research Co., 1986. 2 vol.
(Ref CT 104 S55 1986).
A comprehensive source of ca. 16,000 sources. International with coverage of all time periods. Divided into the three sections of international, national and area, and vocational. Brief annotations.

Stephen, Leslie and Sidney Lee, eds. *Dictionary of National Biography*. London: Oxford University Press, 1908–1990. 28 vol. plus supplements.
(Carrier Lib Storage DA 28 D4).
Covers deceased people of British ancestry. There is a "missing persons" volume. Supplements bring coverage up through 1990. See *Oxford Dictionary of National Biography* below.

Who Was Who in America: A Companion Volume to Who's Who in America. Chicago: Marquis, Who's Who, 1897– .
(Ref E 176 W46).
Historical volume covering 1607–1896.

K. ANNUALS/YEARBOOKS

Britannica Book of the Year. Chicago: Encyclopedia Britannica, 1939– .
(Ref AE 5 E364).
An encyclopedia yearbook. With *The New International Year Book* (see below).

Congressional Quarterly Almanac. Annual. Washington, DC: Congressional Quarterly, 1961– .
(Ref JK 1 C66).
An outstanding source for United States government information, especially useful to determine Congress's activities during a given year. Data includes all recorded votes in Congress.

Editorials on File. New York: Facts on File, 1974– .
(Ref D 839 E3).
Editorials from throughout the United States, topically arranged. Each topic has a brief background essay to set the stage for the editorials.

Facts on File Yearbook... New York: Facts on File, 1943– .
(Ref D 410 F3).
A weekly news updating service. Published in the United States.

Keesing's Record of World Events. London: Longman, 1931– .
(Ref D 410 K4).
A weekly news updating service. Published in Great Britain.

The New International Year Book. New York: Dodd, Mead and Co., 1908–31; New York, London: Funk & Wagnalls Co., 1965.
(Ref AE 5 N5532).
An annual having reference material for the years covered.

The World Almanac and Book of Facts. New York: Newspaper Enterprise Association, 1923–.
(Ref AY 67 N5 W7).

L. PRIMARY SOURCES

Finding Primary Sources in Library Catalogs

When using most library catalogs, the best way to find primary sources is to do an advanced search. Change "Any Word" in the pull-down menu to "Subject Word" and type "sources" in the search box. Combine this with a keyword or subject word in the next search box. For example, the following search will retrieve primary source material related to the history of the Byzantine Empire.

Advanced Word Search

Subject Word:	sources	and
Any Word:	history and byzantine	

Although "sources" is the standard subdivision for primary sources, it does not always appear in the subject heading. These are other words you may try instead of "sources" to find primary documents:

Press conferences	Interviews
Correspondence	Registers
Personal narratives	Diaries

In *WorldCat,* choose "Subject" from the drop-down box, combining key-words with one of the above subdivisions (sources, interviews, etc.). For example, to find primary sources on Winston Churchill, you might try a Subject search for: winston churchill sources. *WorldCat* will look for all three words; e.g., "Winston and Churchill and sources" in the Subject field of a record.

Note: In a perfect world, all primary sources will show one of the designators above in the subject headings for the item described. However, since this is not always the case, you may wish to try searching for keywords or phrases such as "documents," "diary," "letters," or "documentary history" if you are not finding what you need by limiting your search to *subject* words.

The following three sections highlight databases and tangible collections of primary sources.

Public Access Databases (freely available to all)

American Memory.
(From the Library of Congress at http://memory.loc.gov/).
This rich and well-organized site gives the researcher access to an ever-growing set of digitized primary source collections from the Library of

Congress and other scholarly institutions. Collections available here include the following:

■ Born in Slavery: Slave Narratives from the Federal Writers' Project, 1936–1938.

■ "California as I Saw It": First-Person Narratives from California's Early Years, 1949–1900.

■ The Emergence of Advertising in America: 1850–1920.

■ Sunday School Books: Shaping the Values of Youth in 19th Century America.

■ Band Music from the Civil War Era.

Abraham Lincoln Papers at the Library of Congress. Washington, DC: Library of Congress, 2000. (http://memory.loc.gov/ammem/alhtml/malhome.html)

A Compilation of the Messages and Papers of the Presidents, 1789–1902.
(http://onlinebooks.library.upenn.edu/webbin/gutbook/lookup?num=10894).
(J 81 B96 1903).
Covers George Washington up through August 1902 (first part of Theodore Roosevelt's administration).

The Encyclopedia of Diderot and d'Alembert.
(http://www.hti.umich.edu/d/did/index.html).
A scholarly project to translate the famous eighteenth-century encyclopedia into English and post it on the web.

EuroDocs: Primary Historical Documents from Western Europe.
(http://eurodocs.lib.byu.edu).

German History Sources.
(http://www.csustan.edu/History/Faculty/Weikart/gerhist.htm).

Internet History Sourcebooks Project.
(http://www.fordham.edu/halsall/).
Paul Halsall's rich website that compiles and organizes collections of public domain and copy-permitted historical texts on all historic periods from antiquity to the present.

Napoleonica.org.
(http://www.napoleonica.org/us).

Records of an English Village [Earls Colne, 1400–1750].
(http://linux02.lib.cam.ac.uk/earlscolne/intro/index.htm, with coverage for 1375 to 1854).
A wonderful collection of primary documents (from the church and state) from one village in England over the course of four centuries.

The War of the Rebellion: A Compilation of the Official Records of the Union and Confederate Armies. 1880–1901. 70 vol. in 128.
(E 464 U61 1971).
(Online at *The Making of America* website at Cornell http://cdl.library.cornell.edu/moa. This online version does not include the supplement.)
Essential source for Civil War research. Often referred to as *Official Records* or *OR*. The federal government attempted to publish all available major reports and correspondence. There is an index in the reference collection. This is

also available in microfiche in the Library of American Civilization collection at LAC 22140-22174 and on a CD-ROM, available at the Reference Desk. In 100 volumes, a *Supplement to the Official Records of the Union and Confederate Armies* is available at E 464 U61 1971 supp.

Weekly Compilation of Presidential Documents. 1993– .
   (http://www.access.gpo.gov/nara/nara003.html).
   This website compiles presidential documents until they are gathered together into the series, *Public Papers of the Presidents of the United States* (see below).

Library Subscription Databases

Archive of Americana.
   A cluster of collections reflecting the history of the United States through its congressional publications, popular newspapers, and commercial publishing. The databases included may be searched individually or as a set:

- American State Papers, 1789–1838. Legislative and Executive Documents.

- U.S. Congressional Serial Set, 1817–1980. These are the reports, documents, and journals of the U.S. Congress.

- Early American Newspapers.

- Early American Imprints (Evans [1639–1800] and Shaw-Shoemaker [1801–1819]).

- American Broadsides and Ephemera.

Historic Documents. 1972– . Annual.
   (Online Library Database and at E 839.5 H57 in Ref and Stacks).
   Major primary source material with international coverage. Documents can be speeches, treaties, court opinions, reports, etc. Each document has an introduction setting it in perspective. Valuable for historical research since the early 1970s.

Times Digital Archive, 1785–1985. Detroit, MI: Thomson Gale.
   (http://www.galegroup.com/Times/index.htm).
   Two hundred years of the *London Times* online, including all advertisements and illustrations.

Tangible Collections

Africa Through Western Eyes. Marlborough, England: Adam Matthew Publications, 1999–present
   (http://www.adam-matthew-publications.co.uk/digital_guides/).
   There are several microfilm collections that reproduce primary sources owned by various U.S. and UK libraries. In addition to *Africa Through Western Eyes,* there is *Japan Through Western Eyes at this website.*

The American Revolution in Context. London: World Microfilms Publications, 1984.
   (Microfilm).

The Annals of America. Chicago: Encyclopaedia Britannica, Inc., 1968. 20 vol. (Ref E 173 A793).
An excellent source for over 2,000 documents, which are printed chronologically. A separate two-volume conspectus provides historical context for the documents.

Archives Parlementaires de 1787 à 1860: Recueil Complet des Débats Législatifs & Politiques . . . Paris: Librairie administrative de P. Dupont, 1862.
(Microfiche).
Records of the meetings of legislative bodies of the French Revolution.

The Aristocracy, the State, and the Local Community [1477–1828]: The Hastings Collection of Manuscripts from the Huntington Library in California. Brighton, England: Harvester, 1986–.
(Microfilm).
This set of 39 microfilm rolls has a two-volume paper guide. Content includes the correspondence of the Hastings family from 1477–1701.

Commager, Henry S., ed. *Documents of American History.* 9th ed. Appleton-Century-Crofts, 1973.
(Ref E 173 C66 1973).
Chronologically arranged, the documents range from the age of discovery to 1973. Some of the ca. 700 documents are complete while others are excerpts from the full text. Each document is introduced with background information and includes references to additional sources.

Congressional Proceedings.
The following four titles cover the official proceedings of the U.S. Congress. A digital edition of congressional proceedings, beginning with the Continental Congress in 1774 and continuing through the 1875 *Congressional Record,* is available to the public at the American Memory website, (http:// memory .loc.gov/ammem/amlaw/lawhome.html).

- *Journals of the Continental Congress.* 1774–1789.
- *The Annals of Congress of the United States.* 1789–1824.
- *Register of Debates.* 1824–1837.
- *The Congressional Globe . . .* 1833–1873.
- *Congressional Record: Proceedings and Debates of the Congress.* 1873– .
- *GPO Access* (library subscription database) for 1994 to present.

Douglass, David C., ed. *English Historical Documents.* New York: Oxford University Press, 1951–1977. 13 vol. (DA 26 E55).
A masterful collection covering England from ca. 500 to 1914. The subject coverage is broad and the documents have introductions and bibliographies. Volumes 6–7, covering 1559–1659, were never published.

Draper Manuscripts. (Microfilm).
Primary documents collected by Lyman Draper covering the history of the trans-Allegheny West from mid-eighteenth century into the early 1800s.

Early Encounters in North America. Alexandria, VA: Alexander Street Press, 2005 (http://www.alexanderstreet2.com/eenalive/index.html).

This is a series of major early narratives that are edited with introductions and commentary. English-language text with narratives from Vikings, Columbus, English, French, Dutch, and Spanish writings. Coverage begins with 985 and concludes at 1708.

Great Britain. Foreign Office. *British and Foreign State Papers.* London: n.p., 1841–1934. (Microfiche).

The standard source on British foreign relations for the period covered. Treaties, correspondence, and other documentation is included. Indexed.

Israel, Fred L., ed. *Major Peace Treaties of Modern History, 1648–1967.* New York: Chelsea House Pub., 1967–80. 4 vol.
(Ref JX 121 .I8).

Begins with the Peace of Westphalia (1648). Each section contains a commentary. Index in vol. 4.

Kesaris, Paul, ed. *Vietnam National Security Council Histories.* Frederick, MD: University Publications of America, 1981. (Microfilm).

A guide accompanies the collection. Also called *The War in Vietnam.*

Lester, Robert E. and Gary Hoag, eds. *Civil War Unit Histories: Regimental Histories and Personal Narratives.* Bethesda, MD: University Publications of America, 1990. (Microfiche).

Library of American Civilization or, The Microbook Library of American Civilization. Chicago: Library Resources, Inc., 1971–72. (Ultrafiche).

This massive collection of some 20,000 titles on ultrafiche covers American civilization up to World War I. The "call number" is a 5-digit number prefaced by "LAC," e.g., LAC 16459; all LAC fiche are filed numerically by this number. Printed author, title, and subject indexes are available.

MacGregor, Morris J. and Bernard C. Nalty, eds. *Blacks in the United States Armed Forces.* Wilmington, DE: Scholarly Resources, 1977. (Microfilm).

From Colonial times to Vietnam.

The Papers of Albert Gallatin. Philadelphia: Historic Publications, 1970. (Microfilm).
Public Papers of the Presidents of the United States. Office of the Federal Register, U.S. National Archives and Records Administration (NARA), 1929–present. (J 80 A283). Also found online through the National Archives and Record Administration website (http://www.gpoaccess.gov/pubpapers/index.html).

This series began with Herbert Hoover. The Franklin Roosevelt years were never published.

Records of the Confederate States of America. Washington, DC: Library of Congress Photoduplication Service, 1967. (Microfilm).

Ca. 18,500 records from the Confederate government are microfilmed. A guide to the sources is available.

Roosevelt, Franklin D. *Complete Presidential Press Conferences of Franklin D. Roosevelt.* New York: Da Capo Press, 1972. 25 vol. (E 806 R7424 1972).

Schomburg Center Clipping File. Alexandria, VA: Chadwick Healey, 1989. (Microfiche).
Over 14,000 microfiche covering the twentieth-century African-American experience, primarily through newspaper and magazine clippings. A print guide is available.

Southern Historical Society Papers. Millwood, NY: Kraus Reprint Co., 1977. (E 483.7 S76 1977).
The Southern response to the Official Records of *The War of the Rebellion*, this collection includes reminiscences, memoirs, battle reports, Confederate government minutes, etc. Indispensable for serious Civil War research. The index, *An Index-Guide to the Southern Historical Society Papers, 1876–1959* is at Ref E 483.7 1977 index.

Southern Women and Their Families in the 19th Century, Papers and Diaries. Bethesda, MD: University Publications of America, 1991. (Microfilm).
Copies of records held at UNC (Chapel Hill) and at William & Mary.

Stampp, Kenneth, ed. *Records of Ante-bellum Southern Plantations from the Revolution to the Civil War*. Bethesda, MD: University Publications of America, 1994. (Microfilm).

Voices from Ellis Island. Frederick, MD: University Publications of America, 1987. (Microfiche).
An oral history of American immigration. This series consists of 185 microfiche with a printed guide.

Women's Journals of the 19th Century, Part 1, The Women's Penney Paper and Woman's Herald, 1888–1893. Marlborough, England: Adam Matthew, 1997–present. Online guide can be found at: (http://www.adam-matthew-publications.co.uk/digital_guides/). (Microfilm).
An important early publication of the women's movement in Britain.

M. GUIDES TO MANUSCRIPTS

DeWitt, Donald L., comp. *Articles Describing Archives and Manuscript Collections in the United States: An Annotated Bibliography*. Westport, CT: Greenwood Press, 1997. (Ref CE 3022 A2 D478 1997).
The initial arrangement is by broad subject category. The final two categories list foreign repositories holding U.S.-related records and U.S. repositories holding foreign records. Entries are annotated.

Hamer, Philip M., ed. *A Guide to Archives and Manuscripts in the United States*. New Haven, CT: Yale University Press, 1961.
(Ref CD 3022 A45).
A guide to ca. 1,300 manuscript repositories. It is arranged by state and city. Although dated, Hamer remains valuable because of detailed entries and superior indexing.

The National Union Catalog of Manuscript Collections. Washington, DC: Library of Congress, 1959/61–1993. (Biblio Z 6620 U5 N3). Online version can be found at: (http://www.loc.gov/coll/nucmc/).

The most comprehensive guide to United States manuscript collections. All types and forms of manuscript materials are listed. Entries include a description of the collection, the donor(s), the repository, years of coverage, the collection size, and any finding aids. Cumulative indexes are available. Exhaustive indexing. In the online version, search the RLG database.

United States. National Archives and Records Service. *Guide to the Federal Records in the National Archives of the United States.* Washington, DC: National Archives and Records Administration, 1995. 3 vol.
(Ref CD 3026 1995). (Online at National Archives website http://www.archives.gov/research_room/federal_records_guide/).
A very useful introduction to National Archives collections and guide to their use. Contains information on the scope of holdings of various government agencies, and assists the researcher in determining the Record Group number for the needed records.

United States. National Historical Publications and Records Commission. *Directory of Archives and Manuscript Repositories in the United States.* 2nd ed. Phoenix, AZ: Oryx Press, 1988.
(Ref CD 3020 U54 1988).
Over 4,200 archives and manuscript repositories are featured. Arrangement is by state and city. Contact information along with the collection parameters is noted. Although the index is inadequate, this source is useful, especially for locating a repository in a given geographic area.

N. TREATIES

United States

Bevans, Charles I., ed. *Treaties and Other International Agreements of the United States of America, 1776–1949.* Washington, DC: Government Printing Office, 1968–1976. 13 vols.
(Ref JX 236 1968 A5).
Contains texts of all U.S. treaties through 1949. Vol. 13 is a General Index. Often referred to as *Bevans.* This series is continued by the next entry.

Kavass, Igor I. *A Guide to the United States Treaties in Force.* Buffalo, NY: William S. Hein, 1990. 2 vol.
(Ref JX 236.5 G84 1989).
This edition is a guide and finding aid for the full text of treaties in force as of 1989.

U.S. Department of State. *Treaties in Force.* (Online at State Department website: http://www.state.gov/s/l/treaty/treaties/2006/).
This is the latest official edition. A finding aid, it lists bilateral agreements by country (or organization) and subject, multilateral agreements by subject.

U.S. Department of State. *United States Treaties and Other International Agreements.* Washington, DC: Government Printing Office, 1950–.
(Ref JX 231.A34).

This source is often abbreviated *UST.* Until published in these bound volumes, treaties are published in temporary pamphlets (called "slip treaties").

Multilaterals

Multilaterals Project of The Fletcher School, Tufts University. (Online at: http://fletcher.tufts .edu/multilaterals.html).
Although focusing on the mid-twentieth century and beyond, this website contains the full text of many important historical conventions, as well. Provides links to other useful treaty sites.

O. LAW

Garner, Bryan A., ed. *Black's Law Dictionary.* St. Paul, MN: West Group, 1999.
(Ref KF156 B53 1999).
The best reference work for legal terminology.

Olson, Kent C. *Legal Information: How to Find It, How to Use It.* Phoenix, AZ: Oryx Press, 1999.
(Ref KF 240 .O365 1999).
United States Statutes at Large. Washington, DC: U.S. Government Printing Office, n.d.
(Ref KF50 U52 and in Microforms for 1789–1972).
This work compiles all laws enacted by Congress. At the American Memory website at the Library of Congress (http://memory.loc.gov), the full text of the Statutes is available online for 1789 through 1875 (1st through 43rd Congress). An individual statute is often referred to by Public Law number; e.g., PL 94–142. This denotes a law (the 142nd law) passed during the 94th Congress.

P. DIRECTORIES

Ash, Lee, comp. *Subject Collections: A Guide to Special Book Collections and Subject Emphases as Reported by University, College, Public, and Special Libraries and Museums in the United States and Canada.* 7th ed. New Providence, NJ: R. R. Bowker Co., 1993. 2 vol.
(Ref Z 688 Z2 A8 1993).
A comprehensive directory to libraries having special collections. Arranged by subject. Entries give an account of their collections, their size, and outside availability.

Associations Unlimited. Detroit, MI: Gale Research, 1996I–present. (Online Library Subscription Database can be found at: http://galenet.galegroup.com/ servlet/).

The standard source for American association information. Gives contact information and describes the association's publications and programs.

Directory of Historical Societies and Agencies in the United States and Canada. 15th ed. Madison, WI: American Association for State and Local History, 2002.
(Ref E 172 A538 2002).
A comprehensive directory arranged by state or province and then by city or town. Entries include contact information, when founded, publications, and major programs and collection periods.

Filby, P. W., comp. *Directory of American Libraries with Genealogy or Local History Collections.* Wilmington, DE: Scholarly Resources Inc., 1988.
(Ref CS 47 F56 1988).
A directory to libraries in the United States and Canada with outstanding local history collections. Entries include collection strengths, interlibrary loan possibilities, who can use the library, and contact information. Over 1,300 libraries are featured.

Yearbook of International Organizations. Brussels, Belgium: Union of International Associations, 1949–present. Biennial.
(Ref JX 1904 A4).
Useful for locating information on non–United States organizations. It includes material on addresses, structure and purpose, publications, etc.

Q. BOOK REVIEWS

Unless otherwise noted, all of the following are library subscription databases.

America: History and Life. Santa Barbara, CA: ABC-CLIO, Inc., 1964–present.
Book Review Digest Plus. Bronx, NY: H. W. Wilson Co., 1906–present. (Online, 1905 to present; also in print for 1905–1996).
Indexes book reviews from scholarly and popular sources. Extracts of some reviews are included.

Book Review Index. Detroit, MI: Gale Research Co., 1965–present. (In print form only, 1965 to present).
Farber, Evan Ira and others, eds. *Combined Retrospective Index to Book Reviews in Scholarly Journals. 1886–1974.* Arlington, VA: Carrollton Press, 1979–1982. 15 vol. (In print form only).

JSTOR. New York: JSTOR, 1995–present.
Online at (http://www.jstor.org/) An excellent archive of scholarly journals, beginning with their first volumes. You may limit your search to reviews.

Reviews in American History. Westport, CT: Redgrave Information Resources Corp., 1973–present. (In print form, 1973–1997; online library subscription database).

Wilson OmniFile Full Text Mega. Bronx, NY: H. W. Wilson Co., 1982–present.
(library subscription database)
Selective full text for 1982 onward. Retrospective indexing of Readers'
Guide, Humanities Index, and Social Sciences Index, beginning with
1890. You may limit your search to reviews.

R. PUBLIC OPINION SOURCES

Gallup Poll Tuesday Briefing. Washington, DC: The Gallup Organization, 2002–
present.
Title varies: Gallup Poll Monthly, 1989–2002; Gallup Report, 1981–1989;
and Gallup Opinion Index, 1974–1981. This periodical publishes the results
of Gallup Polls on a recurring basis. Indexed in *PAIS International,* which is a
library subscription database.

The Gallup Poll: Public Opinion 1935–1997. Wilmington, DE: Scholarly Resources, 2000.
3 vol.
(Ref HN 90 P8 G3).
A set for the years 1972–1977 is at Ref HN 90 P8 G32. Over 7,000 poll
results are available in the main set. Arranged chronologically. Indexed.

LexisNexis Academic. Miamisburg, OH: LEXIS-NEXIS, Division of Reed Elsevier,
1998–present. (Online Library Subscription Database).
This electronic resource contains polls and survey information from a variety
of sources (e.g., Gallup, Harris, Roper) beginning with the year 1935 (but
there is thin coverage for the earlier years). From the LexisNexis homepage,
click on Reference in left-hand margin.

S. SPEECHES

Representative American Speeches. New York: H. W. Wilson Co., 1937–present. Annual.
(PS 688 B3).
Major speeches in a wide variety of topics are printed. Useful to obtain the
thinking of a given year or time period.

*Speech Index: An Index to 259 Collections of World Famous Orations and Speeches for Various
Occasions.* 4th rev. ed. 1966. New York: Scarecrow Press, 1966. Supplements up to
1980.
(Ref AI 3 S85).
Coverage is for all time periods and geographic areas.

Vital Speeches of the Day. New York: The City News Publishing Co., 1934–present.
(Periodical)
Full indexing is available online in Academic Search Premier (library sub-
scription database), which also contains PDF files of the speech texts. Limit

your search to the journal, *Vital Speeches of the Day*. An excellent source for speeches since 1934.

T. ORAL HISTORY

Allen, Barbara and William Lynwood Montell. *From Memory to History: Using Oral Sources in Local Historical Research*. Nashville, TN: American Association for State and Local History, 1981. (D 16 A38).

Baum, Willa K. *Transcribing and Editing Oral History*. 2nd ed. Nashville, TN: American Association for State and Local History, 1981. (D 16.14 B38 1981).

Columbia University. Oral History Research Office. *The Oral History Collection of Columbia University*. 4th ed. New York: Oral History Research Office, 1979. (Ref E 169.1 C647 1979).

Havlice, Patricia P. *Oral History: A Reference Guide and Annotated Bibliography*. Jefferson, NC: McFarland, 1985.
(Ref D 16.14 H38 1985).

In the First Person: Index to Letters, Diaries, Oral Histories and Other Personal Narratives. Alexandria, VA: Alexander Street Press, 2007. (Online public database offered by Alexander Street Press at http://www.inthefirstperson.com/).
Search letters, diaries, oral histories, memoirs, and autobiographies within scholarly materials that are freely available on the web and Alexander Street databases. Access thousands of personal narratives in English from archives and repositories everywhere.

Meckler, Alan M. *Oral History Collections*. New York: Bowker, 1975.
(Ref AI 3 M4).

Oral History Index: An International Directory of Oral History Interviews. Westport, CT: Meckler, 1990.
(Ref D16.14 .O74 1990).

Smith, Allen. *Directory of Oral History Collections*. Phoenix, AZ: Oryx Press, 1988.
(D 16.14 S54 1988).

U. STYLE MANUALS

The Chicago Manual of Style. 15th ed. Chicago: University of Chicago Press, 2003.
(Ref Z 253 C57 2003).
This is a style guide for publishers, so it presents many options. Turabian (see below) is based on this, but gives concrete examples for students preparing term papers.

Garner, Diane L. *The Complete Guide to Citing Government Information Resources: A Manual for Writers & Librarians*. rev. ed. Bethesda, MD: Congressional Information Service, 1993.
(Ref J 9.5 G37 1993).
The standard style manual for all types of government documents.

Online! A Reference Guide to Using Internet Sources. (Freely available content from Bedford/ St. Martin's at http://www.bedfordstmartins.com/online/).

Extracts from a printed guide, this handy and helpful web resource gives guidance on citing online sources in the four major citation styles: MLA, Chicago, APA, and CBE.

Turabian, Kate L. *A Manual for Writers of Term Papers, Theses, and Dissertations.* 6th ed. Chicago: University of Chicago Press, 1996.
(Ref LB 2369 T8 1996).
Often simply called "Turabian," this invaluable manual is overdue for an update. Although based on the *Chicago Manual* (see above), Turabian was not updated after the most recent edition of *Chicago* (2003). Very little guidance on electronic sources. See the entry above, *Online! . . .* , for guidance on citing online sources.

A Uniform System of Citation. Cambridge, MA: Harvard Law Review Assn., 2005.
(Ref KF 246 U5 2005).
The standard style manual for legal citations. Title varies.

V. GOVERNMENT DOCUMENT INDEXES

CIS Annual. Washington, DC: Congressional Information Service, 1970 present.
(Abstract/Index, Table 2).
Indexing for Congressional Hearings and the Serial Set, beginning with 1970.

Congressional Information Service. *CIS U.S. Serial Set Index.* Washington: Congressional Information Service, 1975–1978. 36 vol.
(Ref Z 1223 Z9 C65 1975).
The Serial Set is a rich collection of documents compiled under the direction of Congress, and commencing in 1798 (although it was entitled *American State Papers* until 1838). Included are reports of investigations, maps, surveys, statistics. Note in the *Primary Sources* section above (under *Archive of Americana*) that JMU has the digital *U.S. Congressional Serial Set Digital Edition* (library subscription database), which is in progress; to date, it covers 1817 to 1894. The print volumes referenced here index the same years (1789–1969) as the CD-ROM, *Congressional Masterfile 1*, available at the Reference Desk. *LexisNexis Congressional* (see below) and the *CIS Annual* (see above) succeed these sources, beginning with 1970.

GPO Monthly Catalog. Dublin, OH: OCLC Online Computer Library Center, Inc., 1997. (Online Library Subscription Database).
This is the standard indexing source for government documents since 1976. For Serial Set and Hearings materials it lacks the indexing depth of the *CIS Annual.*

Index to U.S. Government Periodicals. Chicago: Infordata International, 1970–1987.
(Abstract).

This indexes journal articles in government document periodicals.

LexisNexis Congressional. Bethesda, MD: Congressional Information Service, 1997–present. (Online Library Subscription Database).
This site has some fifteen categories of full-text government information, with coverage for approximately the past twenty years.

LexisNexis Government Periodicals Index. Bethesda, MD: CIS, 2000–present. (Online Library Subscription Database).
This is the revision of the Index to U.S. Government Periodicals cited above.

Monthly Catalog of United States Government Publications. Washington, DC: Government Printing Office, 1940–present. (Gov Doc Ref Area and online at http://catalog.gpo.gov/F).
This has been published since 1895 and is the standard print indexing tool since 1940.

Poore, Benjamin P. *A Descriptive Catalogue of the Government Publications of the United States, September 5, 1774–March 4, 1881.* Washington, DC: Government Printing Office, 1885. 2 vol.
(Ref Z 1223 A1885d).
This is the earliest effort to publish a guide to government documents. Although difficult to use, it lists the majority of documents printed up to 1881.

United States. Department of the Interior. Division of Documents. *Comprehensive Index to the Publications of the United States Government, 1881–1893.* Washington, DC: Government Printing Office, 1905. 2 vol.
(Ref Z 1223 A 1970).
A continuation of the work by Poore (see above). It does not list all documents.

United States. Superintendent of Documents. *Catalog of the Public Documents of the Congress and of All Departments of the Government of the United States. . . .* Washington, DC: Government Printing Office, 1893–1940.
(Ref Z 1223 A13).
For the years of coverage this index is the most complete recording of government documents ever published. Subject arrangement with complete cataloging information. Known as the *Document Catalog.*

United States. Superintendent of Documents. *Checklist of United States Public Documents 1789–1909, Congressional...* 3rd ed., rev. and enl. Washington, DC: Government Printing Office, 1911.
(Ref Z 1223 A113).
This source indexes documents by agency. It allows the researcher to determine the series that were published by departmental agency. Useful for its providing of Serial Set numbers and historical data on the agencies. A second (index) volume was never published.

W. ADDITIONAL HISTORY HANDOUTS

The following handouts on historical topics are available on the JMU Library web (http://www.lib.jmu.edu), in the *Research Guides* section.

African History
African-American Genealogy
African-American History
Age of Exploration
American Civil War
American Indians
Ancient History
Bibliographies
British History
Byzantine Empire
Census and Demography
Classical History
Diaries
Genealogy
Guides
Historical Geography, America &
    Virginia

Historical Newspapers
Islam
Military History
Public History
History of an English
    Village—Earls Colne
Revolution
Schomburg Clipping File
Southern History
Statistics
Treaties
U.S. History, 1789–1848
Vietnam
Virginiana
World War II

Appendix B

The Death of an Ideal City: Rebuilding London After 1666

JACK SHEEHAN

I n the year 1666, the city of London had already undergone a great amount of turmoil from an outbreak of the plague in the previous year. Adding to this disaster, the city caught fire in September, and the blaze grew to engulf a great number of buildings. These buildings included homes, churches, and public buildings. By the time the fire was extinguished more than half of the city lay in ruin. Life in London came to almost a complete standstill, as the city was prepared to be rebuilt from the ground up. Many architects and city planners worked on the rebuilding of the city over the years that followed. However, a plan to build a unified city of grandeur fell greatly short. Due to the elaborate plans, property laws, general disagreement, and the inability to coalesce the plans into reality, London soon became the ideal city that was never realized.[1]

---

[1] The secondary books dealing with the rebuilding of the city are Elizabeth McKellar, *The Birth of Modern London: The Development and Design of the City, 1660–1720* (New York: St. Martin's Press, 1999); Neil Hanson, *The Great Fire of London in that Apocalyptic Year, 1666* (New York: John Wiley and Sons, 2002); Timothy Baker, *London: Rebuilding the City After the Great Fire* (London: Phillimore, 2000); Walter George Bell, *The Great Fire of London*, 2nd ed (London: The Bodley Head, 1951); Jonathan Barry, *The Tudor and Stuart Town: A Reader in English Urban History 1530–1688* (London: Longman Publishing, 1990). The last source deals with the town structure and physical building. There also are a relevant number of articles on the topic as well, including M. A. R. Cooper, "Robert Hooke's Work as Surveyor for the City of London in the Aftermath of the Great Fire," *Notes and Records of the Royal Society of London* 51, no. 2 (1997): 161–174. See also 52, no. 1 (1998): 25–38 and 52, no. 2 (1998): 205–220; Charles Elliot, "Samuel Pepys' London Chronicles," *Smithsonian* 32, no. 4 (2001): 102–109; Phillippa Glanville, "The Topography of Seventeenth Century London: A Review of Maps," *Urban History Yearbook* (1980): 79–83; Frank T. Melton, "Sir Robert Clayton's Building Projects in London, 1666–1672," *Guildhall Studies in London History* 3, no. 1 (1977): 37–41; Alan Wykes, "The Great Fire of London," *British History Illustrated* 1, no. 1 (1974): 18–27. Other sources include A. L. Beier and Roger Finlay, eds., *London 1500–1700: The Making of the Metropolis* (New York: Longman Group Ltd., 1986);

The city of London before the Great Fire was one that was growing ever greater by the years. There were approximately 200,000 people living in London at the start of the seventeenth century, and the city itself and areas around it were growing. It has been stated that 5 percent of the English population lived in London during this time period. Within 50 years the population of London had almost doubled. The rapid increase in population would soon set London to be the largest city in all of Europe by 1700 with approximately 490,000 inhabitants. The boom brought about a new prestige to London. It also led to a great number of problems in the city that soon culminated in a plague and mass destruction. Only after the mass destruction of the city by fire did the people try to establish the grandeur of being the largest city in Europe within the building structures. It was also the fire that enabled the architects to plan the extravagant city, because they were starting with a blank slate, or so they thought.[2]

London prior to the fire was very dense. It had grown from the old Roman area of the city out into the surrounding lands beyond the walls. There were a great number of buildings within the walls of the city, and this enabled any fire to take hold quickly and spread rapidly throughout a given area. Throughout London's history as a city there were numerous fires; in fact fires destroyed important buildings only a few years after the Great Fire. An account from Narcissus Luttrell's notices states that Pump Court, Wapping, Whitehall, and Hornsey Down all caught fire between 1679 and 1699. So, fire was commonplace, and the Great Fire had a large impact across the entire city. One of the reasons that fire spread so quickly was the town's design. It was built up so much that there was little space for a fire break. The *London Gazette* states that "the commodities were not very rich, yet they were so bulky that they could not well be removed."[3] There were numerous wooden houses, narrow alleys, and narrow streets. All of this led to the danger of having a large fire. In the year prior to

Frank E. Brown, "Continuity and Change in the Urban House: Developments in Domestic Space Organisation in Seventeenth Century London," *Comparative Studies in Society and History* 28 (1986): 558–590; Gregg Carr, *Residence and Social Status: The Development of Seventeenth Century London* (London: Garland Publishing, 1990); Robert Fishman, "The Origins of the Suburban Idea in England," *Chicago History* 13, no. 2 (1984): 26–36; Jack Lindsay, *The Monster City: Defoe's London, 1688–1730* (New York: St. Martin's Press, 1978); Valerie Pearl, "Change and Stability in 17th Century London," *London Journal* 5, no. 1 (1979): 3–34; Keith Wrightson, *English Society 1580–1680* (New Brunswick, NJ: Rutgers University Press, 1982). Another facet that is examined in many sources is the growing population and expansion of London. See Jeremy Boulton, *Neighbourhood and Society: A London Suburb in the Seventeenth Century* (Cambridge and New York: Cambridge University Press, 1987); Michael Power, "Shadwell; the Development of a London Suburban Community in the Seventeenth Century," *The London Journal* 4, no. 1 (1978): 29–46. Primary sources come from Roland Bartel, ed., *London in Plague and Fire, 1665–1666: Selected Source Materials for College Research Papers* (Boston: D.C. Heath and Company, 1957); selected acts from the *Early English Books 1641–1671* Collection; Samuel Pepys, *Diary of Samuel Pepys*, eds. Robert Latham and William Matthews (Berkeley: University of California Press, 1970); John Evelyn, *The Diary of John Evelyn*, ed. W. Bray (London: M. W. Dunne, 1901) and the *London Gazette* (London), 2 September 1666–10 September 1666.

[2]Carr, 11; McKellar, 13; Boulton, 25.

[3]The *London Gazette* (London), 2 September 1666–10 September 1666.

the Great Fire, authority was given to imprison anyone who did not obey the building codes. London was going through a rough time, and it came to a head on 2 September 1666, when a fire began on Pudding Lane and swept throughout the city.[4]

After the fire started, it was fueled on by the dry material that existed due to the drought conditions. The wind also played a major factor in the spreading of the fire. The high winds pushed the fire about the city throughout the time it was ablaze. It was decided that the only way to have any effect on the fire, the buildings in the city had to torn down. This meant that whatever buildings were not being burned immediately were now being destroyed by people trying to stop the fire. The fire finally ended on 6 September, and the inhabitants of London woke up on the seventh to discover the city in ruins.[5]

During the fire, there was a great deal of chaos. People were running from their homes leaving all of their valuables behind. Many of the lower class stayed until the last seconds before they ran to the river and caught boats to get across to the opposite bank. The confusion was heightened with the darkness on the first night, when the fire broke out. The *London Gazette* describes a great amount of yelling and confusion, and nobody knowing quite what to do. People were trying to move their valuables from their homes in the city to areas that were untouched by the fire, such as churches. Mass confusion was present throughout the entire time the fire raged, and then continued for some time afterwards. Soon after the fire, before the embers had even cooled, the people suspected plots of various kinds, and looked to convict someone for what had occurred. The chance appeared in a French Huguenot, who claimed to have started the fire all by himself. He was later convicted and sentenced to death. Even though spots were still burning, the inhabitants now faced a daunting task of rebuilding the entire city from the ground up. Very quickly it was apparent that some had plans to build the city in a new and elaborate style, much different from that of the city in ruins.[6]

In the aftermath of the fire, many different plans were proposed right away. Plans such as Christopher Wren's, Robert Hooke's, and John Evelyn's were submitted within days of the fire. These men who submitted the plans were to become very influential in the rebuilding of the city. In this overall scheme of rebuilding there are multiple steps, and the first step is to survey the city. So, the plans to rebuild were put on hold until a committee was appointed and a survey of the entire area was accomplished. Appointed to the committee were Christopher Wren, who was the head architect; Robert Hooke; and Edward Woodroffe, who died and was replaced by John Oliver—all were appointed as

---

[4]Carr, 14, 16; Baker, 13, 16; Richards, 151; John Evelyn, "Account of the Great Fire of London, 1666," and Narcissus Luttrell, "Notices of Other Fires, 1679–1699," in Andrew Browning, ed., *English Historical Documents 1660–1714* (New York: Oxford University Press, 1953), 498–503; Hanson, 31; Bell, 17. The Luttrell accounts describe various fires through notices, and cover the period 1679–1699.

[5]Pepys, v. 7, 269–272.

[6]Pepys, v. 7, 268, 270, 277; *The London Gazette;* Bell, 23; Wykes, 25; Hanson 59, 170.

surveyors. The survey was taken very seriously by those involved. Proclamations were issued stating that all areas needed to be surveyed, that the rubble should be piled up and area cleared within 15 days, the persons did not need to pay a fee, and the residents could present evidence in their favor. The committee saw the need for stricter regulations in the building codes, wider streets, and a uniform city. These elements, if implemented correctly, would improve the quality of life for all. However, before these elements could be realized, a number of problems would occur.[7]

The first problem was that the city needed to keep functioning; London had become a major metropolitan area that was dependent on commerce. If commerce into and out of London ever stopped, then the city could face financial ruin. This is a driving factor as to why the city of grandeur was never realized. In order to keep the goods flowing, plans had to be implemented very quickly. First, the Royal Exchange was temporarily moved to Gresham College. The building of the new Royal Exchange took priority over any other project. This was due to the fact that it was the central marketplace where all of the commerce flowed in and out of London. Without a Royal Exchange set up, then there would be detrimental problems to the economy of the city. In fact, London may have lost a lot of prestige. There were also many other important buildings necessary to the economy of the city that needed to be rebuilt. Pepys, the great diarist, talks of the fear of the economy crashing by saying, "I spoke with Mr. May, who tells me the design of building the city doth go on apace, and by his description, it will be mighty handsome, and to the satisfaction of the people. But I pray God it come not out too late."[8] Many halls of the major liveries had also been destroyed by the fire. These halls were not of the greatest importance, but symbolized a system that had been in place for centuries. The liveries wanted to maintain control of the trade, but lost power in the shuffle to rebuild. Buildings like Blackwell Hall were rebuilt quickly, because it was a major cloth business that brought in a substantial gain. London at this point had become the largest city in all of Europe, therefore it was also a huge economic center. If London's economy crashed, all of England's may have gone with it very easily. Due to the need to keep the economy of London afloat, the rebuilding and planning of the city took a secondary stance. Functionality soon proceeded over a well-organized, grandiose city that the planners sought. This was the first major sacrifice to the plan of an ideal city. Charles II wrote at the time:

> As no particular man hath sustained any loss or damage by the late terrible and deplorable fire in his fortune or estate, in any degree to be compared with the loss and damage we ourself have sustained, so it is not possible for any man to take the same more to heart, and to be more

---

[7]Cooper, 162–164; Baker, 14; Corporation of London, "By the Order to the Rebuilding of the city," *Early English Books 1641–1700* (London: Printed by James Fletcher, n.d.); Wykes, 25–26.

[8]Pepys, v. 7, 384–385.

concerned and solicitous for the rebuilding this famous city with as much expedition as possible.[9]

With such a strong statement, the fate of London was locked into a quick fix solution for rebuilding the city, and work started on London, using the foundations of buildings from the past.[10]

There was a great amount of hope for the new London. People saw the rebuilding as an opportunity. The planners were going to build a magnificent city, and the people were going to live there. There are maps from the survey done in the 1670s by Ogilby, a renowned cartographer of the time, showing improvements to the city, such as Fleet Canal, before they had been constructed. However, the houses were to be set up in the traditional design and not much different in style, showing little optimism. The only thing to differ was the updated building techniques with some innovations. Some were to be built with the timber framing and then the outside faced with brick, or the more advanced houses with the timber inside two layers of brick. The roofs were no longer thatched, but instead highly pitched and the interiors were to be lit from a lightwell that existed between two joining houses. The ground plans of the houses remained much the same as before the fire. The more expensive the house, the more complicated the ground plan. In the simplest of houses, there would be a shop on the street front with a kitchen and a garden behind it. The upstairs would then include a couple chambers, and above that a garret, where goods were stored. As one rises through the classes, they gained an entry hall, parlor, drinking room, and perhaps stables. The houses of the citizens were rebuilt, and many gained technological advances. However, even in the face of much anticipation for rebuilding, many expressed their woes. Pepys stated on 31 December 1666, "Public matters are in a most sad condition . . . The city less and less likely to be built again, everybody settling elsewhere, and nobody encouraged to trade."[11] Thoughts like these ran through the minds of many, but the population continued to grow after the fire.[12]

Another problem encountered in the building of the ideal city was a large one that was hard to get around. If the new plans were accepted, then the streets had to be resituated. In fact this is one of the main causes as to why none of the rebuilding plans were accepted. However, it became evident in the aftermath of the fire that some restructuring in London was necessary to keep another event like the Great Fire from occurring, or at least to contain it. The answer to this was uniform buildings and wider streets and alleys. So, thus began the rebuilding acts. These acts, the first in 1667, established how the new buildings were to be erected. It gave limitations on the size of the buildings, the height, and the materials. Marc Antonio Giustinian, a Venetian Ambassador, stated on 12 October 1666,

---

[9]Bartel, 98–99. Excerpt from proclamation of Charles II on 13 September 1666. Reprinted from *A Source Book of London History*, ed. by P. Meadows (London: G. Bell, 1914).

[10]Baker, 9–11, 83–84; Pepys, v. 7, 281; Bell, 269, 338.

[11]Pepys, v. 7, 426.

[12]Glanville, 80; McKellar, 160–167; Brown, 570–577; Carr, 11; Boulton, 25.

"In Parliament they discussed the rebuilding of the city, and they decided to make a careful model; that the houses shall all be of stone and the streets thirty-six paces wide."[13] Therefore, the new city was to be completed entirely in brick or stone, and the street on which a building was located would determine its height. The "first sort" houses were to be built in alleys and small streets, and only to be two stories tall. The "second sort" houses were built on streets of note, and were to be three stories. The "third sort" were on principal streets, and were to be four stories. The "merchant mansion houses" were the largest and could not be on the street front and had to be four stories.[14] Many temporary sheds were built after the fire during the rebuilding process. These sheds remained for quite a while, and were only given the allotted time of 7 years to stand, and then they had to be torn down. Certain streets were also slated to be widened. Charles II stated, "Fleet street, Cheapside, Cornhill, and all other eminent and notorious streets, shall be of such a breadth, as may, with God's blessing, prevent mischief that one side may suffer if the other be on fire." This is one of the few areas that the ideas of building an ideal city are formulated into reality. There was strict control on the building materials and the regulations held in place by London.[15]

In the restructuring of London there were many different disputes that arose. The plan for an ideal city had been eradicated soon after building had begun, but this did not mean that elements could not be incorporated into the building of the new city. Roads were being widened to allow traffic to flow easier and provide a fire break. There were immediate problems in trying to widen the streets. Many people owned property on either side of the street, and they did not want to relinquish their holdings to the government or to the city of London. This led to many property disputes, however the city just took the land it needed, and only after the fact thought about reimbursing the people for the land they had lost. One man was reimbursed £700 after his land was taken away to build a road. In addition to the disputes with the city, there were also disputes among the people. All of the land in the city had to be surveyed, and was done so by

---

[13]Public Record Office, "Marc Antonio Giustinian, Venetian Ambassador in France, to Doge and Senate," 12 October 1666, *Calendar of State Papers and Manuscript, Relating to English Affairs, Existing in the Archives and Collections in Venice, and in Other Libraries of Northern Italy 1202–[1675]* (September 1666–November 1666) (London, 1864), no. 87, 86.

[14]The mansion houses had to be pushed back from the street in order to have room for a courtyard leading up to the house.

[15]Baker, 5–8; Robert Hanson, "Where as in and by the additional act of Parliament for rebuilding the city of London, it is enacted that the Lord Mayor and Court of Alderman shall be and are thereby empowered and required to cause all and every the sheds, shops, and other buildings . . . to be taken down and removed," *Early English Books 1641–1700* (London: printed by Andrew Clark, n.d.); Sir William Hooker, "This court taking into their consideration, that the utmost time appointed for taking down and removing all such sheds, shops, and other like buildings, which have been erected since the late dismal fire," *Early English Books 1641–*1700 (London: printed by Andrew Clark, n.d.). The two previous sources are documentation from Parliament that announce to the city to tear down temporary buildings. Bell, 250–251; Bartel, 99. From Sept 13th Proclamation.

Hooke, Peter Mills, or John Oliver. These surveyors were called to a site after the rubble was cleared away to look for the foundation of the old house, and to declare what the inhabitant had to build on the site, and their property limits. It soon became unlawful to move a stake or boundary stone, and could lead to imprisonment, or a £10 fine. Once the survey was finished, many of the inhabitants were not very pleased with the results, or claimed that others had taken part of their property. These disputes were taken to the Fire Court that had been set up just after the fire, and was the power in all matters of dispute dealing with the fire. It held the power to cancel existing agreements, substitute other agreements, and set up or extend leases. The purpose of the Fire Court was to also help the tenant. During this time the tenant owed nothing to his landlord, and the Fire Court was to maintain this status quo until the buildings were rebuilt and occupied once again. None of the disputes ever materialized into major problems on their own. Only the fact that the disputes were present prevented the construction of the ideal city.[16]

One question came into the minds of many citizens in London almost immediately: how were they going to pay for all of the rebuilding? The king began by asking for donations from the people throughout the kingdom, however this approach was short lived. A more successful answer was found in coal. With the rebuilding act of 1667, a coal tax was instituted that required, as stated by Milward, a Member of Parliament, "one Shilling a cauldron shall be laid upon coal towards the discharge of building."[17] This tax, once the rebuilding was underway, was supposed to bring in the amount of money needed to fund all of the buildings in some way. However the tax was not able to accomplish this. It had to be raised in subsequent acts. In 1671 it was raised by one shilling, making the tax two shillings on every ton, and then again in 1677 it was raised another shilling, making it three shillings per ton. The tax lasted until 1716, and by the end had been reduced to six pence per ton. The coal tax enabled London to be rebuilt without having to spend gross amounts of money from the treasury. It set up a fund from which the building money could be drawn from, but the tax was not fully successful. Due to its implementation as a reaction to the fire, the funds took a good amount of time to start flowing in. Therefore many people had to start rebuilding using what they could personally afford. Parliament tried to provide more aid to the people by letting them cut timber from within 5 miles of London for the price of the land alone. However, more troubles were placed on the inhabitants. An act was passed that if the owner of a property in the city did not build on the land within 3 years, then the land could be seized by the Lord Mayor; this was subsequently pushed back to 4 years. The act put pressure on the people to build quickly after the fire; however there was no money until a couple years after the fire. The people took the initiative and had their property surveyed, often paying a nominal fee for that, even though

---

[16]Cooper, 26, 206–211; Pepys, v. 8, 562–563; Hanson, 175; Bell, 243–244.

[17]John Milward, *The Diary of John Milward*, ed. Caroline Robbins (Cambridge: Cambridge University Press, 1938), 256.

FIGURE 1   The Guild Church of St. Margaret Pattens

it was not required, and then started to rebuild on their own in the hopes that they would be reimbursed later on down the line.[18]

The inhabitants were quick in taking up the effort to rebuild their city. However, this hastiness led to the failure of realizing any sort of ideal plan. The people had to take up their own personal work. There was no large corporation that rebuilt all of London; it was the individual residents themselves. The effect was that it gave the city a nonuniform appearance, while at the same time tying all of the buildings together through the strong supervision of the surveyors and the rebuilding acts. It is this element that made London a great city to the visual eye. The design of the public buildings by one architect, Wren, creates a backdrop that is cohesive in nature. The 51 churches that were rebuilt after the fire all incorporated the same architectural style, but each had features that were significant to the individual. The steeple on every church was unique, yet it still incorporated the aspects that were congruent throughout the entire city. When looking at the designs of the steeples, one can see the similarities across the entire city. Take St. Margaret Pattens' steeple (Figure 1) and St. Bride Fleet Street's steeple (Figure 2) into comparison.

---

[18]*Cal. State Papers Venetian*, 87. Baker, 6–7; Milward, 256; Cooper, 30–32; Bell, 245.

© Hulton Archive/Getty Images

FIGURE 2 St. Bride's Fleet Street

The third and first respectively according to height, these steeples are entirely different designs. However, it is clear that they mirror each other. The large articulated spires reaching upwards, the baroque ornamentation, and the way both are sectioned off into smaller parts as the eye travels upward show great unity in features. The churches were one of the only parts of the city that gained substantial funds during the rebuilding. Many times the livery companies began to rebuild their halls based on their own funds. The companies employed the mass of construction workers who migrated into the city looking for jobs. The companies were not able to finance the buildings due to the civil war, and loss of rent income. This meant that a large number of the halls were domestic in size, and the liveries had to allow more members to join, in order to gain the proper amount of money. The financial burden had been complicated for the liveries since before the fire. The companies could no longer restrict foreign trade as well as they had done in the past, and because of this, many needed some sort of financial aid, but the only thing to help was the coal tax, and that was primarily spent on the churches, St. Paul's Cathedral, and other public buildings.[19]

---

[19]Cooper, 1, 27–28, 31–32, 207–209; Melton, 37–39, 41; Baker, 10–11, 114, 181–182.

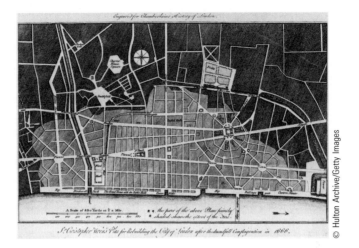

© Hutton Archive/Getty Images

FIGURE 3   Christopher Wren's Plan for Rebuilding London

Looking at London, there are the buildings, the streets, and the overall layout of the city. The last topic is what was denied from the rebuilding. Many plans were presented within a few days or a week of the fire, but none were accepted for the city. There are a number of reasons, but a major one is the complexity of the plans presented. All of the plans that were presented required for the city to be entirely leveled, hence no old foundations to build from, and then new streets to be built along with completely new buildings. It has already been shown that the delegates and people of the city felt there was not enough time for this, and that there was no money for such an extensive rebuilding. However, it is very interesting to view the plans that Wren and others envisioned for the perfect city.[20]

Wren's plan (Figure 3) was the first to be presented, and it incorporates many aspects seen in the modern day city. The plan was focused around public squares. There would be central areas from which a person could go anywhere in the city. Wren stuck to four ideas when designing his ideal city. The first was to leave the royal Exchange on its present site. The second was to make St Paul's significance worthy of the size of London.[21] The third was to improve London Bridge and have four different streets converge there, and the fourth was to clear the river bank to create a large public area, like a park. The main focus in Wren's plan was accessibility to all corners of the city. The streets are aligned in a customized grid pattern with two major highways in the center of London converging and meeting on the west side. St Paul's Cathedral in this plan becomes the central focus. Wren's plan did away with the old historical highways that ran throughout

---

[20]Bell, 230–242.

[21]This aspect appeared in the completion of the city after the fire anyway. Wren designed St Paul's to be a magnificent church. Construction lasted from 1675–1710, and it cost £747,000 of the coal tax. It was the most expensive building that was undertaken, and Wren saw his idea and design of making St Paul's worthy of a large metropolis come to life.

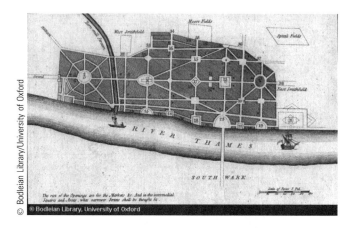

FIGURE 4 John Evelyn's Plan for Rebuilding London

the city by routing them through different areas. He also focused on the beautification of the city. Old ditches were beautiful canals in his design. Wren also moved buildings like Guildhall and the post office. This plan is very elaborate and interesting to view from a modern perspective, but it is far different from the London that was built after the Great Fire, and the London that exists today.[22]

Another plan presented in the wake of the fire was drawn by John Evelyn (Figure 4). Evelyn's plan differed greatly from Wren's, but it also used an arrangement of public squares. Evelyn planned five major squares to be built in a line going across the center of the city. In each of these squares he placed a building of importance: St. Paul's, Mansion House, or St. Dunstan's East. Evelyn moved the Royal Exchange to the waterside and incorporated a number of piazzas there. He also had a grid design with major roads traversing diagonally and meeting at St. Paul's. The Guildhall in this plan receives a good amount of attention and it makes the building very important. It is in a single smaller square on the northern part of the city. This is a place of power and prestige. The entire area burned was to be rebuilt in brick. This was done to ensure that it would survive a long time, and to enhance its visual appearance. The design that Evelyn produced is one that is very sound, and highlights the significance of the important buildings. Evelyn himself presented his plan with high hopes, stating in his diary:

> I presented his Majesty with a survey of the ruins, and a plot for a new city, with a discourse on it; whereupon, after dinner, his Majesty sent for me into the Queen's bed-chamber, her Majesty and the Duke only being present. They examined each particular, and discoursed on them for near an hour, seeming to be extremely pleased with what I had so early thought on.[23]

---

[22]Bell, 230–235; Wykes, 26–27.

[23]Evelyn, 26.

This shows the hope and anticipation that the planners held early on in the rebuilding of the city.[24]

The third plan presented was Robert Hooke's. This plan was very utilitarian, and would become the predecessor to many modern metropolitan areas. The roads in Hooke's plan run in straight lines from east to west, and then have streets crosscutting from north to south. This is a perfect grid design, and it does not bring emphasis to any one area. It sets the entire city up in blocks that are useful, but not in any way a beautification of the city. Hooke thought that the design of the city should be finished first instead of just building on the foundations.[25]

Even though none of the plans were undertaken, London was still rebuilt to a better standard than it had held previously. The roads were now wider, the houses safer, and the streets cleaner. The social impacts of the fire and fear of what was to happen to the city had driven the people to their breaking points. The people did not seek a magnificent work for themselves; instead they sought a functioning economic area that was safe from any more tragedy. It is this mindset that forced Parliament, the King, and city officials to rebuild the area in a manner that incorporated safety precautions and also speediness. Although fires still struck the city on a regular basis, no significant damage was done to London until the mid-twentieth century. More important than the actual design of London as it stands today are the thoughts and ideas that the committee of men in the latter half of the seventeenth century dreamed of for how the city would look. So, whether the city was built according to the ideal plans or not, the seeds of progressive city planning had been planted, and it would not be long before others noticed; but the dream of an ideal city of London died within a year of the fire.

---

[24]Bell, 235–238; Evelyn, 30.

[25]Bell, 239–242.

BIBLIOGRAPHY

I.   Primary Sources

Bartel, Roland ed., *London in Plague and Fire 1665–1666: Selected Source Materials for College Research Papers.* Boston: D.C. Heath and Company, 1957.

This is a collection of reprinted primary materials. The material in the book covers the plague and the fire of London. These documents are inclusive of contemporary newspapers, letters, and Royal Acts and Proclamations.

Browning, Andrew ed., *English Historical Documents 1660–1714.* New York: Oxford University Press, 1953.

This book contains a large number of reprinted primary documents throughout Restoration England. It has Royal Acts, as well as a great number of personal accounts of events happening throughout the period.

Corporation of London. *By the order to the rebuilding of the city . . .* London: James Fletcher. Guildhall Library Collection: *Early English Books, 1641–1700.*

The proclamation that sets the outline for the surveying of the city. It constricts the time citizens have to clear their land of rubble, and proposes how the surveying of the city was to occur.

Evelyn, John. *The Diary of John Evelyn.* Edited by William Bray. Vol. 2. London: M. Walter Dunn, 1901.

A recording of the events surrounding John Evelyn's life from 1620 to 1706. Covers major events to happen throughout the time. Evelyn was very close to the Royal Court and carried out a number of tasks for the city of London.

Great Britain. Public Records Office. *Calendar of State Papers and Manuscripts, Relating to English Affairs, Existing in the Archives and Collections in Venice, and in Other Libraries of Northern Italy 1202–[1675].* (September 1666–November 1666) London: Longman, Green, Longman, Roberts, and Green, 1864.

A large archive of the accounts of the Venetian diplomats to England. The diplomats write about the events that are occurring throughout the country, and the acts that are being passed in Parliament. This is a great source and covers a large span of time.

Hanson, Robert. *Where as in and by the additional act of Parliament for rebuilding the city of London, it is enacted that the Lord Maior and Court of Alderman shall be and are thereby empowered and required to cause all and every shed, shops, and other buildings . . . to be taken down and removed . . .* London: Printed by Andrew Clark. Guild Hall Library Collection: *Early English Books, 1641–1700.*

This is an Act of Parliament from 1673 that states all temporary sheds must be torn down by a certain date.

Hooker, William. *This court taking into their consideration that the utmost time appointed for taking down and removing all such sheds, shops, and other like buildings, which have been*

erected since the late dismal fire . . . London: Printed by Andrew Clark. Guild Hall
Library Collection: *Early English Books,* 1641–1700.

An act from 1674 dealing with the problem of still having temporary buildings on
the land where the city was being rebuilt.

Latham, Robert ed. *The Illustrated Pepys: Extracts From the Diary.* Berkeley: University of
California Press, 1978.

This book contains selected excerpts from the Latham edited version of Pepys's
diary. There are numerous illustrations that coincide with the dates that are featured. This is a great supplement to the Latham edition of the diary.

Milward, John. *The Diary of John Milward.* Edited by Caroline Robbins. Cambridge:
Cambridge University Press, 1938.

Milward was a Member of Parliament from Derbyshire. The work spans from September 1666 to May 1668. There is a significant amount of information dealing
with the actions in Parliament at the time. The diary is well organized with a great
number of notes and detailing on what topics each date covers.

Pepys, Samuel. *The Diary of Samuel Pepys.* Edited by Robert Latham and William
Matthews. Vols. 7 and 8. Berkeley: University of California Press, 1972.

A major source in the study of the Restoration period. Pepys held a position in
the court and wrote down his daily occurrences, as well as his thoughts of people
and events that happened throughout England at the time.

The *London Gazette.* London: Printed by Tho. Newcomb. Monday 2 September–10
September 1666.
Website by David Cornfield. "The Great Fire of London." (http://www.adelpha.
com/~davidco/History/fire1.htm).

The website contains a copy of the original newspaper that was published right
after the Great Fire. Contains a contemporary account of what happened during
the fire, and provides insight to the reaction of the people living in the city.

II. Secondary Sources

Baker, Timothy. *London: Rebuilding the City After the Great Fire.* London: Phillimore, 2000.

One of the best sources on rebuilding the city of London. It is divided into two
separate sections. The first section gives a great deal of information on the major
players and acts; the second gives graphic illustrations of the plans for the public
buildings and churches that were rebuilt.

Barry, Jonathan ed., *The Tudor and Stuart Town: A Reader in English Urban History 1530–
1688.* London: Longman Publishing, 1990.

This is one of the best introductory works on the subject of towns and cities during the time period. It consists of numerous articles that cover a range of topics in
a range of areas. Gives a good starting point to research in the period.

Beier, A. L. and Roger Finlay, eds. *London 1500–1700: The Making of the Metropolis.* New York: Longman Group Ltd., 1986.

A collection of essays on the topic of the growth of London throughout the period. The essays range from economic to social ideas. There are numerous figures for population as well as an essay by itself demonstrating the growth. Uses a good deal of demographic history.

Bell, Walter George. *The Great Fire of London,* 2nd ed. London: The Bodley Head, 1951.

A detailed account of what happened during the fire of London, what burned, what survived, and how the fire spread. The book then goes into the aftermath and rebuilding after the fire. This is an informative source that also contains appendices of typed primary sources.

Boulton, Jeremy. *Neighbourhood and Society: A London Suburb in the Seventeenth Century.* Cambridge and New York: Cambridge University Press, 1987.

This book is on the topic of a suburb on the south bank of the Thames. It gives details into the life that people lived and how the area was laid out. Strongly demographic with good primary sources to back it up.

Brown, Frank E. "Continuity and Change in the Urban House: Developments in Domestic Space Organisation in Seventeenth Century London." *Comparative Studies in Society and History* 28 (1986): 558–590.

This article shows the way that the houses in the seventeenth century were laid out in floor plans and street grids. There are illustrations to back the points, as well as use of statistics to show the number and nature of households.

Carr, Gregg. *Residence and Social Status: The Development of Seventeenth Century London.* London: Garland Publishing, 1990.

This book is a sociological study of the population of London. Gives various details about life throughout the seventeenth century, and how it affected the people. Largely demographic sections on populations and the movement of people.

Cooper, M. A. R. "Robert Hooke's Work as Surveyor for the City of London in the Aftermath of the Great Fire." *Notes and Records of the Royal Society of London* 51, no. 2 (1997): 161–174; also 52, no. 1 (1998): 25–38 and 52, no. 2 (1998): 205–220.

The article is separated into three different sections—the first dealing with the initial survey of Hooke, the second with the certification of lands taken away for new streets, and the third with the settlements of disputes due to rebuilding. In each section the author shows how important Hooke was to the rebuilding of London.

Elliot, Charles. "Samuel Pepys' London Chronicles." *Smithsonian* 32, no. 4 (2001): 102–109.

This article goes into studying Pepys's writings in his diary and how they affected modern research and understanding. It also gives insight into Pepys himself, and how he lived his daily life through the writings or innuendos in the writings.

Fishman, Robert. "The Origins of the Suburban Idea in England." *Chicago History* 13, no. 2 (1984): 26–36.

The article examines the growth of suburbs, especially around London. Includes the factors leading to the growth and the reasons behind the growth in the seventeenth century. It also examines the architectural styles used in the suburbs.

Glanville, Phillippa. "The Topography of Seventeenth Century London; A Review of Maps." *Urban History Yearbook* (1980): 79–83.

The article looks at two different maps from the period of the Restoration that show the expansion and rebuilding after the fire. The first, Ogilby's, is hard to match the dates and other records to what is shown. The second, Morgan's, shows the great expansion into the suburbs.

Hanson, Neil. *The Great Fire of London in that Apocalyptic Year, 1666.* New York: John Wiley and Sons, 2002.

This book gives a great narrative of what occurred during the fire of London. It gives insight into the reactions of the people, and the reactions of the King and Parliament. The book goes into depth about the repercussions of the fire, as well as the trials afterward.

Hudson, Nicholas. "Samuel Johnson, Urban Culture and the Geography of Postfire London." *SEL Studies in English Literature 1500–1900* 42, no. 3 (2002): 577–600.

The article examines how Samuel Johnson, the writer, viewed the city of London. It looks to further ideas of development in the eighteenth century, and the missed opportunities from the seventeenth century.

Lindsay, Jack. *The Monster City: Defoe's London, 1688–1730.* New York: St. Martin's Press, 1978.

This book deals mainly with the social aspects of the city of London. It goes through the fashions of the day as well as the people. It gives a nice mindset of the people at the time especially in regards to the common events that occurred.

McKellar, Elizabeth. *The Birth of Modern London: The Development and Design of the City, 1660–1720.* New York: St. Martin's Press, 1999.

The book deals with the rebuilding of the city and how its ideals were influenced. It goes into the designs of the common houses and the layout of the city. The book pushes the idea that due to the fire, London was brought to the forefront of city planning, and it had a large impact throughout the centuries.

Melton, Frank T. "Sir Robert Clayton's Building Projects in London, 1666–1672." *Guildhall Studies in London History* 3, no. 1 (1977): 37–41.

This article goes through the records of Sir Robert Clayton and shows that at this time the larger capitalists played a small role in the rebuilding of London. Instead, it was more of the small artisans and residents who rebuilt their homes.

Pearl, Valerie. "Change and Stability in 17th Century London." *London Journal* 5, no. 1 (1979): 3–34.

A work that shows the changing society throughout the seventeenth century. Tells that there is a great need for urban centralization to supersede the multiple minor authorities of the past. A great focus on the ever growing city.

Power, Michael. "Shadwell; the Development of a London Suburban Community in the Seventeenth Century." The *London Journal* 4, no. 1 (1978): 29–46.

This article looks at a small suburban community in London. The area did not start to grow until 1669, and continued until 1699. Shows the growth of London and the usefulness of, and unification, of the strong community.

Reddaway, T. F. *The Rebuilding of London After the Great Fire*. London: Edward Arnold and Co., 1951.

This is an important book that is on many bibliographies in other works pertaining to this subject. The work deals with the different city plans and acts that were put into effect after the fire struck London. It gives detailed descriptions of how the city buildings changed, and the overall look of the city.

Richardson, John. *The Annals of London: A Year-by-Year Record of a Thousand Years of History*. Berkeley: University of California Press, 2000.

This book gives a brief account of what occurred in London every year from 1065–1999. Gives the dates when buildings were rebuilt and major events that happened. A good number of visuals are incorporated.

Wrightson, Keith. *English Society 1580–1680*. New Brunswick, NJ: Rutgers University Press, 1982.

About the people of England throughout the seventeenth century. Goes through sections about family structure and social relations, then population and order in the community. It gives background on the lives of people at the time.

Wykes, Alan. "The Great Fire of London." *British History Illustrated* 1, no. 1 (1974): 18–27.

Tells of the amount of destruction wrought by the fire. Then goes into information about the rebuilding acts and the restrictions imposed upon the structures. Also gives details as to how the original plans of rebuilding were never realized. Illus.

III. Illustrations

Figure 1—The Guild Church of St. Margaret Pattens, London, taken from http://www.stmargaretpattens.org/.

Figure 2—St. Bride's Fleet Street taken from http://www.ourpasthistory.com/london/st_brides.htm.

Figure 3—Christopher Wren's Plan for Rebuilding London taken from http://www.oldlondonmaps.com/viewspages/0345.html.

Figure 4—John Evelyn's Plan for Rebuilding London taken from http://www.bodley.ox.ac.uk/guides/maps/lonfire.gif.

Index

A

Abraham Lincoln Papers at the Library of Congress, 155
Abstracts:
   to identify most important sources, 36
   online, 28
Academic Search Premier, 165
Accuracy, 92
Adams, James T., 149
Adams, John, 67–68
Africa:
   Africa Through Western Eyes, 156
   A Bibliography of the Negro in Africa and America, 138
   Encyclopedia of African History, 145
   Index Africanus, 134
   International Historical Statistics: Africa, Asia & Oceania, 1750–2000, 149
   subject bibliographies for, 24
Africa Through Western Eyes, 156
Agreement (in writing), 89
Ahistorical perspectives, 4, 42
Allen, Barbara, 164
Allen, James P., 149
America: History and Life, 28, 36, 133, 163
America at the Polls: A Handbook of American Presidential Election Statistics, 1920–1964 (Richard M. Scammon), 148
America Votes, 147–149
American Council of Learned Societies History E-Book Project, 38
American Counties, The Origins of Names, Dates of Creation and Organization, Area, Population, Historical Data, and Published Sources (Joseph Nathan Kane), 144
American Diaries: An Annotated Bibliography of Published American

Diaries and Journals (Laura Arksey), 134
American Foreign Relations Since 1600 (Robert L. Beisner), 126
American Historical Association, 23, 25, 103
American Historical Association's Guide to Historical Literature, The (Mary B. Norton), 137
American Memory website (Library of Congress), 154–155
   photographic evidence on, 74
   for primary sources, 29
   quality of, 38
   Thomas Jefferson Papers on, 67
   U.S. Congress records on, 69
American National Biography, 151
American Newspapers 1821–1936: A Union List of Files Available in the United States and Canada (Winifred Gregory), 140
American Revolution in Context, The, 156
Ancient history:
   Année Philologique, l', 133
   Barrington Atlas of the Greek and Roman World, 150
   Brill's New Pauly: Encyclopaedia of the Ancient World: Antiquity, 146
   Civilization of the Ancient Mediterranean: Greece and Rome, 146
   Introduction to Ancient History, 126
Annales school, 9–11
Annals of America, The, 157
Annals of Congress of the United States, The, 157
Annotated bibliographies, 51–55, 111, 116
Annotations (reference works), 22
Annuals, 154–155
Appendices, 122
Archive of Americana, 156

Archives Parlementaires de 1787 à 1860: Recueil Complet des Débats Législatifs & Politiques, 157
Aristocracy, the State, and the Local Community, The (1477–1828): The Hastings Collection of Manuscripts from the Huntington Library in California, 157
Arksey, Laura, 134
Articles:
   bibliography citations for, 114
   footnotes for, 106–107
   scholarly (*see* Journal articles)
Articles Describing Archives and Manuscript Collections in the United States: An Annotated Bibliography (Donald L. DeWitt), 159
Artifacts:
   evaluating, 65
   as primary evidence, 76–77
Asamani, J. O., 134
Asia:
   Bibliography of Asian Studies, 134
   Encyclopedia of Asian History, 145
   International Historical Statistics: Africa, Asia & Oceania, 1750–2000, 149
   subject bibliographies for, 24
Associations Unlimited, 161–162
Atlas of American History (James T. Adams), 149
Atlas of Rockingham County, Virginia, An: From Actual Surveys (J. M. Lathrop), 150
Atlas of the British Empire (C. A. Bayly), 150
Atlas of the Historical Geography of the United States (Charles O. Paullin), 150
Atlases, historical, 149–152
Audience:
   effective writing for, 87
   for historical writing, 82
   identifying, 37

Audience (*continued*)
  of primary sources, intended vs.
    unintended, 58–59
Authors:
  of primary evidence, 57–58
  qualifications of, 37–39
  understanding point of view of, 44
Autobiographies, as primary
  evidence, 68

B

Background information, 5–6
Balay, Robert, 22, 126
Barker, Felix, 149
Barraclough, Geoffrey, 149–150
Barrington Atlas of the Greek and
  Roman World (Richard J. A.
  Talbert), 149–150
Baum, Willa K., 164
Bayly, C. A., 150
Beard, Charles, 7, 8
Becker, Carl, 7, 8
Beers, Henry P., 132–133
Beisner, Robert L., 126
Bengtson, Hermann, 126
Bentley, Michael, 146
Berkshire Encyclopedia of World History
  (William H. McNeill), 141
Besterman, Theodore, 22, 132
Bevans, Charles I., 160
Bibliographic essays, 53, 112,
  116–120
Bibliographic Index, 22–23, 133
Bibliographic note cards, 51–55
Bibliographie Annuelle de l'Histoire de
  France du Cinquième Siècle à
  1958, 134
Bibliographies in American History,
  1942–1978: Guide to Materials
  for Research (Henry P. Beers),
  132–133
Bibliographies in History: An Index to
  Bibliographies in History Journals
  and Dissertations, 133
Bibliographies of bibliographies:
  guides to, 22–23
  reference works of, 132–133
Bibliography(-ies), 111–120
  annotated, 51–55, 111, 116
  article citations, 114
  bibliographic essays, 112, 116–120
  book citations, 113
  checking, 122
  electronic source citations, 115
  government publication citations,
    114–115
  guidelines for, 112
  interview citations, 116
  manuscript collection citations, 116
  national, 138–139
  print vs. online, 25
  reference works of, 133–139
  selected, 111
  for Sheehan's student paper,
    180–184
  standard, 111
  subject, 23–25

types of, 111–112
unpublished dissertation/thesis
  citations, 115–116
usefulness of, 38
video citations, 116
Bibliography of American County
  Histories, A (P. William Filby),
  135
Bibliography of American Historical
  Societies (Appleton P. C. Griffin),
  136
Bibliography of Asian Studies, 134
Bibliography of British History, 134–135
Bibliography of the Negro in Africa and
  America, A (Monroe N. Work),
  138
Bibliography of United States—Latin
  American Relations Since 1810, A
  (David F. Trask), 137
Biographical Dictionaries and Related
  Works: An International Bibliogra-
  phy of More Than 16,000
  Collective Biographies (Robert B.
  Slocum), 153
Biographical Dictionary of the United
  States Congress, 1774-present, 151
Biography(-ies), 34, 151–153
Biography and Genealogy Master Index,
  151
Biography Index, 151
Biography Resource Center, 151
Black Access: A Bibliography of
  Afro-American Bibliographies
  (Richard Newman), 133
Black Biography, 1790–1950: A
  Cumulative Index (Randall K.
  Burkett), 151–152
Black history:
  A Bibliography of the Negro in Africa
    and America, 138
  Black Access: A Bibliography of
    Afro-American Bibliographies, 131
  Black Biography, 1790–1950: A
    Cumulative Index, 151–153
  Black History: A Guide to Civilian
    Records in the National Archives, 130
  Blacks in the United States Armed
    Forces, 160
Black History: A Guide to Civilian
  Records in the National Archives
  (Debra L. Newman), 129–130
Blacks in the United States Armed Forces
  (Morris J. MacGregor and
  Bernard C. Nalty), 158
Black's Law Dictionary (Bryan A.
  Garner), 161
Blazek, Ron, 126
Bloch, Marc, 9
Block-indented quotations, 103
Body (of essay), 94–95
Bola, Lucian, 148
Book Review Digest, 36
Book Review Index, 164
Book reviews, 36, 46, 162
  comment on sources in, 49
  heading of, 47
  identification of appropriate
    audience in, 50
  length of, 47

quality of work comments in, 50
reference works of, 164
summary of, 48
text of, 47–48
writing, 46–51
Books, 5
  bibliography citations for, 113
  footnotes for, 104–106
Boolean searches, 26
Boyd, Kelly, 147
Brainstorming, 18
Braudel, Fernand, 9
Brigham, Clarence S., 139
Brill's New Pauly: Encyclopaedia of the
  Ancient World: Antiquity (Hubert
  Canick and Helmut Schneider),
  146
Britannica Book of the Year, 153
British and Foreign State Papers (Great
  Britain, Foreign Office), 158
British Diaries: An Annotated Biblio-
  graphy of British Diaries Written
  Between 1442 and 1942 (William
  Matthews), 136
British Historical Statistics (B. R.
  Mitchell), 149
British Museum, Department of
  Printed Books, 139
Burnham, W. Dean, 148
Burns, Richard Dean, 144
Burton, Dennis A., 130
Butler, L. J., 126

C

Calendars, 31
Canada:
  abstract collections for, 36
  America: History and Life, 133
  American Newspapers 1821–1936:
    A Union List of Files Available in
    the United States and Canada, 140
  Bibliographies in History: An Index to
    Bibliographies in History Journals
    and Dissertations, 133
  book reviews related to, 36
  Directory of Historical Societies and
    Agencies in the United States and
    Canada, 162
  International Historical Statistics: The
    Americas, 1750–2000, 149
  National Archives, 29
  online journal articles/reviews, 28
  Subject Collections: A Guide to
    Special Book Collections and
    Subject Emphases as Reported by
    University, College, Public, and
    Special Libraries and Museums in
    the United States and Canada, 161
  Union List of Serials in Libraries of the
    United States and Canada, 140
Cancick, Hubert, 146
Cannistraro, Philip V., 142
Cappon, Lester J., 139–140
Carter, Susan, 149
Cartoons, evaluating, 64
Catalog of the Public Documents of the
  Congress and of All Departments of

the Government of the United
States (Superintendent of
Documents), 166
Catalogs, online, 25–27, 30
Cayton, Mary Kupiec, 143
Census data, 71
  Historical Census Browser, 148
  Statistical Abstract of the United
  States, 148–149
Center for History and New Media,
  George Mason University, 55
Central question (see Hypotheses)
Central Statistical Office, Great
  Britain, 150
Checklist of United States Public
  Documents 1789–1909, Congres-
  sional (Superintendent of
  Documents), 166
Chicago Manual of Style, The, 99, 103,
  104, 164
Choosing topics, 17–18
Chronological organization, 94–95
Ciment, James, 143
CIS Annual, 165
CIS U.S. Serial Set Index (Congres-
  sional Information Service), 165
Citation footnotes, 100
Civil War Unit Histories: Regimental
  Histories and Personal Narratives
  (Robert E. Lester and Gary
  Hoag), 158
Civilization of the Ancient Mediterra-
  nean: Greece and Rome (Michael
  Grant and Rachel Kitzinger),
  146
Clarity:
  of arguments, 122
  of writing, 87
"Clio's Neglected Tools: A
  Taxonomy of Reference Works
  for American History"
  (Lawrence B. de Graaf),
  126–127
CODOH (Committee for Open
  Debate on the Holocaust), 39
Collections:
  articles in, 107, 114
  tangible, 156–159
Columbia Companion to British History,
  The (Juliet Gardiner), 142
Columbia University Oral History
  Research Office, 164
Combined Retrospective Index to Book
  Reviews in Scholarly Journals
  (Evan Ira Farber), 162
Combined Retrospective Index to Journals
  in History, 36, 134–135
Commager, Henry S., 157
Committee for Open Debate on the
  Holocaust (CODOH), 39
Companion to Historiography (Michael
  Bentley), 146
Comparative history, 14, 15
Compilation of the Messages and Papers
  of the Presidents, A, 155
Complete Guide to Citing Government
  Information Resources, The: A
  Manual for Writers & Librarians
  (Diane L. Garner), 164

Complete Presidential Press Conferences
  of Franklin D. Roosevelt (Franklin
  D. Roosevelt), 158
Comprehensive Index to the Publications
  of the United States Government,
  1881–1893 (Department of the
  Interior, Division of
  Documents), 166
Concise writing, 87
Concluding sentences, 88
Conclusions:
  of essays, 95
  information in, 40–41
Confederate Research Sources: A Guide
  to Archives Collections (James C.
  Neagles), 129
Congress of the United States:
  Annals of Congress of the United
  States, The, 157
  Archive of Americana, 156
  Biographical Dictionary of the United
  States Congress, 1774-present, 151
  Catalog of the Public Documents of the
  Congress and of All Departments of
  the Government of the United
  States, 166
  Checklist of United States Public
  Documents 1789–1909, Congres-
  sional, 166
  CIS Annual, 165
  CIS U.S. Serial Set Index, 165
  The Congressional Globe, 157
  Congressional Proceedings, 157
  Congressional Quarterly Almanac,
  153
  Congressional Record: Proceedings and
  Debates of the Congress, 157
  GPO Access, 157
  A Guide to Research Collections of
  Former Members of the United
  States House of Representatives,
  131
  Guide to Research Collections of
  Former Senators, 1789–1995,
  131
  Guide to Research Collections of
  Former United States Senators,
  1789–1995, 130
  Guide to the Records of the United
  States House of Representatives at
  the National Archives, 1789–
  1989, 131
  The Historical Atlas of United States
  Congressional Districts, 1789–
  1983, 150
  Journals of the Continental Congress,
  1774–1789, 157
  LexisNexis Congressional, 166
  Members of Congress: A Bibliography,
  135
  Senators of the United States, 130
Congressional committees:
  bibliography citations for reports
  of, 115
  bibliography citations for
  testimony before, 114
  footnotes for reports of, 108
  footnotes for testimony before,
  108

Guide to the Records of the United
  States House of Representatives at
  the National Archives, 1789–
  1989, 131
Congressional debates:
  bibliography citations for, 115
  Congressional Record: Proceedings and
  Debates of the Congress, 157
  footnotes for, 108
  Register of Debates, 157
Congressional Globe, The, 157
Congressional Information Service,
  165
Congressional Proceedings, 157
Congressional Quarterly Almanac, 154
Congressional Record: Proceedings and
  Debates of the Congress, 157
Connelly, Owen, 142
Consensus view of history, 8
Context:
  historical, 4–6, 34–35, 41
  historiographical, 6, 35, 42–45
Conversation, writing as, 15
Cook, Bernard, 141–142
Cooke, Jacob Ernest, 143
Correspondence:
  Aristocracy, the State, and the Local
  Community, The [1477–1828]:
  The Hastings Collection of Manu-
  scripts from the Huntington Library
  in California, 157
  footnotes for, 106
  as primary evidence, 66–68
Coulter, Edith M., 133
Court records, as primary evidence,
  69
Coutts, Brian E., 21–22
Critical reading, 39–41
Crosby, Everett U., 126
Crowley, Sean, 47–51
Cultural history, 12–14
  Encyclopedia of American Cultural &
  Intellectual History, 143
  Encyclopedia of Latin American
  History and Culture, 145
Curiosity, topics originating from,
  17–18
Current, Richard N., 143–144
Current Biography Yearbook, 152

D

Databases:
  ICPSR, 148
  library subscription, 156, 163
  online, 27–31
  public access, 154–156
  subject, 23–25
Datapedia of the United States, 1790–
  2000: America Year by Year
  (George Thomas Kurian), 148
de Graaf, Lawrence B., 126
"Death of an Ideal City, The:
  Rebuilding London After 1666"
  (Jack Sheehan), 168–184
  annotated bibliography of, 116
  bibliographic essay of, 117–120
  bibliography of, 23, 180–184

"Death of an Ideal City, The: Rebuilding London After 1666" (Jack Sheehan) (*continued*)
conclusion of, 40–41
first paragraph of, 85–86
footnotes of, 101–102, 111
and forms of writing, 93
interpretation of primary evidence in, 77–80
as narrative, 91
online resources for, 30
text of, 170–181
thesis of, 40
DeConde, Alexander, 144
Department of the Interior, Division of Documents, 166
Derrida, Jacques, 12
Description, 91–92
Descriptive Catalogue of the Government Publications of the United States, A (Benjamin P. Poore), 166
Dewald, Jonathan, 142
Dewey, John, 7
DeWitt, Donald L., 127, 160
Diaries:
  American Diaries: An Annotated Bibliography of Published American Diaries and Journals, 134
  British Diaries: An Annotated Bibliography of British Diaries Written Between 1442 and 1942, 136
  In the First Person: Index to Letters, Diaries, Oral Histories and Other Personal Narratives, 164
  as primary evidence, 68
  Southern Women and Their Families in the 19th Century, Papers and Diaries, 159
Dictionaries, 34, 141–146
Dictionary of American Biography, 152
Dictionary of American History (Stanley I. Kutler), 144–145
Dictionary of Concepts in History (Harry Ritter), 147
Dictionary of Historic Documents (George Childs Kohn), 146
Dictionary of National Biography (Leslie Stephen and Sidney Lee), 153
Dictionary of the Middle Ages (Joseph R. Strayer), 146
Dictionary of the Russian Revolution (George Jackson), 142
Diplomatic history, 13
Directories, 161–162
Directory of American Libraries with Genealogy or Local History Collections (P. W. Filby), 162
Directory of Archives and Manuscript Repositories in the United States (National Historical Publications and Records Commission), 160
Directory of Historical Societies and Agencies in the United States and Canada, 162
Directory of Oral History Collections (Allen Smith), 164
Dissertation Abstracts, 134–135
Document Catalog, 166

Documenting the American South, 30
Documents of American History (Henry S. Commager), 157
Douglass, David C., 157
Draft essays, 95–96
Draper, Lyman, 157
Draper Manuscripts, 157
Durkheim, Émile, 11

E

Early Encounters in North America, 158
"Early writing" stage, 82
EBSCO, 25
Echard, William E., 143
Economic history, 13
  Encyclopedia of American Economic History: Studies of the Principal Movements and Ideas, 145
  Encyclopedia of the Great Depression and the New Deal, 143
Economic Interpretation of the Constitution of the United States, An (Charles Beard), 8
Edited primary sources, 66
Edited works:
  bibliography citations for, 113
  footnotes for, 106
Editing, 90, 96–97
Editions (of books):
  in bibliography, 113
  specifying, 106
Editorials on File, 153
Editors as authors:
  bibliography citations for, 113
  footnotes for, 105
Electronic sources:
  bibliography citations for, 115
  footnotes for, 108–109
  (*See also* Online research)
E-mail messages:
  bibliography citations for, 115
  footnotes for, 108
Embree, Ainslie T., 146
Empire and colonialism, history of, 13
Encyclopedia Judaica, 146
Encyclopedia of African History (Kevin Shillington), 145
Encyclopedia of American Cultural & Intellectual History (Mary Kupiec Cayton and Peter W. Williams), 143
Encyclopedia of American Economic History: Studies of the Principal Movements and Ideas (Glenn Porter), 145
Encyclopedia of American Foreign Policy (DeConde, Burns, and Logevall), 144
Encyclopedia of American Political History: Studies of the Principal Movements and Ideas (Jack Greene), 144
Encyclopedia of American Social History (Cayton, Gorn, and Williams), 143
Encyclopedia of Asian History (Ainslie T. Embree), 145

Encyclopedia of Diderot and d'Alembert, The, 155
Encyclopedia of Eastern Europe from the Congress of Vienna to the Fall of Communism (Richard Frucht), 142
Encyclopedia of Historians and Historical Writing (Kelly Boyd), 147
Encyclopedia of Islam and the Muslim World (Richard C. Martin), 146
Encyclopedia of Latin American History and Culture (Barbara A. Tenenbaum), 145
Encyclopedia of Local History (Carol Kammen and Norma Prendergast), 144
Encyclopedia of Southern History, The (David C. Roller and Robert W. Twyman), 145
Encyclopedia of the American Civil War: A Political, Social and Military History (David S. and Jeanne T. Heidler), 144
Encyclopedia of the American Presidency (Leonard W. Levy and Louis Fisher), 145
Encyclopedia of the Confederacy (Richard N. Current), 143–144
Encyclopedia of the Great Depression and the New Deal (James Ciment), 143
Encyclopedia of the Holocaust (Israel Gutman), 142
Encyclopedia of the North American Colonies (Jacob Ernest Cooke), 143
Encyclopedia of the United States in the Nineteenth Century (Paul Finkelman), 144
Encyclopedia of U.S. Foreign Relations (Bruce W. Jentleson and Thomas G. Paterson), 144
Encyclopedia of World Environmental History (Shepard Krech III), 141
Encyclopedia of World History, The: Ancient, Medieval, and Modern Chronologically Arranged (Peter N. Stearns), 141
Encyclopedia of World History (William L. Langer), 142
Encyclopedias, 34, 141–147
Endnotes, checking, 122
England:
  English Historical Documents, 157
  Historical Dictionary of Stuart England, 143
  The History of London in Maps, 149
  Records of an English Village, 155
English Historical Documents (David C. Douglass), 157
Essays:
  bibliographic, 53, 112, 116–120
  historiographic, 120–121
  requirements for producing, 15
  short informal, 83–84
  (*See also* Writing history)
EuroDocs: Primary Historical Documents from Western Europe, 155

Europe:
  dictionaries/encyclopedias/
    handbooks for, 141–143
  *Encyclopedia of Eastern Europe from
    the Congress of Vienna to the Fall
    of Communism,* 142
  Encyclopedia of the Holocaust, 142
  *EuroDocs: Primary Historical
    Documents from Western Europe,*
    155
  *Europe 1450 to 1789: Encyclopedia
    of the Early Modern World,* 142
  Europe Since 1945: An Encyclopedia,
    141–142
  The Harper Atlas of World History, 150
  Historical Atlas, 150
  *International Historical Statistics:
    Europe, 1750–2000,* 149
  *Medieval Studies: A Bibliographical
    Guide,* 126
  subject bibliographies for, 24
  World War II in Europe, 145
  (See also specific countries)
*Europe 1450 to 1789: Encyclopedia of
  the Early Modern World* (Jonathan
  Dewald), 142
Europe Since 1945: An Encyclopedia
  (Bernard Cook), 141–142
Evaluation of sources:
  online, 38–39
  primary, 57–65
  secondary, 35–36, 44 *(See also*
    Reading of secondary sources)
"Everyman His Own Historian"
  (Carl Becker), 8
Evidence:
  cherry-picking of, 11
  discerning patterns from, 10
  limited, 3
  misuse of, 2
  primary, 6 *(See also* Primary
    sources/evidence)
  testing, 5
  testing hypotheses against, 10–11
  testing theories against, 45
Expanded Academic ASAP, 135
Expert opinions, relying on, 46
Explanatory footnotes, 100, 111

F

Facts on File Yearbook, 153
Farber, Evan Ira, 162
Febvre, Lucien, 9
Filby, P. W., 162
Filby, P. William, 135
Films, evaluating, 64–65
Finkelman, Paul, 145
First draft, 95–96
First paragraph (of a paper), 84–87
Fisher, Louis, 146
Footnotes, 99–111
  approaches to, 101–103
  for books, 104–106
  checking, 122
  citation, 100
  for electronic sources, 108–109
  explanatory, 100, 111

  for government publications,
    107–108
  historiographic, 45–46, 85–86,
    100–101, 110
  for indirect sources (quoted in), 110
  for interviews, 109
  for manuscript collections, 109
  and plagiarism, 103
  purposes of, 100
  and quality of source, 37–38
  style formats for, 103–110
  types of, 100–101
  for unpublished dissertations/
    theses, 109
  for videos, 109
Ford, P., 127
*Foreign Affairs Bibliography: A Selected
  and Annotated List of Books on
  International Relations,* 135
Foreign relations:
  *American Foreign Relations Since
    1600,* 126
  *A Bibliography of United States—Latin
    American Relations Since 1810,* 137
  British and Foreign State Papers, 158
  *Encyclopedia of American Foreign
    Policy,* 144
  *Encyclopedia of U.S. Foreign
    Relations,* 144
  *Foreign Affairs Bibliography: A
    Selected and Annotated List of
    Books on International Relations,*
    135
  *Treaties and Other International
    Agreements of the United States of
    America, 1776–1949,* 160
  *U.S. Foreign Relations A Guide to
    Information Sources,* 130
Foucault, Michel, 12
France:
  *Archives Parlementaires de 1787 à
    1860: Recueil Complet des Débats
    Législatifs & Politiques,* 157
  *Bibliographie Annuelle de l'Histoire de
    France du Cinquième Siècle à
    1958,* 134
  *Historical Dictionaries of French
    History,* 142
  *Historical Dictionary of France from
    the 1815 Restoration to the Second
    Empire,* 142
  *Historical Dictionary of Napoleonic
    France, 1799–1815,* 142
  *Historical Dictionary of the French
    Second Empire, 1852–1870,* 142
Friedel, Frank B., 135
Fritze, Ronald H., 21–22, 127, 143
*From Memory to History: Using Oral
  Sources in Local Historical Research*
  (Barbara Allen and William
  Lynwood Montell), 164
Frucht, Richard, 142

G

*Gallup Poll, The: The Public Opinion
  1935–1997,* 163
Gallup Poll Tuesday Briefing, 163
Garner, Bryan A., 161

Geertz, Clifford, 11–12
Gender historians, 45
*General Catalogue of Printed Books to
  1944* (British Museum,
  Department of Printed Books),
  139
Geostat Center, 71
German History Sources, 155
Germany:
  Encyclopedia of the Holocaust, 142
  German History Sources, 155
Global Books in Print, 139
*Global Encyclopedia of Historical
  Writing, A* (D. R. Woolf), 147
Global history, 14
*Gorbachev Bibliography, The, 1985–
  1991: A Listing of Books and
  Articles in English on Perestroika in
  the USSR* (Joseph L.
  Wieczynski), 138
Gorn, Elliott J., 143
Government documents/
  publications:
  bibliography citations for, 114–115
  *The Complete Guide to Citing Gov-
    ernment Information Resources: A
    Manual for Writers & Librarians,* 166
  footnotes for, 107–108
  *Government Publications and Their
    Use,* 130
  indexes of, 165–166
  *Introduction to United States Govern-
    ment Information Sources,* 129
  *Monthly Catalog of United States
    Government Publications,* 166
  as primary sources/evidence,
    68–69
  *Using Government Information
    Sources: Electronic and Print,* 130
*Government Publications and Their
  Use* (Laurence F. Schmeckebier),
  130
GPO Access, 159
GPO Monthly Catalog, 165
Grammar, 121
Grant, Michael, 146
Great Britain:
  Atlas of the British Empire, 150
  Bibliography of British History, 134
  British and Foreign State Papers, 158
  *British Diaries: An Annotated Bib-
    liography of British Diaries Written
    Between 1442 and 1942,* 136
  British Historical Statistics, 149
  *The Columbia Companion to British
    History,* 142
  Dictionary of National Biography, 153
  *General Catalogue of Printed Books to
    1944,* 138
  *A Guide to British Documents and
    Records in the University of
    Virginia Library,* 132
  *A Guide to the Sources of British
    Military History,* 127
  *Historic Town: Maps and Plans of
    Towns and Cities in the British
    Isles, With Historic Commentaries
    From Earliest Times to 1800,* 150
  Modern British History, 126

Great Britain (*continued*)
 Reader's Guide to British History, 128
 *The Royal Historical Society Biblio-
  graphy*, 137
 Statistical Digest of the War, 149
 Times Digital Archive, 156
 *Women's Journals of the 19th century,
  Part 1, The* Women's Penny
  Paper *and* Woman's Herald,
  1888–1893, 159
 (*See also* England)
*Great Historians of the Modern Age: An
 International Dictionary* (Lucian
 Bola), 147
Greece:
 *Barrington Atlas of the Greek and
  Roman World*, 150
 *Civilization of the Ancient Mediter-
  ranean: Greece and Rome*, 146
Griffin, Appleton P. C., 135
*Guide to Archives and Manuscripts in the
 United States, A* (Philip M.
 Hamer), 159
*Guide to British Documents and Records
 in the University of Virginia
 Library, A* (Sharon Vandercook),
 132
Guide to Historical Literature (American
 Historical Association), 23, 25
*Guide to Manuscripts in the Presidential
 Libraries, A* (Dennis A. Burton),
 129
*Guide to Parliamentary Papers, A: What
 They Are, How to Find Them,
 How to Use Them* (P. Ford), 127
*Guide to Pre-Federal Records in the
 National Archives, A* (National
 Archives and Records Service),
 131–132
*Guide to Records in the National
 Archives of the United States
 Relating to American Indians*
 (Edward E. Hill), 128
Guide to Reference Books (Robert
 Balay), 22, 126
*Guide to Research Collections of Former
 Members of the United States
 House of Representatives, A*, 131
*Guide to Research Collections of Former
 Senators, 1789–1995*, 131
*Guide to Research Collections of Former
 United States Senators, 1789–
 1995: A Listing of Archival
 Repositories Housing the Papers of
 Former Senators, Related
 Collections, and Oral History
 Interviews*, 130
*Guide to the Federal Records in the
 National Archives of the United
 States* (National Archives and
 Records Service), 160
*Guide to the Records of the United States
 House of Representatives at the
 National Archives, 1789–1989*
 (National Archives and Records
 Administration), 131
*Guide to the Sources of British Military
 History, A* (Robin D. Higham),
 127

*Guide to the Study of the United States
 of America, A*, 138
*Guide to the Study of United States
 History Outside the U.S.,
 1945–1980* (Lewis Hanke), 127
*Guide to the United States Treaties in
 Force, A* (Igor I. Kavass), 159
Guides:
 to historical literature, 126–132
 to reference books/bibliographies
  of bibliographies, 22–23
 standard, 21–22
*Guides to Archives and Manuscript
 Collections in the United States: An
 Annotated Bibliography* (Donald
 L. DeWitt), 127

H

Halsall, Paul, 155
Hamer, Philip M., 159
*Handbook for Research in American
 History: A Guide to Bibliographies
 and Other Reference Works*
 (Francis P. Prucha), 130
Handbook of Latin American Studies,
 136
Handbooks, 141–146
Hanke, Lewis, 127
Hardy, Lyda M., 127
Harper Atlas of World History, The, 150
Harper's Weekly, 72
Harrison, Brian, 152
Hartz, Louis, 8
Harvard Guide to American History
 (Frank B. Friedel), 135
Havlice, Patricia P., 164
Hefner, Loretta, 127
Hegel, Georg Wilhelm Friedrich, 7
Hessenbruch, Arne, 127
Higham, Robin, 128
Hill, Edward E., 128
*Historian's Toolbox, The: A Student's
 Guide to the Theory and Craft of
 History* (Robert C. Williams),
 147
Historic Documents, 156
*Historic Town: Maps and Plans of Towns
 and Cities in the British Isles, With
 Historic Commentaries From
 Earliest Times to 1800* (M. D.
 Lobel), 150
Historical Abstracts, 28, 36, 136
Historical Atlas (William R. Shepherd),
 150
*Historical Atlas of United States
 Congressional Districts, The,
 1789–1983* (Kenneth C.
 Martis), 150
Historical atlases, 149–151
*Historical Bibliographies: A Systematic
 and Annotated Guide* (Edith M.
 Coulter), 133
Historical Census Browser, 148
Historical context:
 defined, 34
 as imperative in study of past, 4
 reading of secondary sources for, 41

from secondary sources, 5–6,
  34–35
Historical dictionaries, 34, 141–146
Historical Dictionaries of French History
 series, 142
Historical Dictionary of Fascist Italy
 (Philip V. Cannistraro), 142
*Historical Dictionary of France from the
 1815 Restoration to the Second
 Empire* (Edgar Leon Newman),
 142
Historical Dictionary of Modern Spain
 (Robert W. Kern), 143
*Historical Dictionary of Napoleonic
 France, 1799–1815* (Owen
 Connelly), 142
Historical Dictionary of Stuart England
 (Ronald H. Fritze), 143
*Historical Dictionary of the French
 Second Empire, 1852–1870*
 (William E. Echard), 142
Historical interest, topics originating
 in, 18
Historical knowledge, limits on, 2–4
Historical literature, guides to,
 126–132
Historical periodization, 14–15
*Historical Statistics of the United States:
 Earliest Times to the Present* (Susan
 Carter), 148
Historical writing:
 following World War II, 8
 history of, 6–10
 (*See also* Writing history)
Historicism, 3–4, 7
Historiographic essays, 120–121
Historiographic footnotes, 45–46,
 85–86, 100–101, 110
Historiographical context:
 reading of secondary sources for,
  42–45
 from secondary sources, 6, 35
Historiography:
 Companion to Historiography, 146
 defined, 6, 35, 120
 Dictionary of Concepts in History, 147
 *Encyclopedia of Historians and His-
  torical Writing*, 147
 *A Global Encyclopedia of Historical
  Writing*, 147
 *Great Historians of the Modern Age:
  An International Dictionary*, 147
 *The Historian's Toolbox: A Student's
  Guide to the Theory and Craft of
  History*, 147
 *Historiography: An Annotated Bib-
  liography of Journal Articles, Books,
  and Dissertations*, 147
 importance of understanding, 6
 Marxist, 8–9
 reference works for, 147–148
 *The Study of History: A Bibliogra-
  phical Guide*, 147
*Historiography: An Annotated Biblio-
 graphy of Journal Articles, Books,
 and Dissertations* (Susan K.
 Kinnell), 147
History, 1–15
 ahistorical perspectives of, 4

approaches to, 3–4, 14–15
defined, 1
of historical writing, 6–10
hypotheses in study of, 10–11
as interpretation, 1, 2, 6–10, 42
and limits on knowledge of past, 2–4
misuse of, 2
point of view in, 4–5
primary sources of, 6
public's image of, 10
requirements for producing essays on, 15
secondary sources of, 5–6
types of, 13–14
use of theory in study of, 11–12
History and Bibliography of American Newspapers 1690–1820 (Clarence S. Brigham), 139
History Matters, 30
History of London in Maps, The (Felix Barker), 150
H-Net Online Reviews, 32
Hoag, Gary, 159
Hobsbawm, Eric J., 44
Hofstadter, Richard, 8
How to Research Elections (Fenton S. Martin), 128
How to Research the Supreme Court (Fenton S. Martin), 128–129
Humanities Index, 27–28
Hypotheses, 10–11
testing evidence against, 5
theories in development of, 11–12

I

ICPSR, 148
Imagination, topics originating in, 18
Immigration:
    The Immigration History Research Center: A Guide to Collections, 129
    Voices from Ellis Island, 159
    We the People: An Atlas of America's Ethnic Diversity, 149
In the First Person: Index to Letters, Diaries, Oral Histories and Other Personal Narratives, 164
Index Africanus (J. O. Asamani), 134
Index Islamicus, 136
Index to U.S. Government Periodicals, 165–166
Index-Guide to the Southern Historical Society Papers, An, 159
Indexing and abstracting services, 133–138
Indirect sources (quoted in), footnotes for, 110
Intellectual history, 13
    Encyclopedia of American Cultural & Intellectual History, 143
Intended audiences, 58–59
Intentional sources, 57
Interlibrary loan services, 26
International Historical Statistics: Africa, Asia & Oceania, 1750–2000 (B. R. Mitchell), 149

International Historical Statistics: Europe, 1750–2000 (B. R. Mitchell), 150
International Historical Statistics: The Americas, 1750–2000 (B. R. Mitchell), 150
Internet:
    information access via, 56
    quality of resources on, 38 (*See also* Online research)
Internet History Sourcebooks Project, 30, 156
Interpretation, 92–93
    in historical writing, 82
    history as, 1, 2, 6–10, 42 (*See also* Historiographical context; Historiography)
    latitude in, 43
Interviews:
    bibliography citations for, 116
    evaluating, 62–63
    footnotes for, 109
    as primary evidence, 72–73
Introduction to Ancient History (Hermann Gengtson), 126
Introduction to United States Government Information Sources (Joe Morehead), 129
Introductions:
    in essays, 94
    information in, 40, 44
Inventories, as primary sources/evidence, 69, 70
Islamic countries:
    Encyclopedia of Islam and the Muslim World, 147
    Index Islamicus, 136
Israel, Fred L., 159
Italy:
    Barrington Atlas of the Greek and Roman World, 152
    Civilization of the Ancient Mediterranean: Greece and Rome, 147
    Historical Dictionary of Fascist Italy, 143

J

Jackson, George, 143
Japan Through Western Eyes, 156
Jentleson, Bruce W., 144
Jewish studies:
    Encyclopedia Judaica, 146
Journal articles
    Bibliographies in History: An Index to Bibliographies in History Journals and Dissertations, 133
    bibliography citations for, 114
    Expanded Academic ASAP, 135
    footnotes for, 106–107
    Index Africanus, 134
    Index to U.S. Government Periodicals, 165–166
    knowledge of journals printing, 32
    online databases of, 27–28
    online text of, 27–28
    peer-reviewed, 27, 37
Journal of American History, 136

Journal Storage Project (JSTOR), 28, 162
Journals of the Continental Congress, 1774–1789, 157
JSTOR (*see* Journal Storage Project)

K

Kammen, Carol, 144
Kane, Joseph Nathan, 144
Kavass, Igor I., 160
Keesing's Record of World Events, 153
Kern, Robert W., 143
Kesaris, Paul, 159
Keyword searches, 25–26
Kinnell, Susan K., 147
Kitzinger, Rachel, 146
Knowledge, limits on, 2–4
Kohn, George Childs, 146
Krech, Shepard, III, 141
Kuhn, Thomas, 10
Kurian, George Thomas, 148

L

Labor History Archives in the United States: A Guide for Researching and Teaching (Daniel J. Leab), 128
Language:
    of primary evidence, 60–61
    use of, in writing, 88–89
Larned, Josephus N., 136
Larsen, John C., 128
Lathrop, J. M., 150
Latin America:
    A Bibliography of United States—Latin American Relations Since 1810, 137
    Encyclopedia of Latin American History and Culture, 145
    Handbook of Latin American Studies, 136
    International Historical Statistics: The Americas, 1750–2000, 149
    subject bibliographies for, 24
Law(s):
    as primary evidence, 69
    reference works for, 161
Leab, Daniel J., 128
Lee, Lloyd, 136
Legacy of Conquest (Patricia Nelson Limerick), 43
Legal Information: How to Find It, How to Use It (Kent C. Olson), 161
Lester, Robert E., 158
Levy, Leonard W., 145
LexisNexis Academic, 163
LexisNexis Congressional, 166
LexisNexis Government Periodicals Index, 166
LibDex, 25
Liberal Tradition in America, The (Louis Hartz), 8
Library catalogs:
    finding primary sources in, 154–156
    online, 25–27, 30
    WorldCat, 139

Library of American Civilization or, The Microbook Library of American Civilization, 158
Library of Congress, The: A Guide to Genealogical and Historical Research (James C. Neagles), 129
Library subscription databases, 156, 163
Limerick, Patricia Nelson, 43
Limits:
of evidence, 3
on knowledge of past, 2–4
Lincove, David A., 136
Linguistic turn, 12, 44–45
Listserv messages:
bibliography citations for, 115
footnotes for, 108
Literature of American History, The: A Bibliographical Guide (Josephus N. Larned), 136
Literature review (*see* Reading of secondary sources)
Literature search (*see* Research trail)
Loades, David, 128
Lobel, M. D., 151
Local history, 14
An Atlas of Rockingham County, Virginia, An: From Actual Surveys, 150
American Counties, The Origins of Names, Dates of Creation and Organization, Area, Population, Historical Data, and Published Sources, 144
A Bibliography of American County Histories, 135
Directory of American Libraries with Genealogy or Local History Collections, 162
Encyclopedia of Local History, 144
Historic Town: Maps and Plans of Towns and Cities in the British Isles, With Historic Commentaries From Earliest Times to 1800, 150
From Memory to History: Using Oral Sources in Local Historical Research, 164
Rockingham: An Annotated Bibliography of a Virginia County, 137
United States Local Histories in the Library of Congress: A Bibliography, 138
Locating sources (*see* Research trail)
Logevall, Frederick, 144
London Gazette, 30
London Times, 156

M

Major Peace Treaties of Modern History, 1648–1967 (Fred L. Israel), 158
Making of the English Working Class, The (Edward P. Thompson), 8–9
Manual for Writers of Term Papers, Theses, and Dissertations, A (Kate L. Turabian), 99, 103–104, 166–167

Manuscript collections:
bibliography citations for, 116
footnotes for, 109
guides to, 159–160
Guides to Archives and Manuscript Collections in the United States, 127
Special Collections in the Library of Congress: A Selective Guide, 131
Maps, as primary sources/evidence, 74–76
Martin, Fenton S., 128–129
Martin, Richard C., 146
Martis, Kenneth C., 150
Marx, Karl, 7, 11
Marxism, 8–11, 44
Matthew, H. C. G., 152
Matthews, William, 136
McNeill, William H., 141
Meckler, Alan M., 164
Medieval Studies: A Bibliographical Guide (Everett U. Crosby), 126
Members of Congress: A Bibliography (Robert U. Goehlert), 135
Memoirs, as primary sources/ evidence, 68
Memory, popular, 2
Meyer, Michael, 137
Microform collections, 31
Middle Ages:
Dictionary of the Middle Ages, 146
Middle East:
Encyclopedia of Islam and the Muslim World, 146
Index Islamicus, 136
subject bibliographies for, 24–25
Military history, 13
The American Revolution in Context, 156
Archives Parlementaires de 1787 à 1860: Recueil Complet des Débats Législatifs & Politiques, 157
Blacks in the United States Armed Forces, 158
Civil War Unit Histories: Regimental Histories and Personal Narratives, 158
Encyclopedia of the American Civil War: A Political, Social and Military History, 144
A Guide to the Sources of British Military History, 127
Researching World War I: A Handbook, 128
Southern Historical Society Papers, 159
Statistical Digest of the War, 149
Vietnam National Security Council Histories, 158
The War of the Rebellion: A Compilation of the Official Records of the Union and Confederate Armies, 155–156
The West Point Atlas of American Wars, 151
World War II in Europe, Africa, and the Americas, with General Sources, 136

Miller, Gordon W., 137
Misuse of history, 2
Mitchell, B. R., 149
Mitchell, Darci, 110
Modern British History A Guide to Study and Research (L. J. Butler), 126
Modernization theory, 11
Money, comparing values of, 31–32
Monographs, 5, 34 (*See also* Books)
Montell, William Lynwood, 164
Monthly Catalog of United States Government Publications, 166
Moody, Marilyn K., 131
Moody, Suzanna, 129
Morehead, Joe, 129
Muccigrosso, Robert, 129, 152
Multilateral treaties, 159
Multilaterals Project of The Fletcher School, Tufts University, 161
Multiple-citation footnotes, 101–103
Multivolume works:
bibliography citations for, 113
footnotes for, 106

N

Napoleonica.org, 155
NARA (*see* National Archives and Records Adminstration)
Narration (in writing), 90–92
Narrative:
In the First Person: Index to Letters, Diaries, Oral Histories and Other Personal Narratives, 164
perception of history as, 6
Narrowing topics, 18
Nast, Thomas, 64
National Archives and Records Administration (NARA), 29, 130
National Archives and Records Service, 130–131, 161
National Archives of Canada/ Archives nationales du Canada, 29
National bibliographies and verification sources, 138–139
National Cyclopedia of American Biography, The, 152
National Historical Publications and Records Commission, 160
National history, 14
National Union Catalog of Manuscript Collections, The, 159
National Union Catalog Pre-56 Imprints, The (NUC), 139
Nazi Era, The, 1919–1945: A Select Bibliography of Published Works from the Early Roots to 1980, 137
Neagles, James C., 129
New International Year Book, The, 153
New Left view of history, 9, 10
New Serials Titles: A Union List of Serials Commencing Publication After December 31, 1949, 140
New York Times: Historical, 153
New York Times Obituary Index, The, 153

Newman, Debra L., 129–130
Newman, Edgar Leon, 142
Newman, Richard, 133
Newsgroup messages:
  bibliography citations for, 115
  footnotes for, 108
*Newspaper Indexes: A Location and
  Subject Guide for Researchers*
  (Anita C. Milner), 140
Newspapers:
  *American Newspapers 1821–1936:
  A Union List of Files Available in
  the United States and Canada,*
  140
  Archive of Americana, 156
  bibliography citations for articles
  in, 114
  citing articles from, 107
  Editorials on File, 153
  *History and Bibliography of American
  Newspapers 1690–1820,* 139
  New York Times: Historical, 153
  *Newspaper Indexes: A Location and
  Subject Guide for Researchers,*
  140
  *Newspapers in Microform: Foreign
  Countries, 1948–1983,* 141
  as primary sources/evidence, 72
  reference works for, 139–141
  Schomburg Center Clipping File,
  159
  United States Newspaper Program,
  141
  Virginia Newspapers 1821–1935,
  139
  *Newspapers in Microform: Foreign
  Countries, 1948–1983,* 141
Nonfiction narrative, history as, 10
Nonhistorical perspectives, 4
Norton, Mary B., 137
Notes on sources:
  bibliographic note cards, 51–55
  developing method for, 21
  (*See also* Footnotes)
Note-taking software, 55
*NUC (The National Union Catalog
  Pre-56 Imprints),* 139

O

Objectivity, 5
Oceania:
  *International Historical Statistics:
  Africa, Asia & Oceania, 1750–
  2000,* 149
OED (*Oxford English Dictionary*), 31
Official Records (OR), 155–156
Old Bailey proceedings, 69
Olson, Kent C., 161
On the Structure of Scientific Revolutions
  (Thomas Kuhn), 10
*Online! A Reference Guide to Using
  Internet Sources,* 164
Online research:
  book review sites, 36
  for correspondence, 67
  databases and catalogs, 25–28
  evaluation of sources, 38–39

  listservs for, 32
  *Online! A Reference Guide to Using
  Internet Sources,* 164–165
  for primary/secondary sources,
  28–31
  printed, 34
  and review of printed materials, 25
  text of journal articles, 28
Opening paragraph (of a paper),
  84–87
OR (*Official Records*), 155–156
*Oral History: A Reference Guide and
  Annotated Bibliography* (Patricia P.
  Havlice), 164
Oral history, reference works for,
  164
*Oral History Collection of Columbia
  University, The* (Columbia
  University Oral History
  Research Office), 164
Oral History Collections (Alan M.
  Meckler), 164
*Oral History Index: An International
  Directory of Oral History
  Interviews,* 164
Oral presentations of work, 97–98
Oral primary evidence:
  evaluating, 62–63
  interviews, 72–73
Organization (in writing), 88, 93–95
Oxford Dictionary of National Biography
  (H. C. G. Matthew and Brian
  Harrison), 152
Oxford English Dictionary (OED), 31

P

Page numbering, 122
Paintings:
  evaluating, 63
  as primary evidence, 73–74
PAIS International, 165
Palacký, František, 7
PAO (see Periodical Archive Online)
Papers of Albert Gallatin, The, 158
Paragraphs, 88
Parallel construction (in writing), 89
Past:
  historians' views of, 7–10
  limits on knowledge of, 2–4
Paterson, Thomas G., 144
Paullin, Charles O., 150
Peer review:
  for beginning researchers, 83
  process of, 37
Peer-reviewed journals, 27
Periodic Index Online (PIO), 27
Periodical Archive Online (PAO), 27, 28
Periodicals:
  Index to U.S. Government Periodicals,
  165–166
  *LexisNexis Government Periodicals
  Index,* 166
  *New Serials Titles: A Union List of
  Serials Commencing Publication
  After December 31, 1949,* 140
  as primary sources/evidence, 72
  reference works for, 139–141

  Schomburg Center Clipping File, 160
  The Serials Directory, 140
  The Standard Periodical Directory,
  140
  *Ulrichsweb.com Ulrich's international
  periodicals directory,* 140
  *Union List of Serials in Libraries of the
  United States and Canada,* 141
Periodization, historical, 14–15
Personal correspondence, 66–68
  *In the First Person: Index to Letters,
  Diaries, Oral Histories and Other
  Personal Narratives,* 164
*Personal Papers of Supreme Court
  Justices, The: Descriptive Guide*
  (Alexandra K. Wigdor), 132
Perspectives, ahistorical, 4
Persuasion, 93
Philosophy of history, 7
Photographs:
  evaluating, 63
  as primary sources/evidence,
  73–74
Physical primary evidence:
  artifacts, 76–77
  evaluating, 65
PIO (Periodic Index Online), 27
Plagiarism, 55, 103
Plischke, Elmer
Point of view, 4–5
  in primary evidence, 58
  understanding, 44
Political history, 13
  *Encyclopedia of American Political
  History: Studies of the Principal
  Movements and Ideas,* 144
  *Encyclopedia of the American Civil
  War: A Political, Social and
  Military History,* 144
Poole, William Frederick, 137
Poole's Index to Periodical Literature
  (William Frederick Poole), 137
Poore, Benjamin P., 168
Popular magazines, articles in:
  bibliography citations for, 114
  footnotes for, 107
Popular memory, 2
Porter, Glenn, 145
Positivism, 3, 7
Positivists, 3
Postmodern theory, 10, 12
Precise word choice, 89
Prefaces, information in, 40, 44
Preliminary reviews of secondary
  sources, 36–38
Prendergast, Norma, 144
Presentism, 4, 42
Presidential Ballots, 1836–1892
  (W. Dean Burnham), 148
Presidential Elections Since 1789, 148
Presidential Libraries and Collections
  (Fritz Veit), 130
Presidential papers:
  bibliography citations for, 114
  *A Compilation of the Messages and
  Papers of the Presidents,* 155
  footnotes for, 107
  *A Guide to Manuscripts in the
  Presidential Libraries,* 130

Presidential papers (*continued*)
  Presidential Libraries and Collections, 130
  Public Papers of the Presidents of the United States, 158
  Records of the Presidency: Presidential Papers and Libraries from Washington to Reagan, 130
  Weekly Compilation of Presidential Documents, 156
Presidential Vote, The, 1986–1932 (Edgar E. Robinson), 148
Primary sources/evidence, 56–80
  access to, 56
  artifacts, 76–77
  autobiographies, 68
  correspondence, 66–68
  defined, 57
  diaries, 68
  edited, 66
  evaluating, 57–65
  footnoting, 100
  government documents, 68–69
  identifying, 56
  intentional vs. unintentional, 57
  inventories, 69, 70
  in library catalogs, 155–161
  maps, 74–76
  memoirs, 68
  microform collections of, 31
  newspapers, 72
  online, 28–31, 56
  oral, 62–63, 72–73
  periodicals, 72
  photographs, 73–74
  physical, evaluating, 65
  published, 66
  secondary sources based on, 34
  selected, 66
  statistical records, 71
  in student paper example, 77–80
  unpublished, 66
  visual, evaluating, 63–65
  wills, 69–71
  written, evaluating, 57–62
Problems of historical inquiry, 4–5
Progressive school, 7–8
Project Muse, 28
Proofreading, 90, 121
Prospectus, 18–20, 82–83
Protestant Ethic and the Spirit of Capitalism, The (Max Weber), 11
Prucha, Francis, 130
Public access databases, 156–157
Public history, 14
Public opinion sources, reference works for, 164–165
Public Papers of the Presidents of the United States, 158
Published correspondence:
  bibliography citations for, 113
  footnotes for, 106
Published primary sources, 66
Punctuation, 90
Purpose:
  of primary evidence, 59–60
  in writing, 82

Q

Quatannens, Jo Anne, 130
Quotations, 89–90
  block-indented, 103
  footnoting, 101

R

Ranke, Leopold von, 7
Reader's Guide to British History (David Loades), 128
Reader's Guide to the History of Science (Arne Hessenbruch), 127
Reading of secondary sources, 39–46
  critical, 39–41
  for historical context, 6, 41
  for historiographical context, 42–45
  for sources used, 45–46
  as wise starting point for analysis, 33
Reconstruction in the United States: An Annotated Bibliography (David A. Lincove), 136
Records of an English Village, 155
Records of Ante-bellum Southern Plantations from the Revolution to the Civil War (Kenneth Stampp), 159
Records of Earls Colne, The, 30
Records of the Confederate States of America, 158
Records of the Presidency: Presidential Papers and Libraries from Washington to Reagan (Frank L. Schick), 130
Reference Sources in History: An Introductory Guide (Fritze, Coutts, and Vyhnanek), 21–22, 127
Reference works, 125–167
  abstracts of, 36
  annuals, 153–154
  availability of, 31–32
  bibliographies of bibliographies, 132–133
  bibliographies/indexing and abstracting services, 133–138
  biography, 151–153
  book reviews, 162–163
  dictionaries, 141–146
  directories, 141–146
  encyclopedias, 142–143
  government document indexes, 165–166
  guides to, 22–23
  guides to historical literature, 126–132
  handbooks, 141–146
  handouts on historical topics (JMU), 167
  historical atlases, 149–151
  historiography, 146–151
  law, 161
  manuscript guides, 159–160
  national bibliographies and verification sources, 138–139
  newspaper/periodical sources, 139–141
  oral history, 164

  primary sources, 154–159
  public opinion sources, 163
  speeches, 163–164
  statistical sources and tables, 147–149
  style manuals, 164–165
  treaties, 160–161
  yearbooks, 153–154
Regional history, 14
  The Encyclopedia of Southern History, 145
  Records of Ante-bellum Southern Plantations from the Revolution to the Civil War, 159
  Researcher's Guide to Archives and Regional Sources, 128
  Southern Women and Their Families in the 19th Century, Papers and Diaries, 159
  Virginia Historical Index, 137
Register of Debates, 157
Relativism, 10
Religious history, 13
  Encyclopedia Judaica, 146
  Encyclopedia of Islam and the Muslim World, 146
  Index Islamicus, 136
Representative American Speeches, 164
Research:
  after first draft is done, 96
  online (*see* Online research)
  time spent in writing vs., 81
Research Guide to American Historical Biography (Robert Muccigrosso), 152
Research trail, 20–32
  basic guides to reference books, 22–23
  beginning scholarly analysis with, 33
  bibliographies of bibliographies, 22–23
  defined, 20
  information-recording process for, 21
  purposes of, 20–21
  reference sources available for use, 31–32
  research databases/online catalogs, 25–28
  scholarly journals in area of interest, 32
  standard guides, 21–22
  standard subject bibliographies/databases, 23–25
  websites/digitized databases for sources, 28–31
  (*See also* Reference works)
Researcher's Guide to Archives and Regional Sources (John C. Larsen), 128
Researching World War I: A Handbook (Robin Higham), 128
Reviews:
  book, 36
  by peers, 27, 37
  of possible secondary sources, 36–38
  reliance on, 46

Reviews in American History, 162
Revision of writing, 96–97
Richards, Michael D., 130
Richardson, R. C., 147
Ritter, Harry, 147
Robinson, Edgar E., 148
Robinson, James Harvey, 7, 8
Rockingham: An Annotated Bibliography of a Virginia County (Gordon W. Miller), 137
Roller, David C., 145
Romantic Movement, 7
Rome:
　Barrington Atlas of the Greek and Roman World, 150
　Civilization of the Ancient Mediterranean: Greece and Rome, 146
Roosevelt, Franklin D., 158
Royal Historical Society Bibliography, The, 137
Run-on sentences, 88
Russia:
　Dictionary of the Russian Revolution, 142

S

Scammon, Richard M., 148
Schick, Frank L., 130
Schmeckebier, Laurence F., 130–131
Schneider, Helmut, 146
Scholarly articles, 5, 34 (*See also* Journal articles)
Scholarly presses/journals, 37
　Combined Retrospective Index to Book Reviews in Scholarly Journals, 162
　JSTOR, 162
Schomburg Center Clipping File, 159
Science, history of:
　Reader's Guide to the History of Science, 127
Scientific endeavor, history as, 3, 7
Scribe (software), 55
Search engines, 56
Sears, Jean L., 131
Secondary sources, 33–55
　annotated bibliography of, 51–55
　availability of, 33
　beginning scholarly analysis with, 33
　bibliographic note cards for, 51–55
　careful review of, 33–34
　defined, 5, 34
　evaluating online sources, 38–39
　evaluating usefulness of, 35–36
　footnoting, 100
　historical context provided by, 34–35
　historiographical context provided by, 35
　online, 28–31
　preliminary review of, 36–38

reading, 39–46
　types of, 34
　types of information in, 5–6
　writing review of, 46–51
Selected bibliographies, 111
Selected primary sources, 66
Senators of the United States, a Historical Bibliography: A Compilation of Works by and about Members of the United States Senate (Jo Anne Quatannens), 130
Sentence fragments, 88
Sentences, 88
Serials Directory, The, 140
Sheehan, Jack, 23, 30, 40–41, 45–46, 53, 77–80, 85–86, 91, 93, 101–102, 111, 116, 117–120, 168–184
Shepherd, William R., 150
Shillington, Kevin, 145
Short informal essays, 83–84
Short-title footnotes, 105
Significance of primary sources, 61–62
Single author books:
　bibliography citations for, 113
　footnotes for, 104–105
Skepticism, 10
Slavens, Thomas P., 131
Slocum, Robert B., 153
Smith, Allen, 164
Social history, 10, 13–14
　Encyclopedia of American Social History, 143
　Encyclopedia of the American Civil War: A Political, Social and Military History, 144
Social sciences:
　Social Sciences Index, 27–28
　Sources of Information in the Social Sciences: A Guide to the Literature, 132
Social scientific approach, 10
Software, note-taking, 55
Sources:
　intentional vs. unintentional, 57
　primary, 6 (*See also* Primary sources/evidence)
　search for (*see* Research trail)
　secondary, 5–6 (*See also* Secondary sources)
Sources of Information for Historical Research (Thomas P. Slavens), 131
Sources of Information in the Social Sciences: A Guide to the Literature (William H. Webb), 132
Southern Historical Society Papers, 159
Southern Women and Their Families in the 19th Century, Papers and Diaries, 159
Spain:
　Historical Dictionary of Modern Spain, 143
　Special Collections in the Library of Congress: A Selective Guide, 131

Speech Index: An Index to 259 Collections of World Famous Orations and Speeches for Various Occasions, 163
Speeches:
　as primary evidence, 69
　reference works for, 163
Stampp, Kenneth, 159
Standard bibliographies, 111
Standard guides, 21–22
Standard Periodical Directory, The, 140
Statistical Abstract of the United States (United States Bureau of the Census), 148
Statistical Digest of the War (Great Britain, Central Statistical Office), 149
Statistical sources and tables:
　as primary sources/evidence, 71
　reference works for, 147–149
Statistical Yearbook (United Nations), 149
Stearns, Peter N., 141
Strayer, Joseph R., 146
Study of History, The: A Bibliographical Guide (R. C. Richardson), 147
Style manuals:
　for footnote form, 103–110
　list of, 164–165
Subject bibliographies/databases, 23–25
Subject Collections: A Guide to Special Book Collections and Subject Emphases as Reported by University, College, Public, and Special Libraries and Museums in the United States and Canada (Lee Ash), 161
Subjectivity, 5
Summaries, 84
Superintendent of Documents, U.S., 166
Supreme Court:
　How to Research the Supreme Court, 128
　The Personal Papers of Supreme Court Justices: Descriptive Guide, 132
　The U.S. Supreme Court: A Bibliography, 129
Supreme Court decisions:
　bibliography citations for, 115
　footnotes for, 108
Swem, Earl G., 137

T

Tables (statistical), reference works for, 147–149
Talbert, Richard J. A., 150
Tangible collections, 156–159
Tax records, 71
Tenenbaum, Barbara A., 145
Term Paper Resource Guide to Twentieth-Century United States History (Robert Muccigrosso), 129

Term Paper Resource Guide to Twentieth-Century World History (Michael D. Richards), 130
Testimony before congressional committees:
  bibliography citations for, 114
  footnotes for, 108
Textbooks, 34
Thematic approach to history, 14, 15
Thematic organization, 94–95
Theory(-ies), 10, 11
  author's use of, 44–45
  postmodern, 10
  testing evidence against, 5, 45
Thesaurus, 88
Thesis, 11
  at prospectus stage, 19
  statement of, 40
They Voted for Roosevelt: The Presidential Vote, 1932–1944 (Edgar E. Robinson), 148
"Thick descriptions" of cultures, 12
Third person, writing in, 88–89
Thompson, Edward P., 8–9
Time periods, identification with, 14–15
Times Digital Archive, 158
Times History of the World, The (Geoffrey Barraclough), 149
Title page, 122
Tone of primary evidence, 60–61
"Top rail bias," 13
Topic sentences, 88
Topics:
  choosing, 17–18
  knowledge of journals related to, 32
Transcribing and Editing Oral History (Willa K. Baum), 164
Translated works citations, 106, 113
Trask, David F., 137
Treaties:
  Major Peace Treaties of Modern History, 1648–1967, 158
  reference works for, 160–161
Treaties and Other International Agreements of the United States of America, 1776–1949 (Charles I. Bevans), 160
Treaties in Force (U.S. Department of State), 160
Truth, claims of, 10
Turabian, Kate L., 99, 103–104, 166–167
Turner, Frederick Jackson, 43
Twyman, Robert W., 145

U

Ulrichsweb.com Ulrich's international periodicals directory, 140
Undergraduate research, xii
Uniform System of Citation, A, 165

Unintended audiences, 58–59
Unintentional sources, 57
Union List of Serials in Libraries of the United States and Canada, 140
United Nations, 149
United Nations' website, 69
United States:
  abstract collections for, 36
  America: History and Life, 133
  Atlas of American History, 149
  Atlas of the Historical Geography of the United States, 150
  Bibliographies in American History, 1942–1978, 132
  Bibliographies in History: An Index to Bibliographies in History Journals and Dissertations, 133
  Bibliography of American Historical Societies, 135
  book reviews related to, 36
  census data, 71
  "Clio's Neglected Tools," 126
  Confederate Research Sources, 129
  Datapedia of the United States, 1790–2000: America Year by Year, 148
  dictionaries/encyclopedias/handbooks for, 141–146
  Dictionary of American History, 144–145
  Directory of Historical Societies and Agencies in the United States and Canada, 162
  Documents of American History, 157
  Draper Manuscripts, 157
  Editorials on File, 153
  Encyclopedia of the American Presidency, 145
  Encyclopedia of the Confederacy, 143
  Encyclopedia of the North American Colonies, 143
  Encyclopedia of the United States in the Nineteenth Century, 144
  Guide to Records in the National Archives of the United States Relating to American Indians, 128
  A Guide to the Study of the United States of America, 138
  Guide to the Study of United States History Outside the U.S., 1945–1980, 127
  Guides to Archives and Manuscript Collections in the United States, 127
  Handbook for Research in American History: A Guide to Bibliographies and Other Reference Works, 130
  The Harper Atlas of World History, 150
  Harvard Guide to American History, 135
  Historical Census Browser, 148

Historical Statistics of the United States: Earliest Times to the Present, 148
How to Research Elections, 128
The Immigration History Research Center: A Guide to Collections, 129
International Historical Statistics: The Americas, 1750–2000, 149
Introduction to United States Government Information Sources, 129
Journal of American History, 136
Labor History Archives in the United States, 128
The Literature of American History: A Bibliographical Guide, 136
online journal articles/reviews, 28
online primary sources locators for, 29, 30
Reconstruction in the United States: An Annotated Bibliography, 136
Statistical Abstract of the United States, 148–149
statistical sources/tables for, 147–149
subject bibliographies for, 25
Term Paper Resource Guide to Twentieth-Century United States History, 129
treaties of, 160–161
United States History: A Selective Guide to Information Sources, 126
United States Statutes at Large, 161
We the People: An Atlas of America's Ethnic Diversity, 149
Women in U.S. History: A Resource Guide, 127
The WPA Historical Records Survey: A Guide to the Unpublished Inventories, Indexes, and Transcripts, 127
Writings on American History, 138
(*See also* specific topics, e.g.: Foreign relations)
United States Bureau of the Census, 148–149
United States History: A Selective Guide to Information Sources (Ron Blazek), 126
United States Local Histories in the Library of Congress: A Bibliography, 138
United States Newspaper Program, 141
United States Statutes at Large, 161
United States Treaties and Other International Agreements (U.S. Department of State), 159
University presses, 37
Unpublished dissertations/theses:
  bibliography citations for, 115–116
  footnotes for, 108, 109
Unpublished primary sources, 66
U.S. Department of State, 160

U.S. Foreign Relations A Guide to Information Sources (Elmer Plischke), 130

U.S. Supreme Court, The: A Bibliography (Fenton S. Martin), 129

Using Government Information Sources: Electronic and Print (Jean L. Sears and Marilyn K. Moody), 131

USSR:
  The Gorbachev Bibliography, 1985–1991: A Listing of Books and Articles in English on Perestroika in the USSR, 138

V

Valley of the Shadow, The: Two Communities in the American Civil War, 30

Values, comparing, 31–32

Vandercook, Sharon, 132

Veit, Fritz, 131

Verification sources, 139–140

Videos:
  bibliography citations for, 116
  evaluating, 65
  footnotes for, 109

Vietnam National Security Council Histories (Paul Kesaris), 159

Virginia Historical Index (Earl G. Swem), 138

Virginia Newspapers 1821–1935: A Bibliography with Historical Introduction and Notes (Lester J. Cappon), 140

Visual primary evidence:
  evaluating, 63–65
  maps, 74–76
  microform collections of, 31
  photographs, 73–74

Vital Speeches of the Day, 165

Voice (in writing), 82

Voices from Ellis Island, 160

Voices from the Days of Slavery, 72–73

Volkgeist, 7

Voting:
  America at the Polls: A Handbook of American Presidential Election Statistics, 1920–1964, 149
  America Votes, 148–149
  How to Research Elections, 128–129
  Presidential Ballots, 1836–1892, 149
  Presidential Elections Since 1789, 149
  The Presidential Vote, 1986–1932, 149
  They Voted for Roosevelt: The Presidential Vote, 1932–1944, 149

Vyhnanek, Louis A., 21–22

W

War in Vietnam, The, 158

War of the Rebellion, The: A Compilation of the Official Records of the Union and Confederate Armies, 155

We the People: An Atlas of America's Ethnic Diversity (James P. Allen), 149

Webb, William H., 132

Weber, Max, 11

Websites:
  bibliography citations for, 115
  footnotes for, 108
  (*See also* Online research)

Weekly Compilation of Presidential Documents, 157

West Point Atlas of American Wars, The (West Point Military Academy), 151

Western civilization, study of, 14

Who Was Who in America: A Companion Volume to Who's Who in America, 154

Wigdor, Alexandra K., 132

Williams, Peter W., 143

Williams, Robert C., 147

Wills, as primary sources/evidence, 69–71

Wilson OmniFile Full Text Mega, 138–139, 163

WilsonWeb OmniFile, 36

Witchcraft Bibliography Project, The, 25

Women in U.S. History: A Resource Guide (Lyda J. Hardy), 127

Women's Journals of the 19th century, Part 1, The Women's Penny Paper *and* Woman's Herald, 1888–1893, 159

Woolf, D. R., 147

Word choice, 88–89

World Almanac and Book of Facts, The, 154

World Bibliography of Bibliographies and of Bibliographical Catalogues, Calendars, Abstracts, Digests, Indexes, and the Like, A (Theodore Besterman), 22, 132

World history:
  The American Historical Association's Guide to Historical Literature, 137
  Berkshire Encyclopedia of World History, 141
  Bibliographies in History: An Index to Bibliographies in History Journals and Dissertations, 133
  dictionaries/encyclopedias/handbooks for, 141
  Encyclopedia of World Environmental History, 141
  Encyclopedia of World History, 141
  The Encyclopedia of World History: Ancient, Medieval, and Modern Chronologically Arranged, 141
  Historic Documents, 156
  Historical Abstracts, 136
  Keesing's Record of World Events, 153

The Nazi Era, 1919–1945: A Select Bibliography of Published Works from the Early Roots to 1980, 137

The New International Year Book, 153

Newspapers in Microform: Foreign Countries, 1948–1983, 141

Sources of Information for Historical Research, 131

Statistical Yearbook, 149

Term Paper Resource Guide to Twentieth-Century World History, 130

The Times History of the World, 149–150

in undergraduate studies, 14

World Almanac and Book of Facts, The, 154

A World Bibliography of Bibliographies and of Bibliographical Catalogues, Calendars, Abstracts, Digests, Indexes, and the Like, 132
  (*See also* Ancient history)

World War II in Europe, Africa, and the Americas, with General Sources (Lloyd Lee), 136

World War II in Europe (David T. Zabecki), 143

WorldCat, 25–27, 139, 140, 141, 154

WPA Historical Records Survey, The: A Guide to the Unpublished Inventories, Indexes, and Transcripts (Loretta Hefner), 127

Wright, Edward, 75–76

Writing history, 81–98
  basic approaches to, 90
  beginning process of, 81–82
  as conversation, 15
  descriptive, 91–92
  "early writing" stage of, 82
  editing, 96–97
  effectiveness of, 87–90
  final checklist for, 121–122
  first draft of, 95–96
  first paragraph in, 84–87
  interpretative, 92–93
  narrative, 90–91
  oral presentation of, 97–98
  organization of, 93–95
  peer reviews of, 83
  persuasive, 93
  prospectus for, 82–83
  revisions of, 96–97
  of short informal essays, 83–84
  time spent in research vs., 81
  tips for, 87–90
  (*See also* Historical writing)

Writings on American History, 138

Written primary evidence, 57–62
  audience for, 58–59
  author of, 57–58
  autobiographies, 68
  correspondence, 66–68
  diaries, 68
  government documents, 68–69
  inventories, 69, 70
  memoirs, 68

nce (*continued*)
~~~~62
.ar records, 71
tone and language of, 60–61

wills, 69–71
Wytfliet, Cornelius, 75–76

Y

Yearbook of International Organizations,
   164
Yearbooks, 153–154

Z

Zabecki, David T., 143